John Wolcott Adams

IRVING BACHELLER

ABRAHAM LINCOLN:
A Man for the Ages

A story of the Builders of Democracy

ILLUSTRATED BY
JOHN WOLCOTT ADAMS

the apocryphile press
BERKELEY, CA
www.apocryphile.org

apocryphile press
BERKELEY, CA

Apocryphile Press
1700 Shattuck Ave #81
Berkeley, CA 94709
www.apocryphile.org

This edition first published in 1919 by The Ridgway Company.
Apocryphile Press Edition, 2010.

Printed in the United States of America
ISBN 978-1-93399-88-1

TO

MY DEAR FRIEND AND COMRADE

ALEXANDER GROSSET

I DEDICATE THIS BOOK IN
TOKEN OF MY ESTEEM

A Letter

TO THE AGED AND HONORABLE JOSIAH TRAYLOR FROM
HIS GRANDSON, A SOLDIER IN FRANCE, WHEREIN
THE MOTIVE AND INSPIRATION OF THIS NARRATIVE
ARE BRIEFLY PRESENTED.

In France, September 10, 1915.

Dear Grandfather:

At last I have got mine. I had been scampering towards the stars, like a jack-rabbit chased by barking greyhounds, when a shrapnel shell caught up with me. It sneezed all over my poor bus, and threw some junk into me as if it thought me nothing better than a kind of waste basket. Seems as if it had got tired of carrying its load and wanted to put it on me. It succeeded famously but I got home with the bus. Since then they have been taking sinkers and fish hooks out of me fit only for deep water. Don't worry, I'm getting better fast. I shall play no more football and you will not see me pitching curves and running bases again. No, I shall sit in the grandstand myself hereafter and there will not be so much of me but I shall have quite a shuck on my soul for all that. I've done a lot of thinking since I have been lying on my back with nothing else to do. When your body gets kind of turned over in the ditch it's wonderful how your

A LETTER

mind begins to hustle around the place. Until this thing happened my intellect was nothing more than a vague rumor. I had heard of it, now and then, in college, and I had hoped that it would look me up some time and ask what it could do for me, but it didn't. These days I would scarcely believe that I have a body, the poor thing being upon the jacks in this big machine shop, but my small intellect is hopping all over the earth and back again and watching every move of these high-toned mechanics with their shiny tools and white aprons. My mind and I have kind of got acquainted with each other and I'm getting attached to it. It is quite an energetic, promising young mind and I don't know but I'll try to make a permanent place for it in my business.

I've been thinking of our Democracy and of my coming over here to be chucked into this big jack pot as if my life were a small coin; of all the dear old days of the past I have thought and chiefly how the wonderful story of your life has been woven into mine —threads of wisdom and adventure and humor and romance. I like to unravel it and look at the colors. Lincoln is the strongest, longest thread in the fabric. Often I think of your description of the great, tender hands that lifted you to his shoulder when you were a boy, of the droll and kindly things that he said to you. I have laughed and cried recalling those hours of yours with Jack Kelso and Dr. John Allen and the rude young giant Abe, of which I have heard you tell

A LETTER

*so often as we sat in the firelight of a winter evening.
Best of all I remember the light of your own wisdom as
it glowed upon the story; how you found in Lincoln's
words a prophecy of the great struggle that has come.
Since I have been steering my imagination on its swift,
long flights into the past I have been able to recall
the very words you used: "Lincoln said that a house
divided against itself must fall—that our nation could
not endure part slave and part free, and it was true.
Since then the world has grown incredibly small. The
peoples of the earth have been drawn into one house
and the affairs of each are the concern of all. With
a vain, boastful and unscrupulous degenerate on the
throne of Germany, it is likely to be a house divided
against itself and I fear a greater struggle than the
world has ever seen between the bond and the free.
It will be a bloody contest but of its issue there can be
no doubt because the friends of freedom are the children of light and are many. They will lay all they
have upon its altars. They will be unprepared and
roughly handled for a time but their reserves of material and moral strength which shall express themselves in ready sacrifice, are beyond all calculation.
Only one whose life spans the wide area from Andrew
Jackson to Woodrow Wilson and who has stood with
Lincoln in his lonely tower and watched the flowing
of the tides for three score years and ten, as I have,
can be quite aware of the perils and resources of
Democracy."*

A LETTER

All these and many other things which you have said to me, dear grandfather, have helped me to understand this great thunderous drama in which I have had a part. They have helped me to endure its perils and bitter defeats. It was you who saw clearly from the first that this was the final clash between the bond and the free—an effort of the great house of God to purge itself, and you urged me to go to Canada and enlist in the struggle. For this, too, I thank you. My wounds are dear to me, knowing, as you have made me know, that I have come well by them fighting not in the interest of Great Britain or France or Russia, but in the cause of humanity. It is strange that among these men who are fighting with me I have found only one or two who seem to have a vision of the whole truth of this business.

Now I come to the point of my letter. I have an enlistment to urge upon you in the cause of humanity and there are no wounds to go with it. When I come home, as I shall be doing as soon as I am sufficiently mended, we must go to work on the story of your life so that all who wish to do so may know it as I know it. Let us go to it with all the diaries that you and your father kept, aided by your memory, and give to the world its first full view of the heart and soul of Lincoln. I have read all the biographies and anecdotes of him and yet without the story as you tell it he would have been a stranger to me. After this war, if I mis-

CONTENTS

CONTENTS—*Continued*

A LETTER

take not, Democracy will command the interest of all men. It will be the theme of themes. You tell me that we shall soon get into the struggle and turn the scale. Well, if we do, we shall have to demonstrate a swiftness of preparation and a power in the field which will astonish the world, and when it is all over the world will want to know how this potent Democracy of ours came about. The one name—Lincoln—with the background of your story, especially the background, for the trouble with all the biographies is a lack of background—will be the best answer we could give I think. Of course there are other answers, but, as there are few who dare to doubt, these days, that Lincoln is the greatest democrat since Jesus Christ, if we can only present your knowledge to the world we should do well. Again the great crowd, whom you and I desire to enlighten if we can, do not read biography or history save under the compulsion of the schools, so let us try only to tell the moving story as you have told it to me, with Lincoln striding across the scene or taking the center of the stage just as he was wont to do in your recollection of him. So we will make them to know the giant of Democracy without trying.

Duty calls. What is your answer? Please let me know by cable. Meanwhile I shall be thinking more about it. With love to all the family, from your affectionate grandson,   R. L.

A MAN FOR THE AGES

Property is the fruit of labor; property is desirable; it is a positive good in the world. That some should be rich shows that others may become rich, and hence is just encouragement to industry and enterprise. Let not him who is houseless pull down the house of another, but let him work diligently and build one for himself, thus by example assuring that his own shall be safe from violence when built.

ABRAHAM LINCOLN.

March 21, 1864.

CONTENTS—*Continued*

CONTENTS—*Continued*

A Man for the Ages

BOOK ONE

CHAPTER I

WHICH DESCRIBES THE JOURNEY OF SAMSON HENRY
TRAYLOR AND HIS WIFE AND THEIR TWO CHILDREN
AND THEIR DOG SAMBO THROUGH THE ADIRONDACK
WILDERNESS IN 1831 ON THEIR WAY TO THE LAND
OF PLENTY, AND ESPECIALLY THEIR ADVENTURES
IN BEAR VALLEY AND NO SANTA CLAUS LAND.
FURTHERMORE, IT DESCRIBES THE SOAPING OF THE
BRIMSTEADS AND THE CAPTURE OF THE VEILED
BEAR.

IN the early summer of 1831 Samson Traylor and
his wife, Sarah, and two children left their old home
near the village of Vergennes, Vermont, and began
their travels toward the setting sun with four chairs,
a bread board and rolling-pin, a feather bed and
blankets, a small looking-glass, a skillet, an axe, a pack
basket with a pad of sole leather on the same, a water
pail, a box of dishes, a tub of salt pork, a rifle, a teapot, a sack of meal, sundry small provisions and a
violin, in a double wagon drawn by oxen. It is a
pleasure to note that they had a violin and were not

I

disposed to part with it. The reader must not overlook its full historic significance. The stern, uncompromising spirit of the Puritan had left the house of the Yankee before a violin could enter it. Humor and the love of play had preceded and cleared a way for it. Where there was a fiddle there were cheerful hearts. A young black shepherd dog with tawny points and the name of Sambo followed the wagon or explored the fields and woods it passed.

If we had been at the Congregational Church on Sunday we might have heard the minister saying to Samson, after the service, that it was hard to understand why the happiest family in the parish and the most beloved should be leaving its ancestral home to go to a far, new country of which little was known. We might also have heard Samson answer:

"It's awful easy to be happy here. We slide along in the same old groove, that our fathers traveled, from Vergennes to Paradise. We work and play and go to meetin' and put a shin plaster in the box and grow old and narrow and stingy and mean and go up to glory and are turned into saints and angels. Maybe that's the best thing that could happen to us, but Sarah and I kind o' thought we'd try a new starting place and another route to Heaven."

Then we might have seen the countenance of the minister assume a grave and troubled look. "Samson, you must not pull down the pillars of this temple," he said.

"No, it has done too much for me. I love its faults even. But we have been called and must go. A great empire is growing up in the West. We want to see it; we want to help build it."

The minister had acquired a sense of humor among those Yankees. Years later in his autobiography he tells how deeply the words of Samson had impressed him. He had answered:

"Think of us. I don't know what we shall do without your fun and the music of your laugh at the pleasure parties. In addition to being the best wrestler in the parish you are also its most able and sonorous laugher."

"Yes, Sarah and I have got the laughing habit. I guess we need a touch of misery to hold us down. But you will have other laughers. The seed has been planted here and the soil is favorable."

Samson knew many funny stories and could tell them well. His heart was as merry as *The Fisher's Hornpipe*. He used to say that he got the violin to help him laugh, as he found his voice failing under the strain.

Sarah and Samson had been raised on adjoining farms just out of the village. He had had little schooling, but his mind was active and well inclined. Sarah had prosperous relatives in Boston and had had the advantage of a year's schooling in that city. She was a comely girl of a taste and refinement unusual in the place and time of her birth. Many well favored youths had sought her hand, but, better than others, she liked the big, masterful, good-natured, humorous Samson, crude as he was. Naturally in her hands his timber had undergone some planing and smoothing and his thought had been gently led into new and pleasant ways. Sarah's Uncle Rogers in Boston had kept them supplied with some of the best books and magazines of the time. These they had read aloud with keen enjoyment. Moreover, they remembered what they read and cherished and thought about it.

Let us take a look at them as they slowly leave the village of their birth. The wagon is covered with tent cloth drawn over hickory arches. They are sitting on a seat overlooking the oxen in the wagon front. Tears are streaming down the face of the woman. The man's head is bent. His elbows are resting on his knees; the hickory handle of his ox whip lies across his lap, the lash at his feet. He seems to be looking down at his boots, into the tops of which his trousers have been folded. He is a rugged, blond, bearded man with kindly blue eyes and a rather prominent nose. There is a striking expression of power in the head and shoulders of Samson Traylor. The breadth of his back, the size of his wrists and hands, the color of his face betoken a man of great strength. This thoughtful, sorrowful attitude is the only evidence of emotion which he betrays. In a few minutes he begins to whistle a lively tune.

The boy Josiah—familiarly called Joe—sits beside his mother. He is a slender, sweet-faced lad. He is looking up wistfully at his mother. The little girl Betsey sits between him and her father.

That evening they stopped at the house of an old friend some miles up the dusty road to the north.

"Here we are—goin' west," Samson shouted to the man at the door-step.

He alighted and helped his family out of the wagon.

"You go right in—I'll take care o' the oxen," said the man.

Samson started for the house with the girl under one arm and the boy under the other. A pleasant-faced woman greeted them with a hearty welcome at the door.

"You poor man! Come right in," she said.

"Poor! I'm the richest man in the world," said he. "Look at the gold on that girl's head—curly, fine gold, too—the best there is. She's Betsey—my little toy woman—half past seven years old—blue eyes—helps her mother get tired every day. Here's my toy man Josiah—yes, brown hair and brown eyes like Sarah—heart o' gold—helps his mother, too—six times one year old."

"What pretty faces!" said the woman as she stooped and kissed them.

"Yes, ma'am. Got 'em from the fairies," Samson went on. "They have all kinds o' heads for little folks, an' I guess they color 'em up with the blood o' roses an' the gold o' buttercups an' the blue o' violets. Here's this wife o' mine. She's richer'n I am. She owns all of us. We're her slaves."

"Looks as young as she did the day she was married —nine years ago," said the woman.

"Exactly!" Samson exclaimed. "Straight as an arrow and proud! I don't blame her. She's got enough to make her proud I say. I fall in love again every time I look into her big, brown eyes."

The talk and laughter brought the dog into the house.

"There's Sambo, our camp follower," said Samson. "He likes us, one and all, but he often feels sorry for us because we can not feel the joy that lies in buried bones and the smell of a liberty pole or a gate post."

They had a joyous evening and a restful night with these old friends and resumed their journey soon after daylight. They ferried across the lake at Burlington and fared away over the mountains and through the deep forest on the Chateaugay trail.

Since the Pilgrims landed between the measureless waters and the pathless wilderness they and their descendants had been surrounded by the lure of mysteries. It filled the imagination of the young with gleams of golden promise. The love of adventure, the desire to explore the dark, infested and beautiful forest, the dream of fruitful sunny lands cut with

water courses, shored with silver and strewn with gold
beyond it—these were the only heritage of their sons
and daughters save the strength and courage of the
pioneer. How true was this dream of theirs gathering
detail and allurement as it passed from sire to son!
On distant plains to the west were lands more lovely
and fruitful than any of their vision; in mountains far
beyond was gold enough to gild the dome of the
heavens, as the sun was wont to do at eventide, and
silver enough to put a fairly respectable moon in it.
Yet for generations their eyes were not to see, their
hands were not to touch these things. They were only
to push their frontier a little farther to the west and
hold the dream and pass it on to their children.

Those early years of the nineteenth century held the
first days of fulfillment. Samson and Sarah Traylor
had the old dream in their hearts when they first turned
their faces to the West. For years Sarah had resisted
it, thinking of the hardships and perils in the way of
the mover. Samson, a man of twenty-nine when he
set out from his old home, was said to be "always
chasing the bird in the bush." He was never content
with the thing in hand. There were certain of their
friends who promised to come and join them when, at
last, they should have found the land of plenty. But
most of the group that bade them good-by thought it
a foolish enterprise and spoke lightly of Samson when
they were gone. America has undervalued the brave

souls who went west in wagons, without whose sublime
courage and endurance the plains would still be an
unplowed wilderness. Often we hear them set down
as seedy, shiftless dreamers who could not make a
living at home. They were mostly the best blood of
the world and the noblest of God's missionaries. Who
does not honor them above the thrifty, comfort loving
men and women who preferred to stay at home, where
risks were few, the supply of food sure and sufficient
and the consolations of friendship and religion always
at hand. Samson and Sarah preferred to enlist and
take their places in the front battle line of Civilization.

They had read a little book called *The Country of
the Sangamon.* The latter was a word of the Potta-
watomies meaning land of plenty. It was the name of a
. river in Illinois draining "boundless, flowery meadows
of unexampled beauty and fertility, belted with timber,
blessed with shady groves, covered with game and
mostly level, without a stick or a stone to vex the
plowman." Thither they were bound to take up a
section of government land.

They stopped for a visit with Elisha Howard and
his wife, old friends of theirs, who lived in the village
of Malone, which was in Franklin County, New York.
There they traded their oxen for a team of horses.
They were large gray horses named Pete and Colonel.
The latter was fat and good-natured. His chief interest in life was food. Pete was always looking for

food and perils. Colonel was the near horse. Now and then Samson threw a sheepskin over his back and put the boy on it and tramped along within arm's reach of Joe's left leg. This was a great delight to the little lad.

They proceeded at a better pace to the Black River country, toward which, in the village of Canton, they tarried again for a visit with Captain Moody and Silas Wright, both of whom had taught school in the town of Vergennes.

They proceeded through DeKalb, Richville and Gouverneur and Antwerp and on to the Sand Plains. They had gone far out of their way for a look at these old friends of theirs.

Every day the children would ask many questions, as they rode along, mainly about the beasts and birds in the dark shadows of the forest through which they passed. These were answered patiently by their father and mother and every answer led to other queries.

"You're a funny pair," said their father one day. "You have to turn over every word we say to see what's under it. I used to be just like ye, used to go out in the lot and tip over every stick and stone I could lift to see the bugs and crickets run. You're always hopin' to see a bear or a panther or a fairy run out from under my remarks."

"Wonder why we don't see no bears?" Joe asked.

" 'Cause they always see us first or hear us comin',"

said his father. "If you're goin' to see ol' Uncle Bear ye got to pay the price of admission."

"What's that?" Joe asked.

"Got to go still and careful so you'll see him first. If this old wagon didn't talk so loud and would kind o' go on its tiptoes maybe we'd see him. He don't like to be seen. Seems so he was kind o' shamed of himself, an' I wouldn't wonder if he was. He's done a lot o' things to be 'shamed of."

"What's he done?" Joe asked.

"Ketched sheep and pigs and fawns and run off with 'em."

"What does he do with 'em?"

"Eats 'em up. Now you quit. Here's a lot o' rocks and mud and I got to 'tend to business. You tackle yer mother and chase her up and down the hills a while and let me get my breath."

Samson's diary tells how, at the top of the long, steep hills he used to cut a small tree by the roadside and tie its butt to the rear axle and hang on to its branches while his wife drove the team. This held their load, making an effective brake.

Traveling through the forest, as they had been doing for weeks, while the day waned, they looked for a brookside on which they could pass the night with water handy. Samson tethered, fed and watered their horses, and while Sarah and the children built a fire and made tea and biscuits, he was getting bait and catching fish in the stream.

"In a few minutes from the time I wet my hook a mess of trout would be dressed and sizzling, with a piece of salt pork, in the pan, or it was a bad day for fishing," he writes.

After supper the wagon was partly unloaded, the feather bed laid upon the planks under the wagon roof and spread with blankets. Then Samson sang songs and told stories or played upon the violin to amuse the family. The violin invariably woke the birds in the tree-tops, and some, probably thrushes or warblers or white throated sparrows, began twittering. Now and then one would express his view of the disturbance with a little phrase of song. Often the player paused to hear these musical whispers "up in the gallery," as he was wont to call it.

Often if the others were weary and depressed he would dance merrily around the fire, playing a lively tune, with Sambo glad to lend a helping foot and much noise to the program. If mosquitos and flies were troublesome Samson built smudges, filling their camp with the smoky incense of dead leaves, in which often the flavor of pine and balsam was mingled. By and by the violin was put away and all knelt by the fire while Sarah prayed aloud for protection through the night. So it will be seen that they carried with them their own little theater, church and hotel.

Soon after darkness fell, Sarah and the children lay down for the night, while Samson stretched out with his blankets by the fire in good weather, the loaded musket and the dog Sambo lying beside him. Often the howling of wolves in the distant forest kept them awake, and the dog muttering and barking for hours.

Samson woke the camp at daylight and a merry song was his reveille while he led the horses to their drink.

"Have a good night?" Sarah would ask.

"Perfect!" he was wont to answer. "But when the smudges went out the mosquiters got to peckin' my face."

"Mine feels like a pincushion," Sarah would often answer. "Will you heat up a little water for us to wash with?"

"You better believe I will. Two more hedge hogs last night, but Sambo let 'em alone."

Sambo had got his mouth sored by hedge hogs some time before and had learned better than to have any fuss with them.

When they set out in the morning Samson was wont to say to the little lad, who generally sat beside him: "Well, my boy, what's the good word this morning?" Whereupon Joe would say, parrot like:

"God help us all and make His face to shine upon us."

"Well said!" his father would answer, and so the day's journey began.

Often, near its end, they came to some lonely farmhouse. Always Samson would stop and go to the door to ask about the roads, followed by little Joe and

Betsey with secret hopes. One of these hopes was related to cookies and maple sugar and buttered bread and had been cherished since an hour of good fortune early in the trip and encouraged by sundry good-hearted women along the road. Another was the hope of seeing a baby—mainly, it should be said, the hope of Betsey. Joe's interest was merely an echo of hers. He regarded babies with an open mind, as it were, for the opinions of his sister still had some weight with him, she being a year and a half older than he, but babies invariably disappointed him, their capabilities being so restricted. To be sure, they could make quite a noise, and the painter was said to imitate it, but since Joe had learned that they couldn't bite he had begun to lose respect for them. Still, not knowing what might happen, he always took a look at every baby.

The children were lifted out of the wagon to stretch their legs at sloughs and houses. They were sure to be close behind the legs of their father when he stood at a stranger's door. Then, the night being near, they were always invited to put their horses in the barn and tarry until next morning. This was due in part to the kindly look and voice of Samson, but mostly to the wistful faces of the little children—a fact unsuspected by their parents. What motherly heart could resist the silent appeal of children's faces or fail to understand it? Those were memorable nights for

Sarah and Joe and Betsey.   In a letter to her brother
the woman said:

"You don't know how good it seemed to see a
woman and talk to her, and we talked and talked
until midnight, after all the rest were asleep.   She let
me hold the baby in my lap until it was put to bed.
How good it felt to have a little warm body in my
arms again and feel it breathing!   In all my life I
never saw a prettier baby.   It felt good to be in a real
house and sleep in a soft, warm bed and to eat jelly
and cookies and fresh meat and potatoes and bread and
butter.   Samson played for them and kept them laughing with his stories until bedtime.   They wouldn't take
a cent and gave us a dozen eggs in a basket and a
piece of venison when we went away.   Their name is
Sanford and I have promised to write to them.   They
are good Christian folks and they say that maybe they
will join us in the land of plenty if we find it all we
expect."

They had two rainy, cold days, with a northeast
wind blowing and deep mud in the roads.   The children complained of the cold.   After a few miles' travel
they stopped at an old hunter's camp facing a great
mossy rock near the road.

"Guess we'll stop here for a visit," said Samson.

"Who we goin' to visit?" Joe asked.

"The trees and the fairies," said his father.   "Don't
ye hear 'em askin' us to stop?   They say the wind is
blowin' bad an' that we'd better stop an' make some

good weather. They offer us a house and a roof to cover it and some wood to burn. I guess we'll be able to make our own sunshine in a few minutes."

Samson peeled some bark and repaired the roof and, with his flint and tinder and some fat pine, built a roaring fire against the rock and soon had his family sitting, in its warm glow, under shelter. Near by was another rude framework of poles set in crotches partly covered with bark which, with a little repairing, made a sufficient shelter for Pete and Colonel. Down by a little brook a few rods away he cut some balsams and returned presently with his arms full of the fragrant boughs. These he dried in the heat of the fire and spread in a thick mat on the ground under the lean-to. It was now warm with heat, reflected from the side of the great rock it faced. The light of the leaping flames fell upon the travelers.

"Ye see ye can make yer own weather and fill it with sunshine if ye only know how," said Samson, as he sat down and brushed a coal out of the ashes and swiftly picked it up with his fingers and put it into the bowl of his clay pipe. "Mother and I read in a book that the wood was full o' sunlight all stored up and ready for us to use. Ye just set it afire and out comes the warm sunlight for days like this. God takes pretty good care of us—don't He?"

The heat of other fires had eaten away a few inches of the base of the rock. Under its overhang some one had written with a black coal the words "Bear Valley Camp." On this suggestion the children called for a bear story, and lying back on the green mat of boughs, Samson told them of the great bear of Camel's Hump which his father had slain, and many other tales of the wilderness.

They lived two days in this fragrant, delightful shelter until the storm had passed and the last of their corn meal had been fed to the horses. They were never to forget the comfort and the grateful odors of their camp in Bear Valley.

On a warm, bright day in the sand country after the storm they came to a crude, half finished, frame house at the edge of a wide clearing. The sand lay in drifts on one side of the road. It had evidently moved in the last wind. A sickly vegetation covered the field. A ragged, barefooted man and three scrawny, ill clad children stood in the dooryard. It was noontime. A mongrel dog, with a bit of the hound in him, came bounding and barking toward the wagon and pitched upon Sambo and quickly got the worst of it. Sambo, after much experience in self-defense, had learned that the best way out of such trouble was to seize a leg and hang on. This he did. The mongrel began to yelp. Samson lifted both dogs by the backs of their necks, broke the hold of Sambo and tossed aside the mongrel, who ran away whining.

"That reminds me of a bull that tackled a man over in Vermont," said he. "The man had a club in his hand. He dodged and grabbed the bull's tail and beat him all over the lot. As the bull roared, the man hollered: 'I'd like to know who began this fuss anyway.'"

The stranger laughed.

"Is that your house?" Samson asked.

The man stepped nearer and answered in a low, confidential tone:

"Say, mister, this is a combination poorhouse and idiot asylum. I am the idiot. These are the poor."

He pointed to the children.

"You don't talk like an idiot," said Samson.

The man looked around and leaned over the wheel as if about to impart a secret.

"Say, I'll tell ye," he said in a low tone. "A real, first-class idiot never does. You ought to see my actions."

"This land is an indication that you're right," Samson laughed.

"It proves it," the stranger whispered.

"Have you any water here?" Samson asked.

The stranger leaned nearer and said in his most confidential tone: "Say, mister, it's about the best in the United States. Right over yonder in the edge o' the woods—a spring—cold as ice—Simon-pure water. 'Bout the only thing this land'll raise is water."

"This land looks to me about as valuable as so much sheet lightnin' and I guess it can move just about as quick," said Samson.

The stranger answered in a low tone: "Say, I'll tell

ye, it's a wild cow—don't stand still long 'nough
to give ye time to git anything out of it. I've toiled
and prayed, but it's hard to get much out of it."

"Praying won't do this land any good," Samson
answered. "What it needs is manure and plenty of it.
You can't raise anything here but fleas. It isn't decent
to expect God to help run a flea farm. He knows too
much for that, and if you keep it up He'll lose all
respect for ye. If you were to buy another farm and
bring it here and put it down on top o' this one, you
could probably make a living. I wouldn't like to live
where the wind could dig my potatoes."

Again the stranger leaned toward Samson and said
in a half-whisper: "Say, mister, I wouldn't want you
to mention it, but talkin' o' fleas, I'm like a dog with
so many of 'em that he don't have time to eat. Somebody has got to soap him or he'll die. You see, I
traded my farm over in Vermont for five hundred
acres o' this sheet lightnin', unsight an' unseen. We
was all crazy to go West an' here we are. If it wasn't
for the deer an' the fish I guess we'd 'a' starved to
death long ago."

"Where did ye come from?"

"Orwell, Vermont."

"What's yer name?"

"Henry Brimstead," the stranger whispered.

"Son of Elijah Brimstead?"

"Yes, sir."

Samson took his hand and shook it warmly. "Well, I declare!" he exclaimed. "Elijah Brimstead was a friend o' my father."

"Who are you?" Brimstead asked.

"I'm one o' the Traylors o' Vergennes."

"My father used to buy cattle of Henry Traylor."

"Henry was my father. Haven't you let 'em know about your bad luck?"

The man resumed his tone of confidence. "Say, I'll tell ye," he answered. "A man that's as big a fool as I am ought not to advertise it. A brain that has treated its owner as shameful as mine has treated me should be compelled to do its own thinkin' er die. I've invented some things that may sell. I've been hopin' my luck would turn."

"It'll turn when you turn it," Samson assured him.

Brimstead thoughtfully scuffed the sand with his bare foot. In half a moment he stepped to the wheel and imparted this secret: "Say, mister, if you've any more doubt o' my mental condition, I'm goin' to tell ye that they've discovered valuable ore in my land two miles back o' this road, an' I'm hopin' to make a fortune. Don't that prove my case?"

"Any man that puts his faith in the bowels of the earth can have my vote," said Samson.

Brimstead leaned close to Samson's ear and said in a tone scarcely audible:

"My brother Robert has his own idiot asylum. It's

a real handsome one an' he has made it pay, but I wouldn't swap with him."

Samson smiled, remembering that Robert had a liquor store. "Look here, Henry Brimstead, we're hungry," he said. "If ye furnish the water, we'll skirmish around for bread and give ye as good a dinner as ye ever had in yer life."

Henry took the horses to his barn and watered and fed them. Then he brought two pails of water from the spring. Meanwhile Samson started a fire in a grove of small poplars by the roadside and began broiling venison, and Sarah got out the bread board and the flour and the rolling-pin and the teapot. As she waited for the water she called the three strange children to her side. The oldest was a girl of ten, with a face uncommonly refined and attractive. In spite of her threadbare clothes, she had a neat and cleanly look and gentle manners. The youngest was a boy of four. They were a pathetic trio.

Joe had been telling them about Santa Claus and showing them a jack-knife which had come down the chimney in his pack at Christmas time and describing a dress of his mother's that had gold and silver buttons on it. The little six-year-old girl had asked him many questions about his mother and had stood for some moments looking up into Sarah's face. The girl timidly felt the dress and hair of the woman and touched her wedding ring.

"Come and wash your faces and hands," Joe demanded as soon as the water came.

This they did while he poured from a dipper.

"Nice people always wash before they eat," he reminded them.

Then he showed them his bear stick, with the assurance that it had killed a hedge hog, omitting the unimportant fact that his father had wielded it. The ferocity of hedge hogs was a subject on which he had large information. He told how one of their party had come near getting his skin sewed on a barn door. A hedge hog had come and asked Sambo if he would have some needles. Sambo had never seen a hedge hog, so he said that he guessed he would.

Then the hedge hog said: "Help yourself."

Sambo went to take some and just got his face full of 'em so it looked like a head o' barley. They had to be took out with a pinchers or they'd 'a' sewed his skin on to a barn door. That was their game. They tried to sew everybody's skin on a barn door.

Every night the hedge hog came around and said: "Needles, needles, anybody want some needles."

Now Sambo always answered: "No thank you, I've had enough."

"Where's your mother?" Sarah asked of the ten-year-old girl.

"Dead. Died when my little brother was born."

"Who takes care of you?"

"Father and—God. Father says God does most of it."

"Oh dear!" Sarah exclaimed, with a look of pity.

They had a good dinner of fresh biscuit and honey and venison and eggs and tea. While they were eating Samson told Brimstead of the land of plenty.

After dinner, while Brimstead was bringing the team, one of his children, the blonde, pale, tattered little girl of six, climbed into the wagon seat and sat holding a small rag doll, which Sarah had given her. When they were ready to go she stubbornly refused to get down.

"I'm goin' away," she said. "I'm goin' aw-a-ay off to find my mother. I don't like this place. There ain't no Santa Claus here. I'm goin' away."

She clung to the wagon seat and cried loudly when her father took her down.

"Ain't that enough to break a man's heart?" he said with a sorrowful look.

Then Samson turned to Brimstead and asked:

"Look here, Henry Brimstead, are you a drinking man? Honor bright now."

"Never drink a thing but water and tea."

"Do you know of anybody who'll give ye anything for what you own here?"

"There's a man in the next town who offered me three hundred and fifty dollars for my interest."

"How far is it?"

"Three miles."

"Come along with us and get the money if you can. I'll help ye fit up and go where ye can earn a living."

"I'd like to, but my horse is lame and I can't leave the children."

"Put 'em right in this wagon and come on. If there's a livery in the place, I'll send ye home."

So the children rode in the wagon and Samson and Brimstead walked, while Sarah drove the team to the next village. There the good woman bought new clothes for the whole Brimstead family and Brimstead sold his interest in the sand plains and bought a good pair of horses, with harness and some cloth for a wagon cover, and had fifty dollars in his pocket and a new look in his face. He put his children on the backs of the horses and led them to his old home, with a sack of provisions on his shoulder. He was to take the track of the Traylors next day and begin his journey to the shores of the Sangamon.

Samson had asked about him in the village and learned that he was an honest man who had suffered bad luck. A neighbor's wife had taken his children for two years, but bad health had compelled her to give them up.

"God does the most of it," Sarah quoted from the young girl, as they rode on. "I guess He's saved 'em from the poorhouse to-day. I hope they'll ketch up with us. I'd like to look after those children a little. They need a mother so."

"They'll ketch up all right," said Samson. "We're loaded heavier than they'll be and goin' purty slow. They'll be leavin' No Santa Claus Land to-morrow mornin'. Seems so God spoke to me when that girl said there wa'n't no Santa Claus there."

"No Santa Claus Land is a good name for it," said Sarah.

They got into a bad swale that afternoon and Samson had to cut some corduroy to make a footing for team and wagon and do much prying with the end of a heavy pole under the front axle. By and by the horses pulled them out.

"When ol' Colonel bends his neck things have to move, even if he is up to his belly in the mud," said Samson.

As the day waned they came to a river in the deep woods. It was an exquisite bit of forest with the bells of a hermit thrush ringing in one of its towers. Their call and the low song of the river were the only sounds in the silence. The glow of the setting sun which lighted the western windows of the forest had a color like that of the music—golden. Long shafts of it fell through the tree columns upon the road here and there. Our weary travelers stopped on the rude plank bridge that crossed the river. Odors of balsam and pine and tamarack came in a light, cool breeze up the river valley.

"It smells like Bear Valley," said Sarah.

"What was that poetry you learned for the church party?" Samson asked.

"I guess the part of it you're thinking of is:

> 'And west winds with musky wing
> Down the cedarn alleys fling
> 'Nard and Cassia's balmy smells.' "

"That's it," said Samson. "I guess we'll stop at this tavern till to-morrow."

Joe was asleep and they laid him on the blankets until supper was ready.

Soon after supper Samson shot a deer which had waded into the rapids. Fortunately, it made the opposite shore before it fell. All hands spent that evening dressing the deer and jerking the best of the meat. This they did by cutting the meat into strips about the size of a man's hand and salting and laying it on a rack, some two feet above a slow fire, and covering it with green boughs. The heat and smoke dried the meat in the course of two or three hours and gave it a fine flavor. Delicious beyond any kind of meat is venison treated in this manner. If kept dry, it will retain its flavor and its sweetness for a month or more.

Samson was busy with this process long after the others had gone to bed. When it was nearly finished he left the meat on the rack, the fire beneath it having burned low, crossed the river to the wagon, got his blanket, reloaded his gun and lay down to sleep with the dog beside him.

Some hours later he was awakened by "a kind of a bull beller," as he described it. The dog ran barking across the river. Samson seized the gun and followed him. The first dim light of the morning showed through the tree-tops. Some big animal was growling and roaring and rolling over and over in a clump of bushes near the meat rack. In half a moment it rolled out upon the open ground near Samson. The latter could now see that it was a large black bear engaged in a desperate struggle with the pack basket. The bear had forced his great head into the top of it and its hoop had got a firm hold on his neck. He was sniffing and growling and shaking his head and striking with both fore paws to free himself. Sambo had laid hold of his stub tail and the bear was trying in vain to reach him, with the dog dodging as he held on. The movements of both were so lively that Samson had to step like a dancer to keep clear of them. The bear, in sore trouble, leaped toward him and the swaying basket touched the side of the man. Back into the bushes and out again they struggled, Sambo keeping his hold. A more curious and ludicrous sight never gladdened the eye of a hunter. Samson had found it hard to get a chance to shoot at the noisy, swift torrent of fur. Suddenly the bear rose on his hind legs and let out an angry woof and gave the basket a terrific shaking. In this brief pause a ball

from the rifle went to his heart and he fell. Samson
jumped forward, seized the dog's collar and pulled
him away while the bear struggled in his death throes.
Then the man started for camp, while his great laugh
woke distant echoes in the forest.

"Bear steak for dinner!" he shouted to Sarah and
the children, who stood shivering with fright on the
bridge.

Again his laughter filled the woods with sound.

"Gracious Peter! What in the world was it?" Sarah
asked.

"Well, ye see, ol' Uncle Bear came to steal our
bacon an' the bacon kind o' stole him," said Samson,
between peals of laughter, the infection of which went
to the heart and lips of every member of the family.
"Shoved his head into the pack basket and the pack
basket wouldn't let go. It said: 'This is the first
time I ever swallered a bear, an' if you don't mind
I'll stay on the outside. I kind o' like you.' But the
bear did mind. He didn't want to be et up by a basket. He'd always done the swallerin' himself an' he
hollered an' swore at the basket an' tried to scare it
off. Oh, I tell ye he was awful sassy and impudent to
that old thing, but it hung on and the way he flounced
around, with Sambo clingin' to his tail, and the bear
thinkin' that he was bein' swallered at both ends, was
awful. Come an' see him."

They went to the bear, now dead. Sambo ran ahead
of them and laid hold of the bear's stump of a tail

and shook it savagely, as if inclined to take too much credit upon himself. The hoop of the pack basket had so tight a hold upon the bear's neck that it took a strong pull to get it back over his head. One side of the basket had been protected from the bear's claws by a pad of sole leather—the side which, when the basket was in use, rested on the back of its carrier. His claws had cut nearly through it and torn a carrying strap into shreds.

"I guess he'd 'a' tore off his veil if the dog had give him a little more time," said Samson. "Ol' Uncle Bear had trouble at both ends and didn't know which way to turn."

A good-sized piece of bacon still lay in the bottom of the basket.

"I wouldn't wonder if that would taste pretty beary now," said Samson, as he surveyed the bacon. "It's been sneezed at and growled on so much. Betsey, you take that down to the shore o' the river there and wash the bear out of it. I'll skin him while yer mother is gettin' breakfast. There's plenty o' live coals under the venison rack, I guess."

They set out rather late that morning. As usual, Joe stood by the head of Colonel while the latter lapped brown sugar from the timid palm of the boy. Then the horse was wont to touch the face of Joe with his big, hairy lips as a tribute to his generosity. Colonel had seemed to acquire a singular attachment for the boy and the dog, while Pete distrusted both of them. He had never a moment's leisure, anyhow, being always busy with his work or the flies. A few breaks in the pack basket had been repaired with green withes. It creaked with its load of jerked venison when put aboard. The meat of the bear was nicely wrapped in his hide and placed beside it. They sold meat and hide and bounty rights in the next village they reached for thirty long shillings.

"That cheers up the ol' weasel," Samson declared, as they went on.

"He got a hard knock after we met the Brimsteads," said Sarah.

"Yes, ma'am! and I'm not sorry either. He's got to come out of his hole once in a while. I tell ye God kind o' spoke to us back there in No Santa Claus Land. He kind o' spoke to us."

After a little silence, Sarah said: "I guess He's apt to speak in the voices of little children."

His weasel was a dried pig's bladder of unusual size in which he carried his money. Samson had brought with him a fairly good quantity of money for those days. In a smaller bladder he carried his tobacco.

Farther on the boy got a sore throat. Sarah bound a slice of pork around it and Samson built a camp by the roadside, in which, after a good fire was started, they gave him a hemlock sweat. This they did by steeping hemlock in pails of hot water and, while the patient sat in a chair by the fireside, a blanket was spread about him and pinned close to his neck. Under the blanket they put the pails of steaming hemlock tea. After his sweat and a day and night in bed, with a warm fire burning in front of the shanty, Joe was able to resume his seat in the wagon. They spoke of the Brimsteads and thought it strange that they had not come along.

On the twenty-ninth day after their journey began they came in sight of the beautiful green valley of the Mohawk. As they looked from the hills they saw the roof of the forest dipping down to the river shores and stretching far to the east and west and broken, here and there, by small clearings. Soon they could see the smoke and spires of the thriving village of Utica.

CHAPTER II

AT Utica they bought provisions and a tin trumpet for Joe, and a doll with a real porcelain face for Betsey, and turned into the great main thoroughfare of the north leading eastward to Boston and westward to a shore of the midland seas. This road was once the great trail of the Iroquois, by them called the Long House, because it had reached from the Hudson to Lake Erie, and in their day had been well roofed with foliage. Here the travelers got their first view of a steam engine. The latter stood puffing and smoking near the village of Utica, to the horror and amazement of the team and the great excitement of those in the wagon. The boy clung to his father for fear of it.

Samson longed to get out of the wagon and take a close look at the noisy monster, but his horses were rearing in their haste to get away, and even a short stop was impossible. Sambo, with his tail between his legs, ran ahead, in a panic, and took refuge in some bushes by the roadside.

"What was that, father?" the boy asked when the horses had ceased to worry over this new peril.

"A steam engyne," he answered. "Sarah, did ye get a good look at it?"

"Yes; if that don't beat all the newfangled notions I ever heard of," she exclaimed.

"It's just begun doin' business," said Samson.

"What does it do?" Joe asked.

"On a railroad track it can grab hold of a house full o' folks and run off with it. Goes like the wind, too."

"Does it eat 'em up?" Joe asked.

"No. It eats wood and oil and keeps yellin' for more. I guess it could eat a cord o' wood and wash it down with half a bucket o' castor oil in about five minutes. It snatches folks away to some place and drops 'em. I guess it must make their hair stand up and their teeth chatter."

"Does it hurt anybody?" Joe asked hopefully.

"Well, sir, if anybody wanted to be hurt and got in its way, I rather guess he'd succeed purty well. It's powerful. Why, if a man was to ketch hold of the tail of a locomotive, and hang on, it would jerk the toe nails right off him."

Joe began to have great respect for locomotives.

Soon they came in view of the famous Erie Canal,

hard by the road. Through it the grain of the far West had just begun moving eastward in a tide that was flowing from April to December. Big barges, drawn by mules and horses on its shore, were cutting the still waters of the canal. They stopped and looked at the barges and the long tow ropes and the tugging animals.

"There is a real artificial river, hundreds o' miles long, hand made of the best material, water tight, no snags or rocks or other imperfections, durability guaranteed," said Samson. "It has made the name of DeWitt Clinton known everywhere."

"I wonder what next!" Sarah exclaimed.

They met many teams and passed other movers going west, and some prosperous farms on a road wider and smoother than any they had traveled. They camped that night, close by the river, with a Connecticut family on its way to Ohio with a great load of household furniture on one wagon and seven children in another. There were merry hours for the young, and pleasant visiting between the older folk that evening at the fireside. There was much talk among the latter about the great Erie Canal.

So they fared along through Canandaigua and across the Genesee to the village of Rochester and on through Lewiston and up the Niagara River to the Falls, and camped where they could see the great water flood and hear its muffled thunder. When nearing the latter they overtook a family of poor Irish emigrants, of the name of Flanagan, who shared their camp site at the Falls. The Flanagans were on their way to Michigan and had come from the old country three years before and settled in Broome County, New York. They, too, were on their way to a land of better promise. Among them was a rugged, freckled, red-headed lad, well along in his teens, of the name of Dennis, who wore a tall beaver hat, tilted saucily on one side of his head, and a ragged blue coat with brass buttons, as he walked beside the oxen, whip in hand, with trousers tucked in the tops of his big cow-hide boots. There was also a handsome young man in this party of the name of John McNeil, who wore a ruffled shirt and swallow-tail coat, now much soiled by the journey. He listened to Samson's account of the Sangamon country and said that he thought he would go there. He had traded hats on the way with Dennis, who had been deeply impressed by the majestic look of the beaver and had given a silver breast pin and fifteen shillings to boot.

A jolly lad was Dennis, who danced jigs, on a flat rock by the riverside, as Samson played *The Irish Washerman* and *The Fisher's Hornpipe*. In the midst of the fun a puff of wind snatched the tall beaver hat from his head and whirled it over the side of the cliff into the foliage of a clump of cedars growing out of the steep cliff-side, ten feet or so below its top. Before any one could stop him the brave Irish lad had scrambled down the steep to the cedars—a place of some peril, for they hung over a precipice more than a hundred feet deep above the river. He got his treasure, but Samson had to help him back with a rope.

The latter told of the veiled bear, and when the story was finished he said to the Irish lad: "It will not do you any harm to remember that it is easier to get into trouble than to get out of it. In my opinion one clean-hearted Irish boy is worth more than all the beaver hats in creation."

Sarah gave the Irish family a good supply of cookies and jerked venison before she bade them good-by.

When our travelers left, next morning, they stopped for a last look at the great Falls.

"Children," said Samson, "I want you to take a good look at that. It's the most wonderful thing in the world and maybe you'll never see it again."

"The Indians used to think that the Great Spirit was in this river," said Sarah.

"Kind o' seems to me they were right," Samson remarked thoughtfully. "Kind o' seems as if the great spirit of America was in that water. It moves on in the way it wills and nothing can stop it. Everything in its current goes along with it."

"And only the strong can stand the journey," said Sarah.

These words were no doubt inspired by an ache in

her bones. A hard seat and the ceaseless jolting of the wagon through long, hot, dusty days had wearied them. Even their hearts were getting sore as they thought of the endless reaches of the roads ahead. Samson stuffed a sack with straw and put it under her and the children on the seat. At a word of complaint he was wont to say:

"I know it's awful tiresome, but we got to have patience. We're goin' to get used to it and have a wonderful lot of fun. The time'll pass quick—you see."

Then he would sing and get them all laughing with some curious bit of drollery. They spent the night of July third at a tavern in Buffalo, then a busy, crude and rapidly growing center for the shipping east and west. Next day there was to be a great celebration of the Fourth of July in Buffalo and our travelers had stopped there to witness it. The bells began to ring and the cannon to bomb at sunrise. It was a day of great excitement for the west-bound travelers. The horses trembled in their stalls. Sambo took refuge in Colonel's manger and would not come out.

There were many emigrants on their way to the far West in the crowd—men, women and children and babies in arms—Irish, English, Germans and Yankees. There were also well dressed, handsome young men from the colleges of New England going out to be missionaries "between the desert and the sown."

Buffalo, on the edge of the midland seas, had the

flavor of the rank, new soil in it those days—and
especially that day, when it was thronged with rough
coated and rougher tongued, swearing men on a holiday, stevedores and boatmen off the lakes and rivers
of the middle border—some of whom had had their
training on the Ohio and Mississippi.   There was
much drunkenness and fighting in the crowded streets.
Some of the carriers and handlers of American commerce vented their enthusiasm in song.

In Samson's diary was the refrain of one of these
old lake songs, which he had set down, as best he
could, after the event:

"Then here's three cheers for the skipper an' his crew,
    Give 'er the wind an' let 'er go, for the boys'll put
        'er through;
I thought 'twould blow the whiskers right off o' you
        an' me,
    On our passage up from Buffalo ·to Milwaukee-ee."

Each of these rough men had dressed to his own
fancy.   Many wore fine boots of calf skin with red
tops, drawn over their trousers, and high heels and
blue and red shirts and broad brimmed straw hats.   A
long haired man, in buckskin leggings and moccasins,
with a knife at his belt and too much whisky beneath
it, amused a crowd by a loud proclamation of his own
reckless and redoubtable character and a louder appeal
for a chance to put it in action.   It was a droll bit of
bragging and merely intended, as the chronicler in-
forms us, to raise a laugh.

"Here I be half man an' half alligator," he shouted. "Oh, I'm one o' yer tough kind, live forever an' then turn into a hickory post. I've just crept out o' the ma'shes of ol' Kentuck. I'm only a yearlin', but cuss me if I don't think I can whip anybody in this part o' the country. I'm the chap that towed the Broadhorn up Salt River where the snags was so thick a fish couldn't swim without rubbin' his scales off. Cock a doodle doo! I'm the infant that refused his milk before his eyes was open an' called for a bottle o' rum. Talk about grinnin' the bark off a tree—that ain't nothin'. One look o' mine would raise a blister on a bull's heel. Cock a doodle doo! (slapping his thighs). Gol darn it! Ain't there some one that dast come up an' collar me? It would just please my vitals if there was some man here who could split me into shoe pegs. I deserve it if ever a man did. I'll have to go home an' have another settlement with ol' Bill Sims. He's purty well gouged up, an' ain't but one ear, but he's willin' to do his best. That's somethin'. It kind o' stays yer appetite, an' I suppose that's all a man like me can expect in this world o' sorrow."

At this point a tall, raw-boned woman in "a brindle dress" (to quote the phrase of Samson), wearing a large gilt pin just below her collar, with an ortho-graphic design which spelled the name Minnie, approached the hero and boldly boxed his ears.

"Licked at last," he shouted as he picked up his hat,

dislodged by the violence he had suffered, and retired from the scene with a good-natured laugh.

Sarah was a bit dismayed by the behavior of these rough forerunners of civilization.

"Don't worry," said Samson, as they were driving away on the Lake Road next morning. "The lake and river boatmen are the roughest fellers in the West, and they're not half as bad as they look an' talk. Their deviltry is all on the outside. They tell me that there isn't one o' those boys who wouldn't give his life to help a woman, an' I guess it's so."

They had the lake view and its cool breeze on their way to Silver Creek, Dunkirk and Erie, and a rough way it was in those days.

Enough has been written of this long and wearisome journey, but the worst of it was ahead of them—much the worst of it—in the swamp flats of Ohio and Indiana. In one of the former a wagon wheel broke down, and that day Sarah began to shake with ague and burn with fever. Samson built a rude camp by the roadside, put Sarah into bed under its cover and started for the nearest village on Colonel's back.

"I shall never forget that day spent in a lonely part of the woods," the good woman wrote to her brother. "It endeared the children to me more than any day I can remember. They brought water from the creek, a great quantity of which I drank, and bathed my aching head and told me stories and cheered me in

every way they could. Joe had his bear stick handy
and his plans for bears or wolves or Indians. Samson
had made some nails at a smithy in Pennsylvania. Joe
managed to drive one of them through an end of his
bear stick and made, as he thought, a formidable
weapon. With his nail he hoped to penetrate the
bear's eye. He had also put some bacon in the bottom
of the pack basket, knowing the liking of the basket
for bears. My faith in God's protection was perfect
and in spite of my misery the children were a great
comfort. In the middle of the afternoon Samson returned with a doctor and some tools and a stick of
seasoned timber. How good he looked when he came
and knelt by my bed and kissed me! This is a hard
journey, but a woman can bear anything with such a
man. The doctor gave me Sapington's fever pills and
said I would be all right in three days, and I was.

"Late that afternoon it began to rain. Samson was
singing as he worked on his wheel. A traveler came
along on horseback and saw our plight. He was a
young missionary going west. Samson began to joke
with him.

" 'You're a happy man for one in so much trouble,'
said the stranger.

"Then I heard Samson say: 'Well, sir, I'm in a fix
where happiness is absolutely necessary. It's like
grease on the wagon wheels—we couldn't go on without it. When we need anything we make it if we can.
My wife is sick and the wagon is broke and it's raining and night is near in a lonesome country, and it
ain't a real good time for me to be down in the mouth
—is it now? We haven't broke any bones or had an

earthquake or been scalped by Indians, so there's some
room for happiness.'

"'Look here, stranger—I like you,' said the man.
'If there's anything I can do to help ye, I'll stop
a while.'"

He spent the night with them and helped mend the
felly and set the tire.

The fever and ague passed from one to another
and all were sick before the journey ended, although
Samson kept the reins in hand through his misery.
There were many breaks to mend, but Samson's in-
genuity was always equal to the task.

One day, near nightfall, they were overtaken by a
tall, handsome Yankee lad riding a pony. His pony
stopped beside the wagon and looked toward the travelers as if appealing for help. The boy was pointing
toward the horizon and muttering. Sarah saw at
once that his mind was wandering in the delirium of
fever. She got out of the wagon and took his hand.
The moment she did so he began crying like a child.

"This boy is sick," she said to Samson, who came
and helped him off his horse. They camped for the
night and put the boy to bed and gave him medicine
and tender care. He was too sick to travel next day.
The Traylors stayed with him and nursed the lad
until he was able to go on. He was from Niagara
County, New York, and his name was Harry Needles.
His mother had died when he was ten and his father

had married again. He had not been happy in his home after that and his father had given him a pony and a hundred dollars and sent him away to seek his own fortune. Homesick and lonely and ill, and just going west with a sublime faith that the West would somehow provide for him, he might even have perished on the way if he had not fallen in with friendly people. His story had touched the heart of Sarah and Samson. He was a big, green, gentle-hearted country boy who had set out filled with hope and the love of adventure. Sarah found pleasure in mothering the poor lad, and so it happened that he became one of their little party. He was helpful and good-natured and had sundry arts that pleased the children. The man and the woman liked the big, honest lad.

One day he said to Samson: "I hope you won't mind if I go along with you, sir."

"Glad to have you with us," said Samson. "We've talked it over. If you want to, you can come along with us and our home shall be yours and I'll do what's right by you."

They fared along through Indiana and over the wide savannas of Illinois, and on the ninety-seventh day of their journey they drove through rolling, grassy, flowering prairies and up a long, hard hill to the small log cabin settlement of New Salem, Illinois, on the shore of the Sangamon. They halted about noon in the middle of this little prairie village, opposite a small

John Wolcott Adams

clapboarded house. A sign hung over its door which bore the rudely lettered words: "Rutledge's Tavern."

A long, slim, stoop-shouldered young man sat in the shade of an oak tree that stood near a corner of the tavern, with a number of children playing around him. He had sat leaning against the tree trunk reading a book. He had risen as they came near and stood looking at them, with the book under his arm. Samson says in his diary that he looked like "an untrimmed yearling colt about sixteen hands high. He got up slow and kept rising till his bush of black tousled hair was six feet four above the ground. Then he put on an old straw hat without any band on it. He reminded me of Philemon Baker's fish rod, he was that narrer. For humliness I'd match him against the world. His hide was kind o' yaller and leathery. I could see he was still in the gristle—a little over twenty—but his face was marked up by worry and weather like a man's. I never saw anybody so long between joints. Don't hardly see how he could tell when his feet got cold."

He wore a hickory shirt without a collar or coat or jacket. One suspender held up his coarse, linsey trousers, the legs of which fitted closely and came only to a blue yarn zone above his heavy cowhide shoes. Samson writes that he "fetched a sneeze and wiped his big nose with a red handkerchief" as he stood surveying them in silence, while Dr. John Allen, who had sat on the door-step reading a paper—a kindly faced man of middle age with a short white beard under his chin—greeted them cheerfully.

The withering sunlight of a day late in August fell upon the dusty street, now almost deserted. Faces at the doors and windows of the little houses were looking out at them. Two ragged boys and a ginger colored dog came running toward the wagon. The latter and Sambo surveyed each other with raised hair and began scratching the earth, straight legged, whining meanwhile, and in a moment began to play together. A man in blue jeans who sat on the veranda of a store opposite, leaning against its wall, stopped whittling and shut his jack-knife.

"Where do ye hail from?" the Doctor asked.

"Vermont," said Samson.

"All the way in that wagon?"

"Yes, sir."

"I guess you're made o' the right stuff," said the Doctor. "Where ye bound?"

"Don't know exactly. Going to take up a claim somewhere."

"There's no better country than right here. This is the Canaan of America. We need people like you. Unhitch your team and have some dinner and we'll talk things over after you're rested. I'm the doctor here and I ride all over this part o' the country. I reckon I know it pretty well."

A woman in a neat calico dress came out of the

door—a strong built and rather well favored woman with blonde hair and dark eyes.

"Mrs. Rutledge, these are travelers from the East," said the Doctor. "Give 'em some dinner, and if they can't pay for it, I can. They've come all the way from Vermont."

"Good land! Come right in an' rest yerselves. Abe, you show the gentleman where to put his horses an' lend him a hand."

Abe extended his long arm toward Samson and said "Howdy" as they shook hands.

"When his big hand got hold of mine, I kind of felt his timber," Samson writes. "I says to myself, 'There's a man it would be hard to tip over in a rassle.' "

"What's yer name? How long ye been travelin'? My conscience! Ain't ye wore out?" the hospitable Mrs. Rutledge was asking as she went into the house with Sarah and the children. "You go and mix up with the little ones and let yer mother rest while I git dinner," she said to Joe and Betsey, and added as she took Sarah's shawl and bonnet: "You lop down an' rest yerself while I'm flyin' around the fire."

"Come all the way from Vermont?" Abe asked as he and Samson were unhitching.

"Yes, sir."

"By jing!" the slim giant exclaimed. "I reckon you feel like throwin' off yer harness an' takin' a roll in the grass."

CHAPTER III

WHEREIN THE READER IS INTRODUCED TO OFFUT'S STORE AND HIS CLERK ABE, AND THE SCHOLAR JACK KELSO AND HIS CABIN AND HIS DAUGHTER BIM, AND GETS A FIRST LOOK AT LINCOLN.

THEY had a dinner of prairie chickens and roast venison, flavored with wild grape jelly, and creamed potatoes and cookies and doughnuts and raisin pie. It was a well cooked dinner, served on white linen, in a clean room, and while they were eating, the sympathetic landlady stood by the table, eager to learn of their travels and to make them feel at home. The good food and their kindly welcome and the beauty of the rolling, wooded prairies softened the regret which had been growing in their hearts, and which only the children had dared to express.

"Perhaps we haven't made a mistake after all," Sarah whispered when the dinner was over. "I like these people and the prairies are beautiful."

"It is the land of plenty at last," said Samson, as they came out-of-doors. "It is even better than I thought."

"As Douglas Jerrold said of Australia: 'Tickle it with a hoe and it laughs with a harvest,'" said Dr.

46

Allen, who still sat in the shaded dooryard, smoking his pipe. "I have an extra horse and saddle. Suppose you leave the family with Mrs. Rutledge and ride around with me a little this afternoon. I can show you how the land lies off to the west of us, and to-morrow we'll look at the other side."

"Thank you—I want to look around here a little," said Samson. "What's the name of this place?"

"New Salem. We call it a village. It has a mill, a carding machine, a tavern, a schoolhouse, five stores, fourteen houses, two or three men of genius, and a noisy dam. You will hear other damns, if you stay here long enough, but they don't amount to much. It's a crude but growing place and soon it will have all the embellishments of civilized life."

That evening many of the inhabitants of the little village came to the tavern to see the travelers and were introduced by Dr. Allen. Most of them had come from Kentucky, although there were two Yankee families who had moved on from Ohio.

"These are good folks," said the Doctor. "There are others who are not so good. I could show you some pretty rough customers at Clary's Grove, not far from here. We have to take things as they are and do our best to make 'em better."

"Any Indians?" Sarah asked.

"You see one now and then, but they're peaceable. Most of 'em have gone with the buffalos—farther west. We have make-believe Indians—some reckless white boys who come whooping into the village, half crazy with drink, once in a while. They're not so bad as they seem to be. We'll have to do a little missionary work with them. The Indians have left their imitators all over the West, but they only make a loud noise. That will pass away soon. It's a noisy land. Now and then a circuit rider gets here and preaches to us. You'll hear the Reverend Stephen Nuckles if you settle in these parts. He can holler louder than any man in the state."

"You bet he can holler some when he gits fixed for it," said Abe, who sat near the open door.

"He's for them that need scarin'. The man that don't need that has to be his own preacher here and sow and reap his own morality. He can make himself just as much of a saint as he pleases."

"If he has the raw material to work with," Abe interposed.

"The self-made saint is the only kind I believe in," said Samson.

"We haven't any Erie Canal to Heaven, with the minister towin' us along," said Abe. "There's some that say it's only fifteen miles to Springfield, but the man that walks it knows better."

The tavern was the only house in New Salem with stairs in it. Stairs so steep, as Samson writes, that "they were first cousins to the ladder." There were four small rooms above them. Two of these were separated by a partition of cloth hanging from the rafters. In each was a bed and bedstead and smaller beds on the floor. In case there were a number of adult guests the bedstead was screened with sheets hung upon strings. In one of these rooms the travelers had a night of refreshing sleep.

After riding two days with the Doctor, Samson bought the claim of one Isaac Gollaher to a half section of land a little more than a mile from the western end of the village. He chose a site for his house on the edge of an open prairie.

"Now we'll go over and see Abe," said Dr. Allen, after the deal was made. "He's the best man with an axe and a saw in this part of the country. He clerks for Mr. Offut. Abe Lincoln is one of the best fellows that ever lived—a rough diamond just out of the great mine of the West, that only needs to be cut and polished."

Denton Offut's store was a small log structure about twenty by twenty which stood near the brow of the hill east of Rutledge's Tavern. When they entered it Abe lay at full length on the counter, his head resting on a bolt of blue denim as he studied a book in his hand. He wore the same shirt and one suspender and linsey trousers which he had worn in the dooryard of the tavern, but his feet were covered only by his blue yarn socks.

It was a general store full of exotic flavors, chiefly those of tea, coffee, whisky, tobacco, muscovado sugar and molasses.   There was a counter on each side. Bolts of cloth, mostly calico, were piled on the far end of the right counter as one entered and the near end held a show case containing a display of cutlery, pewter spoons, jewelry and fishing tackle.   There were double windows on either side of the rough board door with its wooden latch.   The left counter held a case filled with threads, buttons, combs, colored ribbons, and belts and jew's-harps. A balance stood in the middle of this counter.   A chest of tea, a big brown jug, a box of candles, a keg and a large wooden pail occupied its farther end.   The shelving on its side walls was filled by straw hats, plug tobacco, bolts of cloth, pills and patent medicines and paste-board boxes containing shirts, handkerchiefs and underwear. A suit of blue jeans, scythes and snaths, hoes, wooden hand rakes and a brass warming-pan hung from the rafters. At the rear end of the store was a large fireplace. There were two chairs near the fireplace, both of which were occupied by a man who sat in one while his feet lay on the other.   He was sleeping peacefully, his chin resting on his breast.   He wore a calico shirt with a fanciful design of morning-glories on it printed in appropriate colors, a collar of the same material and a red necktie.

Abe laid aside his book and rose to a sitting posture.

"Pardon me—you see the firm is busy," said Abe. "You know Eb Zane used to say that he was never so busy in his life as when he lay on his back with a broken leg. He said he had to work twenty-four hours a day doin' nothin' an' could never git an hour off. But a broken leg is not so bad as a lame intellect. That lays you out with the fever an' ague of ignorance. Jack Kelso recommended Kirkham's pills and poultices of poetry. I'm trying both and slowly getting the better of it. I've learned three conjugations, between customers, this afternoon."

The man sleeping in the chair began snoring and groaning.

"Don't blame Bill," Abe went on. "Any man would have the nightmare in a shirt like that. He went to a dance at Clary's Grove last night and they shut him up in a barrel with a small dog and rolled 'em down hill in it. I reckon that's how he learnt how to growl."

In the laughter that followed the sleeper awoke.

"You see there's quite an undercurrent beneath the placid surface of our enterprise," Abe added.

The sleeper whose name was William Berry rose and stretched himself and was introduced to the newcomer. He was a short, genial man, of some thirty years, with blond, curly hair and mustache. On account of his shortness and high color he was often referred to as the Billberry shortcake. His fat cheeks had a color as definite as that of the blossoms on his shirt, now rather soiled. His prominent nose shared their glow of ruddy opulence. His gray eyes wore a look of apology. He walked rather stiffly as if his legs were rheumatic.

"Mr. Traylor, this is Mr. William Berry," said Dr. Allen. "In this beautiful shirt he resembles a bit of vine-clad sculpture from an Italian garden, but is real flesh and blood and a good fellow."

"I don't understand your high-toned talk," said Berry. "This shirt suits me to a dot."

"It is the pride of New Salem," said the Doctor. "Mr. Traylor has just acquired an interest in all our institutions. He has bought the Gollaher tract and is going to build a house and some fences. Abe, couldn't you help get the timber out in a hurry so we can have a raising within a week? You know the arts of the axe better than any of us."

Abe looked at Samson.

"I reckon he and I would make a good team with the axe," he said. "He looks as if he could push a house down with one hand and build it up with the other. You can bet I'll be glad to help in any way I can."

"We'll all turn in and help. I should think Bill or Jack Kelso could look after the store for a few days," said the Doctor. "I promised to take Mr. Traylor over to Jack Kelso's to-night. Couldn't you come along?"

"Good! We'll have a story-tellin' and get Jack to unlimber his guns," said Abe.

It was a cool evening with a promise of frost in the

air. Jack Kelso's cabin, one of two which stood close together at the western end of the village, was lighted by the cheery blaze of dry logs in its fireplace. There were guns on a rack over the fireplace under a buck's head; a powder horn hanging near them on its string looped over a nail. There were wolf and deer and bear pelts on the floor. The skins of foxes, raccoons and wildcats adorned the log walls. Jack Kelso was a blond, smooth faced, good-looking, merry-hearted Scot, about forty years old, of a rather slight build, some five feet, eight inches tall. That is all that any one knew of him save that he spent most of his time hunting and fishing and seemed to have all the best things, which great men had said or written, on the tip of his tongue. He was neatly dressed in a blue flannel coat and shirt, top boots and riding breeches.

"Welcome! and here's the best seat at the fireside," he said to Samson.

Then, as he filled his pipe, he quoted the lines from Cymbeline:

" 'Think us no churls nor measure our good minds
  By this rude place we live in.'

"My wife and daughter are away for a visit and for two days I've had the cabin to myself. Look, ye worshipers of fire, and see how fine it is now! The homely cabin is a place of beauty. Everything has the color of the rose, coming and going in the flickering shadows. What a heaven it is when the flames are leaping! Here is Hogarth's line of beauty; nothing perpendicular or horizontal."

He took Abe's hand and went on: "Here, ye lovers of romance, is one of the story-tellers of Ispahan who has in him the wisdom of the wandering tribes. He can tell you a tale that will draw children from their play and old men from the chimney corner. My boy, take a chair next to Mr. Traylor."

He took the hand of the Doctor and added: "Here, too, is a man whose wit is more famous than his pills— one produces the shakes and the other cures them. Doctor, you and I will take the end seats."

"My pills can be relied upon but my wit is like my dog, away from home most of the time," said the Doctor.

"Gathering the bones with which you often astonish us," said Kelso. "How are the lungs, Doctor?"

"They're all right. These long rides in the open are making a new man of me. Another year in the city would have used me up."

"Mr. Traylor, you stand up as proud and firm as a big pine," Kelso remarked. "I believe you're a Yankee."

"So do I," said Samson. "If you took all the Yankee out o' me I'd have an empty skin."

Then Abe began to show the stranger his peculiar art in these words:

"Stephen Nuckles used to say: 'God's grace embraces the isles o' the sea an' the uttermost parts o' the earth. It takes in the Esquimaux an' the Hottentots. Some go so fur as to say that it takes in the Yankees but I don't go so fur.' "

Samson joined in the good-natured laughter that followed.

"If you deal with some Yankees you take your life in your hands," he said. "They can serve God or Mammon and I guess they have given the Devil some of his best ideas. He seems to be getting a lot of Yankee notions lately."

"There was a powerful prejudice in Kentucky against the Yankees," Abe went on. "Down there they used to tell about a Yankee who sold his hogs and was driving them to town. On the way he decided that he had sold them too cheap. He left them with his drover in the road and went on to town and told the buyer that he would need help to bring 'em in.

" 'How's that?' the buyer asked.

" 'Why they git away an' go to runnin' through the woods an' fields an' we can't keep up with 'em.'

" 'I don't think I want 'em,' says the buyer. 'A speedy hog hasn't much pork to carry. I'll give ye twenty bits to let me off.' "

"I guess that Yankee had one more hog than he'd counted," said Samson.

"It reminds me of a man in Pope County who raised the biggest hog in Illinois," Abe went on. "It was a famous animal and people from far and near came to see him. One day a man came an' asked to see the hog.

" 'We're chargin' two bits for the privilege now, said the owner.

"The man paid the money and got into his wagon.

" 'Don't you want to see him?' the farmer asked.

" 'No,' said the stranger. 'I've seen the biggest hog in Illinois an' I don't care to look at a smaller one.' "

"Whatever prejudice you may find here will soon vanish," said Kelso, turning to the newcomer. "I have great respect for the sturdy sons of New England. I believe it was Theodore Parker who said that the pine was the symbol of their character. He was right. Its roots are deep in the soil; it towers above the forest; it has the strength of tall masts and the substance of the builder in its body, music in its waving branches and turpentine in its veins. I thought of this when I saw Webster and heard him speak at Plymouth."

"What kind of a looking man is he?" Abe asked.

"A big erect, splendid figure of a man. He walked like a ram at the head of his flock. As he began speaking I thought of that flash of Homer's in the *Odyssey*:

" 'When his great voice went forth out of his breast and his words fell like the winter snows—not then would any mortal contend with Ulysses.' "

'Abe who since his story had sat with a sad face look-ing into the fire now leaned forward, his elbows on his knees, and shook his head with interest while his gray eyes took on a look of animation. The diary speaks often of the "veil of sadness" on his face.

"He is a very great man," Abe exclaimed.

"Have you learned that last noble flight of his in the reply to Hayne as you promised?" Kelso asked.

"I have," said Abe, "and the other day when I was tramping back from Bowlin Green's I came across a drove of cattle and stopped and gave it to them. They all let go of the grass and stood looking. By an' by the bull thought he'd stood it as long as he could an' bellered back at me."

"Good! Now stand up and let us see how you imi- tate the great chief of the Whig clan," said Kelso.

The lank and awkward youth rose and began to speak the lines in a high pitched voice that trembled with excitement. It lowered and steadied and rang out like noble music on a well played trumpet as the channel of his spirit filled with the mighty current of the orator's passion. Then, indeed, the words fell from his lips "like the winter snows."

"They shook our hearts as the wind shakes the branches of a tree," Samson writes in his diary. "The lean, bony body of the boy was transfigured and as I looked at his face in the firelight I thought it was hand-some.

"Not a word was spoken for a minute after he sat

down. I had got my first look at Lincoln. I had seen his soul. I think it was then I began to realize that a man was being made among us 'more precious than fine gold; even a man more precious than the golden wedge of Ophir.' "

The Doctor gazed in silence at the boy. Kelso sat with both hands in his pockets and his chin upon his breast looking solemnly into the fire.

"Thank you, Abe," he said in a low voice. "Something unusual has happened and I'm just a little scared."

"Why?" Abe asked.

"For fear somebody will spoil it with another hog story. I'm a little afraid of anything I can say. I would venture this, that the man Webster is a prophet. In his Plymouth address he hears receding into never returning distance the clank of chains and all the horrid din of slavery. It will come true."

"Do you think so?" Abe asked.

"Surely—there are so many of us who hate it. These Yankees hate it and they and their children are scattering all over the midlands. Their spirit will guide the West. The love of Liberty is the salt of their blood and the marrow of their bones. Liberty means freedom for all. Wait until these babies, coming out here by the wagon load, have grown to manhood. Slavery will have to reckon with them."

"I hate it too," said Abe. "Down the Mississippi I have seen men and women sold like oxen. If I live I'm going to hit that thing on the head some day."

"Do you still want to be a lawyer?" Kelso asked.

"Yes, but sometimes I think I'd make a better blacksmith," said Abe.

"I believe you'd do better with the hammer of argument."

"If I had the education likely I would. I'm trying to make up my mind what's best for me."

"No, you're trying to decide what is best for your friends and your country and for the reign of law and justice and liberty."

"But I think every man acts from selfish motives," Abe insisted.

Dr. Allen demurred as follows:

"The other night you happened to remember that you had overcharged Mrs. Peters for a jug of molasses and after you had closed the store you walked three miles to return the money which belonged to her. Why did you do it?"

"For a selfish motive," said Abe. "I believe honesty is the best policy."

"Then you took that long walk just to advertise your honesty—to induce people to call you 'Honest Abe' as they have begun to do?"

"I wouldn't want to put it that way," said Abe.

"But that's the only way out," the Doctor insisted, "and we knowing ones would have to call you 'Sordid Abe.'"

"There's a hidden Abe and you haven't got acquainted with him yet," Kelso interposed. "We have all caught a glimpse of him to-night. He's the Abe that loves honor and justice and humanity and their great temple of freedom that is growing up here in the new world. He loves them better than fame or fortune or life itself. I think it must have been that Abe whose voice sounded like a trumpet just now and who sent you off to Mrs. Peters with the money. You haven't the chance to know him that we have. Some day you two will get acquainted."

"I don't know how to plead to that indictment," Abe answered. "It looks so serious I shall have to take counsel."

At this moment there was a loud rap on the door. Mr. Kelso opened it and said: "Hello, Eli! Come in."

A hairy faced, bow legged man, bent under a great pack, partly covered with bed ticking, stood in the doorway.

"Hello, Mr. Kelso," the bearded man answered. "The poor vandering Jew has gome back ag'in—hey? I tink I haf to take de hump off my back before I gits in."

Staggering beneath his load he let it down to the ground.

"Bring in your Trojan horse and mind you do not let out its four and twenty warriors until morning. I'll have some bread and milk for you in a minute. Gentlemen, this is my friend Eli—a wandering pioneer of trade."

"I haf a vonderful line o' goods—vonderful! vonderful!" said the Jew, gesturing with both hands. "Silk an' satin! De flowers o' de prairie, de birds o' de air could not show you colors like dem. You vill fall in love. If I do not let you have dem you vill break your hearts. An' I have here one instrument dot make all kind o' music."

"First supper—then open your Trojan horse," said Kelso.

"First I must show my goods," the Jew insisted, "an' I'll bet you take dem all—everyt'ing vat I have in dot pack an' you pay my price an' you t'ank me an' say 'Eli, vat you have to drink?'"

"I'll bet you four bits I don't," said Kelso.

"You are my frient; I vould not take your money like dot so easy. No! It vould not be right. These are Scotch goods, gentlemen—so rare an' beautiful—not'ing like dem in de world."

He began to undo his pack while the little company stood around him.

"Gentlemen, you can see but you can not buy. Only my frient can have dem goods," he went on glibly as he removed the cover of the pack.

Suddenly there was a lively stir in it. To the amazement of all a beautiful girl threw aside the ticking and leaped out of the large wicker basket it had covered. With a merry laugh she threw her arms around Jack Kelso's neck and kissed him.

The men clapped their hands in noisy merriment.

"That's like Bim, isn't it?" said the Doctor.

"Exactly!" Abe exclaimed.

"I stop at David Barney's an' dere she took de goods out o' my pack an' fix up dis job lot fer you," said Eli with a laugh.

"A real surprise party!" the girl exclaimed.

She was a small sized girl, nearing sixteen, with red cheeks and hazel eyes and blonde hair that fell in curls upon her shoulders.

"Mr. Traylor, this is my daughter Bim," said Kelso. "She is skilled in the art of producing astonishment."

"She must have heard of that handsome boy at the tavern and got in a hurry to come home," said the Doctor.

"Ann Rutledge says that he is a right purty boy," the girl laughed as she brushed her curls aside.

She turned to Samson Traylor and asked wistfully, "Do you suppose he would play with me?"

CHAPTER IV

WHICH PRESENTS OTHER LOG CABIN FOLK AND THE
FIRST STEPS IN THE MAKING OF A NEW HOME AND
CERTAIN CAPACITIES AND INCAPACITIES OF ABE.

NEXT morning at daylight two parties went out in
the woods to cut timber for the home of the newcomers. In one party were Harry Needles carrying
two axes and a well filled luncheon pail; Samson with
a saw in his hand and the boy Joe on his back; Abe
with saw and axe and a small jug of root beer and a
book tied in a big red handkerchief and slung around
his neck. When they reached the woods Abe cut a
pole for the small boy and carried him on his shoulder
to the creek and said:

"Now you sit down here and keep order in this
little frog city. If you hear a frog say anything im-
proper you fetch him a whack. Don't allow any nonsense. We'll make you Mayor of Frog City."

The men fell to with axes and saws while Harry
limbed the logs and looked after the Mayor. Their
huge muscles flung the sharp axes into the timber and
gnawed through it with the saw. Many big trees fell
before noon time when they stopped for luncheon.
While they were eating Abe said:

"I reckon we better saw out a few boards this afternoon. Need 'em for the doors. We'll tote a cou-

ple of logs up on the side o' that knoll, put 'em on skids an' whip 'em up into boards with the saw."

Samson took hold of the middle of one of the logs and raised it from the ground.

"I guess we can carry 'em," he said.

"Can ye shoulder it?" Abe asked.

"Easy," said Samson as he raised an end of the log, stepped beneath it and, resting its weight on his back, soon got his shoulder near its center and swung it clear of the ground and walked with it to the knoll-side where he let it fall with a resounding thump that shook the ground. Abe stopped eating and watched every move in this remarkable performance. The ease with which the big Vermonter had so defied the law of gravitation with that unwieldly stick amazed him.

"That thing'll weigh from seven to eight hundred pounds," said he. "I reckon you're the stoutest man in this part o' the state an' I'm quite a man myself. I've lifted a barrel o' whisky and put my mouth to the bung hole. I never drink it."

"Say," he added as he sat down and began eating a doughnut. "If you ever hit anybody take a sledge hammer or a crowbar. It wouldn't be decent to use your fist."

"Don't talk when you've got food in your mouth," said Joe who seemed to have acquired a sense of re-sponsibility for the manners of Abe.

"I reckon you're right," Abe laughed. "A man's

ideas ought not to be mingled with cheese and doughnuts."

"Once in a while I like to try myself in a lift," said
Samson. "It feels good. I don't do it to show off.
I know there's a good many men stouter than I be.
I guess you're one of 'em."

"No, I'm too stretched out—my neck is too far from
the ground," Abe answered. "I'm like a crowbar. If
I can get my big toe or my fingers under anything I
can pry some."

After luncheon he took off his shoes and socks.

"When I'm working hard I always try to give my
feet a rest and my brain a little work at noon time,"
he remarked. "My brain is so far behind the procession I have to keep putting the gad on it. Give me
twenty minutes of Kirkham and I'll be with you
again."

He lay down on his back under a tree with his book
in hand and his feet resting on the tree trunk well
above him. Soon he was up and at work again.

They hewed a flat surface on opposite sides of the
log which Samson had carried and peeled it and raised
its lower end on a cross timber. Then they marked
it with a chalk line and sliced it into inch boards with
a whip saw, Abe standing on top of the log and Samson beneath it. Suddenly the saw stopped. A clear,
beautiful voice flung the music of *Sweet Nightingale*
into the timbered hollow. It halted the workers and
set the woodland ringing. The men stood silent like

those hearing a benediction. The singing ceased. Still they listened for half a moment. It was as if a spirit had passed and touched them.

"It's Bim—the little vixen!" said Abe tenderly. "She's hiding here in the woods somewheres."

Abe straightened up and peered through the bushes. The singing ceased.

"I can see yer curls. Come out from behind that tree—you piece o' Scotch goods!" Abe shouted.

Only silence followed his demand.

"Come on," Abe persisted. "There's a good-looking boy here and I want to introduce you."

"Ask him to see if he can find me," said the voice of the girl from a distance.

Abe beckoned to Harry and pointed to the tree behind which he had seen her hiding. Harry stealthily approached it only to find that she had gone. He looked about for a moment but could not see her. Soon they heard a little call, suggesting elfland trumpets, in a distant part of the wood. It was repeated three or four times; each time fainter and farther. They saw and heard no more of her that day.

"She's an odd child and as pretty as a spotted fawn, and about as wild," said Abe. "She's a kind of a first cousin to the bobolink."

When they were getting ready to go home that afternoon Joe got into a great hurry to see his mother. It seemed to him that ages had elapsed since he had seen her—a conviction which led to noisy tears.

Abe knelt before him and comforted the boy. Then he wrapped him in his jacket and swung him in the air and started for home with Joe astride his neck.

Samson says in his diary: "His tender play with the little lad gave me another look at the man Lincoln."

"Some one proposed once that we should call that stream the Minnehaha," said Abe as he walked along. "After this Joe and I are going to call it the Minneboohoo."

The women of the little village had met at a quilting party at ten o'clock with Mrs. Martin Waddell. There Sarah had had a seat at the frame and heard all the gossip of the countryside. The nimble fingered Ann Rutledge—a daughter of the tavern folk—had sat beside her. Ann was a slender, good-looking girl of seventeen with blue eyes and a rich crown of auburn hair and a fair skin well browned by the sunlight. She was the most dexterous needle worker in New Salem. It was Mrs. Peter Lukins, a very lean, red haired woman with only one eye which missed no matrimonial prospect—who put the ball in play so to speak.

"Ann, if Honest Abe gits you, you'll have to spend the first three months makin' a pair o' breeches for him. It'll be a mile o' sewin'."

"I reckon she'd have to spend the rest o' her life keepin' the buttons on 'em," said Mrs. John Cameron.

"Abe doesn't want me and I don't want Abe so I reckon some other girl will have to make his breeches," said Ann.

"My lord! but he's humbly," said Mrs. Alexander Ferguson.

"Han'some is that han'some does," Mrs. Martin Waddell remarked. "I don't know anybody that does han'somer."

"Han'some is that han'some looks I say," Mrs. Lukins continued with a dreamy look in her eye.

"I like a man that'll bear inspection—up an' a comin' an' neat an' trim as a buck deer," Mrs. Ferguson confessed.

"An' the first ye know he's up an' a goin'," said Mrs. Samuel Hill. "An then all ye have to look at is a family o' children an' the empty bread box."

"Wait until Abe has shed his coat an' is filled out a little. He'll be a good-lookin' man an' I wouldn't wonder," Mrs. Waddell maintained.

"If Abe lives he'll be a great man, I think," said Mrs. Dr. Allen. "I forgot how he looked when I heard him talking the other night at the debate in the schoolhouse about the flogging of sailors with the cat o' nine tails. He has a wonderful gift. If I were Ann I should be proud of his friendship and proud to go with him to the parties."

"I am," said Ann meekly, with her eyes upon her work. "I love to hear him talk, too."

"Oh, land o' mercy! He's good company if you only use your ears," Mrs. Ferguson remarked. "Mis' Traylor, where did you git your man?"

"At Vergennes. We were born in the same neighborhood and grew up together," said Sarah.

"Now there's the kind of a man! Stout as a buffalo an' as to looks I'd call him, as ye might say, real copasetic." Mrs. Lukins expressed this opinion solemnly and with a slight cough. Its last word stood for nothing more than an indefinite depth of meaning. She added by way of drawing the curtain of history: "I'll bet *he* didn't dilly dally long when he made up his mind. I reckon he were plum owdacious."

"What a pretty pattern this is!" said Sarah with a sudden shift of front.

Mrs. Lukins was not to be driven from the Elysian fields so easily and forthwith she told the story of her own courtship.

A bountiful dinner of stewed venison and chicken pie and tea and frosted cake was served, all hands turning in to help with the table and the cleaning up. While they were eating Sarah told of her long journey and their trials with fever and ague.

"It's the worst part of going west but it really isn't very dangerous," said Mrs. Dr. Allen.

"Nine scoops o' water in the holler o' the hand from a good spring for three mornin's before sunrise an' strong coffee with lemon juice will break the ager every time," said Mrs. Lukins. "My gran' mammy used to say it were better than all the doctors an' I've tried it an' know what it'll do."

"I suppose if you got ten scoops it would be no good," said Sarah with a laugh in which Mrs. Allen and some of the others joined.

Mrs. Lukins looked offended. "When I'm takin' medicine I always foller directions," said she.

So the day passed with them and was interrupted by the noisy entrance of Joe, soon after candlelight, who climbed on the back of his mother's chair and kissed her and in breathless eagerness began to relate the history of his own day.

That ended the quilting party and Sarah and Mrs. Rutledge and Ann joined Samson and Abe and Harry Needles who were waiting outside and walked to the tavern with them.

John McNeil, whom the Traylors had met on the road near Niagara Falls and who had shared their camp with them, arrived on the stage that evening. He was dressed in a new butternut suit and clean linen and looked very handsome. Samson writes that he resembled the pictures of Robert Emmet. With fine, dark eyes, a smooth skin, well moulded features and black hair neatly brushed on a shapely head he was not at all like the rugged Abe. In a low tone and very modestly, with a slight brogue on his tongue he told of his adventures on the long, shore road to Michigan. Ann sat listening and looking into his face as he talked. Abe came in, soon after eight o'clock, and was introduced to the stranger. All noted the contrast between the two young men as they greeted each other. Abe sat down for a few minutes and looked sadly into the fire but said nothing.   He rose presently, excused himself and went away.

Soon Samson followed him.   Over at Offut's store he did not find Abe, but Bill Berry was drawing liquor from the spigot of a barrel set on blocks in a shed connected with the rear end of the store and serving it to a number of hilarious young Irishmen.   His shirt was soiled.   Its morning-glories had grown dim in a kind of dusty twilight.   The young men asked Samson to join them.

"No, thank you.   I never touch it," he said.

"We'll come over here an' learn ye how to enjoy yerself some day," one of them said.

"I'm pretty well posted on that subject now," Samson answered.

It is likely that they would have begun his schooling at once but when they came out into the store and saw the big Vermonter standing in the candlelight their laughter ceased for a moment.   Bill was among them with a well filled bottle in his hand.

He and the others got into a wagon which had been waiting at the door and drove away with a wild Indian whoop from the lips of one of the young men.

Samson sat down in the candlelight and Abe in a moment arrived.

"I'm getting awful sick o' this business," said Abe.

"I kind o' guess you don't like the whisky part of it," Samson remarked, as he felt a piece of cloth.

"I hate it," Abe went on. "It don't seem respectable any longer."

"Back in Vermont we don't like the whisky business."

"You're right, it breeds deviltry and disorder. In my youth I was surrounded by whisky. Everybody drank it. A bottle or a jug of liquor was thought to be as legitimate a piece of merchandise as a pound of tea or a yard of calico. That's the way I've always thought of it. But lately I've begun to get the Yankee notion about whisky. When it gets into bad company it can raise the devil."

Soon after nine o'clock 'Abe drew a mattress filled with corn husks from under the counter, cleared away the bolts of cloth and laid it where they had been and covered it with a blanket.

"This is my bed," said he. "I'll be up at five in the morning. Then I'll be making tea here by the fireplace to wash down some jerked meat and a hunk o' bread. At six or a little after I'll be ready to go with you again. Jack Kelso is going to look after the store to-morrow."

He began to laugh.

"Ye know when I went out of the tavern that little vixen stood peekin' into the window—Bim, Jack's girl," said Abe. "I asked her why she didn't go in and she said she was scared. 'Who you 'fraid of?' I asked. 'Oh, I reckon that boy,' says she. And honestly her hand trembled when she took hold of my arm and walked to her father's house with me."

Abe snickered as he spread another blanket. "What a cut-up she is! Say, we'll have some fun watching them two I reckon," he said.

The logs were ready two days after the cutting began. Martin Waddell and Samuel Hill sent teams to haul them. John Cameron and Peter Lukins had brought the window sash and some clapboards from Beardstown in a small flat boat. Then came the day of the raising—a clear, warm day early in September. All the men from the village and the near farms gathered to help make a home for the newcomers. Samson and Jack Kelso went out for a hunt after the cutting and brought in a fat buck and many grouse for the bee dinner, to which every woman of the neighborhood made a contribution of cake or pie or cookies or doughnuts.

"What will be my part?" Samson had inquired of Kelso.

"Nothing but a jug of whisky and a kind word and a house warming," Kelso had answered.

They notched and bored the logs and made pins to bind them and cut those that were to go around the fireplace and window spaces. Strong, willing and well trained hands hewed and fitted the logs together. Alexander Ferguson lined the fireplace with a curious mortar made of clay in which he mixed grass for a binder. This mortar he rolled into layers called "cats," each eight inches long and three inches thick. Then he laid them against the logs and held them in

place with a woven network of sticks. The first fire
—a slow one—baked the clay into a rigid stone-like
sheath inside the logs and presently the sticks were
burned away. The women had cooked the meats by an
open fire and spread the dinner on a table of rough
boards resting on poles set in crotches. At noon one
of them sounded a conch shell. Then with shouts of
joy the men hurried to the fireside and for a moment
there was a great spluttering over the wash basins.
Before they ate every man except Abe and Samson
"took a pull at the jug—long or short"—to quote a
phrase of the time.

It was a cheerful company that sat down upon the
grass around the table with loaded plates. Their food
had its extra seasoning of merry jests and loud laughter. Sarah was a little shocked at the forthright direct-
ness of their eating, no knives or forks or napkins
being needed in that process. Having eaten, washed
and packed away their dishes the women went home
at two. Before they had gone Samson's ears caught
a thunder of horses' feet in the distance. Looking
in its direction he saw a cloud of dust in the road and
a band of horsemen riding toward them at full speed.
Abe came to him and said:

"I see the boys from Clary's Grove are coming. If
they get mean let me deal with 'em. It's my respon-
sibility. I wouldn't wonder if they had some of Offut's whisky with them."

The boys arrived in a cloud of dust and a chorus

of Indian whoops and dismounted and hobbled their horses. They came toward the workers, led by burly Jack Armstrong, a stalwart, hard-faced blacksmith of about twenty-two with broad, heavy shoulders, whose name has gone into history. They had been drinking some but no one of them was in the least degree off his balance. They scuffled around the jug for a moment in perfect good nature and then Abe and Mrs. Waddell provided them with the best remnants of the dinner. They were rather noisy. Soon they went up on the roof to help with the rafters and the clapboarding. They worked well a few minutes and suddenly they came scrambling down for another pull at the jug. They were out for a spree and Abe knew it and knew further that they had reached the limit of discretion.

"Boys, there are ladies here and we've got to be careful," he said. "Did I ever tell you what Uncle Jerry Holman said of his bull calf? He said the calf was such a *suckcess* that he didn't leave any milk for the family and that while the calf was growin' fat the children was growin' poor. In my opinion you're about fat enough for the present. Le's stick to the job till four o'clock. Then we'll knock off for refreshments."

The young revelers gathered in a group and began to whisper together. Samson writes that it became evident then they were going to make trouble and says:

"We had left the children at Rutledge's in the care of Ann. I went to Sarah and told her she had better go on and see if they were all right.

" 'Don't you get in any fight,' she said, which shows that the women knew what was in the air.

"Sarah led the way and the others followed her."

Those big, brawny fellows from the grove when they got merry were looking always for a chance to get mad at some man and turn him into a plaything. A victim had been a necessary part of their sprees. Many a poor fellow had been fastened in a barrel and rolled down hill or nearly drowned in a ducking for their amusement. A chance had come to get mad and they were going to make the most of it. They began to growl with resentment. Some were wigging their leader Jack Armstrong to fight Abe. One of them ran to his horse and brought a bottle from his saddle-bag. It began passing from mouth to mouth. Jack Armstrong got the bottle before it was half emptied, drained it and flung it high in the air. Another called him a hog and grappled him around the waist and there was a desperate struggle which ended quickly. Armstrong got a hold on the neck of his assailant and choked him until he let go. This was not enough for the sturdy bully of Clary's Grove. He seized his follower and flung him so roughly on the ground that the latter lay for a moment stunned. Armstrong had got his blood warm and was now ready for action. With a wild whoop he threw off his coat, unbuttoned his right shirt-sleeve and rolled it to the shoulder and declared in a loud voice, as he swung his arm in the air, that he could "out jump, out hop, out run, throw down, drag out an' lick any man in New Salem."

In a letter to his father Samson writes:

"Abe was working at my elbow. I saw him drop his hammer and get up and make for the ladder. I knew something was going to happen and I followed him. In a minute every one was off the roof and out of the building. I guess they knew what was coming. The big lad stood there swinging his arm and yelling like an Injun. It was a big arm and muscled and corded up some but I guess if I'd shoved the calico off mine and held it up he'd a pulled down his sleeve. I suppose the feller's arm had a kind of a mule's kick in it, but, good gracious! If he'd a seen as many arms as you an' I have that have growed up on a hickory helve he'd a known that his was nothing to brag of. I didn't know just how good a man Abe was and I was kind o' scairt for a minute. I never found it so hard work to do nothin' as I did then. Honest my hands kind o' ached. I wanted to go an' cuff that feller's ears an' grab hold o' him an' toss him over the ridge pole. Abe went right up to him an' said:

" 'Jack, you ain't half so bad or half so cordy as ye think ye are. You say you can throw down any man here. I reckon I'll have to show ye that you're mistaken. I'll rassle with ye. We're friends an' we won't

talk about lickin' each other.   Le's have a friendly
rassle.'

"In a second the two men were locked together.
Armstrong had lunged at Abe with a yell.   There was
no friendship in the way he took hold.   He was going
to do all the damage he could in any way he could.
He tried to butt with his head and ram his knee into
Abe's stomach as soon as they came together.   Half
drunk Jack is a man who would bite your ear off.   It
was no rassle; it was a fight.   Abe moved like lightning.   He acted awful limber an' well greased.   In a
second he had got hold of the feller's neck with his
big right hand and hooked his left into the cloth on
his hip.   In that way he held him off and shook him
as you've seen our dog shake a woodchuck.   Abe's
blood was hot.   If the whole crowd had piled on him
I guess he would have come out all right, for when
he's roused there's something in Abe more than bones
and muscles.   I suppose it's what I feel when he speaks
a piece.   It's a kind of lightning.   I guess it's what
our minister used to call the power of the spirit.   Abe
said to me afterwards that he felt as if he was fighting for the peace and honor of New Salem.

"A friend of the bully jumped in and tried to trip
Abe.   Harry Needles stood beside me.   Before I could
move he dashed forward and hit that feller in the middle of his forehead and knocked him flat.   Harry had
hit Bap McNoll the cock fighter.   I got up next to the
kettle then and took the scum off it.   Fetched one of
them devils a slap with the side of my hand that took
the skin off his face and rolled him over and over.
When I looked again Armstrong was going limp.   His

mouth was open and his tongue out. With one hand fastened to his right leg and the other on the nape of his neck Abe lifted him at arm's length and gave him a toss in the air. Armstrong fell about ten feet from where Abe stood and lay there for a minute. The fight was all out of him and he was kind of dazed and sick. Abe stood up like a giant and his face looked awful solemn.

" 'Boys, if there's any more o' you that want trouble you can have some off the same piece,' he said.

"They hung their heads and not one of them made a move or said a word. Abe went to Armstrong and helped him up.

" 'Jack, I'm sorry that I had to hurt you,' he said. 'You get on to your horse and go home.'

" 'Abe, you're a better man than me,' said the bully, as he offered his hand to Abe. 'I'll do anything you say.' "

So the Clary's Grove gang was conquered. They were to make more trouble but not again were they to imperil the foundations of law and order in the little community of New Salem. As they were starting away Bap McNoll turned to Harry Needles and shouted: "I'll git even with you yet—you slab-sided son of a dog."

That is not exactly what he said but it is near enough.

CHAPTER V

IN WHICH THE CHARACTER OF BIM KELSO FLASHES OUT
IN A STRANGE ADVENTURE THAT BEGINS THE WEAV-
ING OF A LONG THREAD OF ROMANCE.

THE shell of the cabin was finished that day. Its
puncheon floor was in place but its upper floor was to
be laid when the boards were ready. Its two doors
were yet to be made and hung, its five windows to be
fitted and made fast, its walls to be chinked with clay
mortar. Samson and Harry stayed that evening after
the rest were gone, smoothing the puncheon floor.
They made a few nails at the forge after supper and
went over to Abe's store about nine. Two of the
Clary's Grove Gang who had tarried in the village sat
in the gloom of its little veranda apparently asleep.
Dr. Allen, Jack Kelso, Alexander Ferguson and Martin Waddell were sitting by its fireside while Abe sat
on the counter with his legs hanging off.

"He's a tough oak stick of a man," Kelso was saying.

"Here he is now," said Dr. Allen. "That lad you
cuffed had to stop at my office for repairs."

"I told you once to use a crowbar if you wanted to
hit anybody, but never to use your hands," said Abe.

"Well there wasn't any time to lose and there was no crowbar handy," said Samson.

"That reminds me of a general who made the boys of his regiment promise to let him do all the swearin'," Abe began. "One day a sergeant got into trouble with a mule team. It was raining hard and the off mule balked. Wouldn't draw a pound. The sergeant got wet to the skin and swore a song of fourteen verses that was heard by half the regiment. The general called him up for discipline.

" 'Young man, I thought it was understood that I was to do all the swearin',' he said.

" 'So it was,' said the sergeant, 'but that swearin' had to be done right away. You couldn't 'a' got there in time to do it if I'd 'a' sent for ye.' "

"I'm sorry we had to have trouble," Samson remarked, after the outburst of appreciation that followed Abe's story. "It's the only spot on the day. I'll never forget the kindness of the people of New Salem."

"The raising bee is a most significant thing," said Kelso. "Democracy tends to universal friendship—each works for the crowd and the crowd for each and there are no favorites. Every community is like the thousand friends of Thebes. Most of its units stand together for the common good—for justice, law and honor. The schools are spinning strands of democracy out of all this European wool. Railroads are to pick them up and weave them into one great fabric. By and by we shall see the ten million friends of America standing together as did the thousand friends of Thebes."

"It's a great thought," said Abe.

"No man can estimate the size of that mighty phalanx of friendship all trained in one school," Kelso went on. "Two years ago the *Encyclopedia Britannica* figured that the population of the United States in 1905 would be 168,000,000 people, and in 1966, 672,-000,000. Wealth, power, science, literature, all follow in the train of light and numbers. The causes which moved the sceptre of civilization from the Euphrates to Western Europe will carry it from the latter to the New World."

"They say that electricity and the development of the steam engine is going to make all men think alike," said Abe. "If that's so Democracy and Liberty will spread over the earth."

"The seed of Universal Brotherhood is falling far and wide and you can not kill it," Kelso continued. "Last year Mazzini said: 'There is only one sun in heaven for the whole earth, only one law for all who people it. We are here to found fraternally the unity of the human race so that, sometime, it may present but one fold and one Shepherd.'"

Then Lincoln spoke again: "I reckon we are near the greatest years in history. It is a privilege to be alive."

"And young," Dr. Allen added.

"Young! What a God's blessed thing is that!" said Kelso and then he quoted from Coleridge:

> " 'Verse, a breeze mid blossoms straying
> Where Hope clung feeding like a bee,
> Both were mine! Life went a maying
> With Nature, Hope and Poesy
> When I was young!'

"Abe, have ye learned the *Cotter's Saturday Night?*"

"Not yet. It's a heavy hog to hold but I'll get a grip on an ear and a hind leg and lift it out o' the pen before long. You see."

"Don't fail to do that. It will be a help and joy to ye."

"Old Kirkham is a hard master," said Abe. "I hear his bell ringing every time I get a minute's leisure. I'm nigh through with him. Now I want to study rhetoric."

"Only schoolmasters study rhetoric," Kelso declared. "A real poet or a real orator is born with all the rhetoric he needs. We should get our rhetoric as we get our oxygen—unconsciously—by reading the masters. Rhetoric is a steed for a light load under the saddle but he's too warm blooded for the harness. He was for the day of the plumed knight—not for these times. No man of sense would use a prancing horse on a plow or a stone boat. A good plow horse is a beautiful thing. The play of his muscles, the power of his stride are poetry to me but when he tries to put on style he is ridiculous. That suggests what rhetoric is apt to do to the untrained intellect. If you've anything to say or write head straight across the field and keep your eye on the furrow. Then comes the sowing and how beautiful is the sower striding across the field in his suit of blue jeans, with that wonderful gesture, so graceful, so imperious! Put him in a beaver hat and broadcloth and polished calfskin and a frilled shirt and you couldn't think of anything more ridiculous!"

In the last diary of Samson Henry Traylor is this entry:

"I went to Gettysburg with the President to-day and sat near him when he spoke. Mr. Everett addressed the crowd for an hour or so. As Kelso would say 'He rode the prancing steel of Rhetoric.' My old friend went straight across the field and his look and gestures reminded me of that picture of the sower which Jack gave us one night long ago in Abe's store. Through my tears I could see the bucket hanging on his elbow and the good seed flying far and wide from his great hand. When he finished the field, plowed and harrowed and fertilized by war, had been sowed for all time. The spring's work was done and well done."

At a quarter of ten the Doctor rose and said:

John Wolcott Adams

"We're keeping Abe from his sleep and wearing the night away with philosophy. I'm going home."

"I came over to see if you could find a man to help me to-morrow," Samson said to Abe. "Harry is going over to do the chinking alone. I want a man to help me on the whipsaw while I cut some boards for the upper flooring."

"I'll help you myself," Abe proposed. "I reckon I'll close the store to-morrow unless Jack will tend it."

"You can count on me," said Jack. "I'm short of sleep anyhow and a day of rest will do me good."

Abe went with his friends to the door beyond which the two boys from Clary's Grove sat as if sound asleep. It is probable, however, that they had heard what Samson had said to Abe.

"Well, I didn't know these wild turkeys were roosting here," Abe laughed. He roused them from their slumbers and said: "Boys, you're trying to saw the day off a little too short. It's got to run till you get to Clary's Grove. Better take those horses home and feed 'em."

The boys got up and yawned and stretched themselves and mounted their horses which had been tied to a bar and rode away in the darkness.

Next morning Abe and Samson set out for the woods soon after daylight.

"I like that boy Harry," said Abe. "I reckon he's got good stuff in him. The way he landed on Bap

McNoll was a caution.   I like to see a feller come right up to the scratch, without an invitation just in the nick o' time, as he did."

"Did you see him jump in?" Samson asked.

"I saw everything some way. I saw you when ye loosened the ear o' John Callyhan. That tickled me. But the way I felt yesterday—honest, it seemed as if I could handle 'em all. That boy Harry is a likely young colt—strong and limber and well put together and broad between the eyes."

"An' gentle as a kitten," Samson added. "There never was a better face on a boy or a better heart behind it. We like him."

"Yes, sir. He's a well topped young tree—straight and sound and good timber. Looks as if that little girl o' Jack's was terribly took up with him. I don't wonder. There are not many boys like Harry around here."

"What kind of a girl is she?" Samson asked.

"Awful shy since the arrow hit her. She don't know what it means yet. She'll get used to that I reckon. She's a good girl and smart as a steel trap. Her father takes her out on the plains with him shooting. She can handle a gun as well as anybody and ride a horse as if she had growed to his back. Every body likes Bim but she has her own way of behaving and sometimes it's awful new-fashioned."

Harry Needles went whistling up the road toward

the new house with sickle, hoe and trowel. As he passed the Kelso cabin he whistled the tune of *Sweet Nightingale*. It had haunted his mind since he had heard it in the woods. He whistled as loudly as ever he could and looked at the windows. Before he had passed Bim's face looked out at him with a smile and her hand flickered back of the panes and he waved his to her. His heart beat fast as he hurried along.

"I'm not so very young," he said to himself. "I wish I hadn't put on these old clothes. Mrs. Traylor is an awful nice woman but she's determined to make me look like a plow horse. I don't see why she couldn't let me wear decent clothes."

Sarah had enjoyed mothering the boy. His health had returned. His cheeks were ruddy, his dark eyes clear and bright, his tall form erect and sturdy. Moreover the affectionate care his new friends had given him and his interest in the girl filled his heart with the happiness which is the rain of youth and without which it becomes an arid desert.

He had helped Alexander Ferguson with the making of the fireplace and knew how to mix the mortar. He worked with a will for his heart was in the new home. It was a fine September morning. The warm sunlight had set the meadow cocks a crowing. The far reaches of the great, grassy plain were dimmed with haze. It was a vast, flowery wilderness, waving and murmuring in the breeze like an ocean. How long

those acres, sown by .the winds of heaven, had waited
for the plowman now arrived!

Harry felt the beauty of the scene but saw and enjoyed more the face of Bim Kelso as he worked and
planned his own house—no cabin but a mansion like
that of Judge Harper in the village near his old home.
He had filled every crevice in the rear wall and was
working on the front when he heard the thunder of
running horses and saw those figures, dim in a cloud
of dust, flying up the road again. He thought of the
threat of Bap McNoll. It occurred to him that he
would be in a bad way alone with those ruffians if
they were coming for revenge. He stepped into the
door of the house and stood a moment debating what
he would best do. He thought of running toward the
grove, which was a few rods from the rear door of the
house, and hiding there. He couldn't bear to run.
Bim and all the rest of them would hear of it. So
with the sickle in his right hand he stood waiting inside the house and hoping they wouldn't stop. They
rode up to the door and dismounted quietly and hobbled their horses. There were five of them who crowded into the cabin with McNoll in the lead.

"Now, you young rooster, you're goin' to git what's
comin' to you," he growled.

The boy faced them bravely and warned them away
with his sickle. They were prepared for such emer-
gencies. One of them drew a bag of bird shot from

his pocket and hurled it at Harry's head. It hit him full in the face and he staggered against the wall stunned by the blow. They rushed upon the boy and disarmed and bore him to the floor. For a little time he knew not what was passing. When he came to, his hands and feet were tied and the men stood near, cursing and laughing, while their leader, McNoll, was draining a bottle. Suddenly he heard a voice trembling with excitement and wet with tears saying:

"You go 'way from here or I'll kill you dead. So help me God I'll kill you. If one o' you touches him he's goin' to die."

He saw Bim Kelso at the window with her gun leveled at the head of McNoll. Her face was red with anger. Her eyes glowed. As he looked a tear welled from one of them and trailed down the scarlet surface of her cheek. McNoll turned without a word and walked sulkily out of the back door. The others crowded after him. They ran as soon as they had got out of the door. She left the window. In a moment the young men were galloping away.

Bim came into the house sobbing with emotion but with her head erect. She stood her gun in a corner and knelt by the helpless boy. He was crying also. Her hair fell upon his face as she looked at the spot of deep scarlet color made by the shot bag. She kissed it and held her cheek against his and whispered: "Don't cry. It's all over now. I'm going to cut these ropes."

It was as if she had known and loved him always. She was like a young mother with her first child. Tenderly she wiped his tears away with her blond, silken hair. She cut his bonds and he rose and stood before her. Her face changed like magic.

"Oh what a fool I've been!" she exclaimed.

"Why so?" he asked.

"I cried and I kissed you and we never have been introduced to each other."

She covered her eyes with her hair and with bent head went out of the door.

"I'll never forget that kiss as long as I live," said the boy as he followed her. "I'll never forget your help or your crying either."

"How I must have looked!" she went on, walking toward her pony that was hitched to a near tree.

"You were beautiful!" he exclaimed.

"Go away from me—I won't speak to you," she said. "Go back to your work. I'll stay here and keep watch."

The boy returned to his task pointing up the inside walls but his mind and heart were out in the sunlight talking with Bim. Once he looked out of the door and saw her leaning against the neck of the pony, her face hidden in his mane. When the sun was low she came to the door and said:

"You had better stop now and go home."

She looked down at the ground and added:

"Please, please, don't tell on me."

"Of course not," he answered. "But I hope you won't be afraid of me any more."

She looked up at him with a little smile. "Do you think I'm afraid of *you?*" she asked as if it were too absurd to be thought of. She unhitched and mounted her pony but did not go.

"I do wish you could raise a mustache," she said, looking wistfully into his face.

Involuntarily his hand went to his lip.

"I could try," he said.

"I can't bear to see you look so terribly young; you get worse and worse every time I see you," she scolded plaintively. "I want you to be a regular man right quick."

He wondered what he ought to say and presently stammered: "I—I—intend to. I guess I'm more of a man than anybody would think to look at me."

"You're too young to ever fall in love I reckon."

"No I'm not," he answered with decision.

"Have you got a razor?" she asked.

"No."

"I reckon it would be a powerful help. You put soap on your lip and mow it off with a razor. My father says it makes the grass grow."

There was a moment of silence during which she brushed the mane of her pony. Then she asked timidly: "Do you play on the flute?"

"No, why?"

"I think it would break my heart. My Uncle Henry plays all day and it makes him look crazy. Do you like yellow hair?"

"Yes, if it looks like yours."

"If you don't mind I'll put a mustache on you just —just to look at every time I think of you."

"When I think of you I put violets in your hair," he said.

He took a step toward her as he spoke and as he did so she started her pony. A little way off she checked him and said:

"I'm sorry. There are no violets now."

She rode away slowly waving her hand and singing with the joy of a bird in the springtime:

"My sweetheart, come along
Don't you hear the glad song
As the notes of the nightingale flow?
Don't you hear the fond tale
Of the sweet nightingale
As she sings in the valleys below—
As she sings in the valleys below?"

He stood looking and listening. The song came to him as clear and sweet as the notes of a vesper bell wandering in miles of silence.

When it had ceased he felt his lip and said: "How

slow the time passes! I'm going to get some shaving soap and a razor."

That evening when Harry was helping Samson with the horses he said:

"I'm going to tell you a secret. I wish you wouldn't say anything about it."

Samson stood pulling the hair out of his card and looking very stern as he listened while Harry told of the assault upon him and how Bim had arrived and driven the rowdies away with her gun but he said not a word of her demonstration of tender sympathy. To him that had clothed the whole adventure with a kind of sanctity so that he could not bear to have it talked about.

Samson's eyes glowed with anger. They searched the face of the boy. His voice was deep and solemn when he said:

"This is a serious matter. Why do you wish to keep it a secret?"

The boy blushed. For a moment he knew not what to say. Then he spoke: "It ain't me so much—it's her," he managed to say. "She wouldn't want it to be talked about and I don't either."

Samson began to understand. "She's quite a girl I guess," he said thoughtfully. "She must have the nerve of a man—I declare she must."

"Yes-sir-ee! They'd 'a' got hurt if they hadn't gone away, that's sure," said Harry.

"We'll look out for them after this," Samson rejoined. "The first time I meet that man McNoll he'll have to settle with me and he'll pay cash on the nail."

Bim having heard of Harry's part in Abe's fight and of the fact that he was to be working alone all day at the new house had ridden out through the woods to the open prairie and hunted in sight of the new cabin that afternoon. Unwilling to confess her extreme interest in the boy she had said not a word of her brave act. It was not shame; it was partly a kind of rebellion against the tyranny of youthful ardor; it was partly the fear of ridicule.

So it happened that the adventure of Harry Needles made scarcely a ripple on the sensitive surface of the village life. It will be seen, however, that it had started strong undercurrents likely, in time, to make themselves felt.

The house and barn were finished whereupon Samson and Harry drove to Springfield—a muddy, crude and growing village with thick woods on its north side —and bought furniture. Their wagon was loaded and they were ready to start for home. They were walking on the main street when Harry touched Samson's arm and whispered:

"There's McNoll and Callyhan."

The pair were walking a few steps ahead of Samson and Harry. In a second Samson's big hand was on McNoll's shoulder.

"This is Mr. McNoll, I believe," said Samson.

The other turned with a scared look.

"What do ye want o' me?" he demanded.

Samson threw him to the ground with a jerk so strong and violent that it rent the sleeve from his shoulder. McNoll's companion who had felt the weight of Samson's hand and had had enough of it turned and ran.

"What do ye want o' me?" McNoll asked again as he struggled to free himself.

"What do I want o' you—you puny little coward," said Samson, as he lifted the bully to his feet and gave him a toss and swung him in the air and continued to address him. "I'm just goin' to muss you up proper. If you don't say you're sorry and mean it I'll put a tow string on your neck and give you to some one that wants a dog."

"I'm sorry," said McNoll. "Honest I am! I was drunk when I done it."

Samson released his prisoner. A number in the crowd which had gathered around them clapped their hands and shouted, "Hurrah for the stranger!"

A constable took Samson's hand and said: "You deserve a vote of thanks. That man and his friends have made me more trouble than all the rest of the drinking men put together."

"And I am making trouble for myself," said Samson. "I have made myself ashamed. I am no fighting man, I was never in such a muss on a public street before and with God's help it will never happen again."

"Where do you live?" the officer asked.

"In New Salem."

"I wish it was here. We need men like you. What part of the East do you hail from?"

"Vermont," Samson answered. "I've just bought land and built a cabin a little west of the village. Came here for a load of furniture."

"I'm a Maine man and a Whig and opposed to slavery and my name is Erastus Wright," said the constable.

"I am a Whig and against slavery," Samson volunteered.

"I could tell that by the look of you," said the constable. "Some day we must sit down together and talk things over."

Samson wrote in his diary:

"On the way home my heart was sore. I prayed in silence that God would forgive me for my bad example to the boy. I promised that I would not again misuse the strength He has given me. In my old home I would have been disgraced by it. The minister would have preached of the destruction that follows the violent man to put him down; the people would have looked askance at me. Deacon Somers would have called me aside to look into my soul, and Judge Grandy and his wife would not have invited me to their parties. Here it's different. A chap who can take the law in his hands and bring the evil man to his senses, even if he has to hit him over the head, is looked up to. That day a number of men and boys increased my shame by following us to the wagon and wanting to shake hands and feel of my muscles and paining my soul with praise. It's a reckless country. You feel it as soon as you get here. In time, I fear, I shall be as headlong as the rest of them. Some way the news of my act has got here from Springfield. Sarah was kind of cut up. Jack Kelso has nicknamed me 'The man with the iron arms,' and Abe, who is a better man every way, laughs at my embarrassment and says I ought to feel honored. For one thing Jack Armstrong has become a good citizen. His wife has foxed a pair of breeches for Abe. They say McNoll has left the country. There has been no deviltry here since that day. I guess the gang is broken up—too much iron in its way."

Sarah enjoyed fixing up the cabin. Jack Kelso had given her some deer and buffalo skins to lay on the floors. The upper room, reached by a stick ladder, had its two beds, one of which Harry occupied. The children slept below in a trundle bed that was pushed under the larger one when it was made up in the morning.

"Some time I'm going to put in a windletrap and get rid o' that stick ladder," Samson had said.

Sarah had all the arts of the New England home maker. Under her hand the cabin, in color, atmosphere and general neatness, would have delighted a higher taste than was to be found on the prairies, save in the brain of Kelso who really had some acquaintance with beauty. To be sure the bed was in one corner, spread with its upper cover knit of gray yarn harmonizing in color with the bark of the log walls. A handsome dark brown buffalo robe lay beside it. The rifle and powder horn were hung above the mantel. The fireplace had its crane of wrought iron.

Every one in the little village came to the house warming.

"There is nothing in America so beautiful as 'this here kind o' thing' when the firelight shines upon it," said Kelso who often indulged in the vernacular of the real ladder climbers.

"Well, of course, it isn't like Boston or New York," Sarah answered.

"Thank God!" Kelso exclaimed. "New York hurts my feelings, so many of its buildings are of grand design and small proportions. Mrs. Traylor, you are lucky to have this beautiful island in an ocean of music. There is music in the look and sound of these meadows—bird music, wind music, the level music of Felician David's Desert. Perhaps you don't know about that and really it doesn't matter. Traylor, tune up your fiddle."

Samson began to play, stopping often to give the hand of welcome to a guest. The people of New Salem were in their best clothes. The women wore

dresses of new calico—save Mrs. Dr. Allen, who wore
a black silk dress which had come with her from her
late home in Lexington.   Bim Kelso came in a dress
of red muslin trimmed with white lace.   Ann Rutledge
also wore a red dress and came with Abe.   The latter
was rather grotesque in his new linsey trousers, of a
better length than the former pair, but still too short.

"It isn't fair to blame the trousers or the tailor," he
had said when he had tried them on.   "My legs are
so long that the imagination of the tailor is sure to
fall short if the cloth don't.   Next time I'll have 'em
made to measure with a ten-foot pole instead of a
yardstick.   If they're too long I can roll 'em up and
let out a link or two when they shrink.   Ever since I
was a boy I have been troubled with shrinking pants."

Abe wore a blue swallow-tail coat with brass buttons, the tails of which were so short as to be well
above the danger of pressure when he sat down.   His
cowhide shoes had been well blackened; the blue yarn
of his socks showed above them.   "These darned socks
of mine are rather proud and conceited," he used to
say.   "They like to show off."

He wore a shirt of white, unbleached cotton, a
starched collar and black tie.

In speaking of his collar to Samson, he said that
he felt like a wild horse in a box stall.

Mentor Graham, the schoolmaster, was there—a
smooth-faced man with a large head, sandy hair and

a small mustache, who spoke by note, as it were. Kelso called him the great articulator and said that he walked in the valley of the shadow of Lindley Murray. He seemed to keep a watchful eye on his words, as if they were a lot of schoolboys not to be trusted. They came out with a kind of self-conscious rectitude.

The children's games had begun and the little house rang with their songs and laughter, while their elders sat by the fire and along the walls talking. Ann Rutledge and Bim Kelso and Harry Needles and John McNeil played with them. In one of the dances all joined in singing the verses:

> I won't have none o' yer' weevily wheat,
>   I won't have none o' yer barley;
> I won't have none o' yer' weevily wheat,
>   To make a cake for Charley.
>
> Charley is a fine young man,
>   Charley is a dandy,
> Charley likes to kiss the girls,
>   Whenever it comes handy.

When a victim was caught in the flying scrimmage at the end of a passage in the game of Prisoners, he or she was brought before a blindfolded judge:

"Heavy, heavy hangs over your head," said the Constable.

"Fine or superfine?" the judge inquired.

"Fine," said the Constable, which meant that the victim was a boy. Then the sentence was pronounced and generally it was this:

"Go bow to the wittiest, kneel to the prettiest and kiss the one that you love best."

Harry was the first prisoner. He went straight to Bim Kelso and bowed and knelt, and when he had risen she turned and ran like a scared deer around the chairs and the crowd of onlookers, some assisting and some checking her flight, before the nimble youth. Hard pressed, she ran out of the open door, with a merry laugh, and just beyond the steps Harry caught and kissed her, and her cheeks had the color of roses when he led her back.

John McNeil kissed Ann Rutledge that evening and was most attentive to her, and the women were saying that the two had fallen in love with each other.

"See how she looks at him," one of them whispered.

"Well, it's just the way he looks at her," the other answered.

At the first pause in the merriment Kelso stood on a chair, and then silence fell upon the little company.

"My good neighbors," he began, "we are here to rejoice that new friends have come to us and that a new home is born in our midst. We bid them welcome. They are big boned, big hearted folks. No man has grown large who has not at one time or another had his feet in the soil and felt its magic power going up into his blood and bone and sinew. Here is a wonderful soil and the inspiration of wide horizons; here are broad and fertile fields. Where the corn grows high you can grow statesmen. It may be that out of one of these little cabins a man will come to carry the torch of Liberty and Justice so high that its light will shine into every dark place. So let no one despise the cabin—humble as it is. Samson and Sarah Traylor, I welcome and congratulate you. Whatever may come, you can find no better friends than these, and of this you may be sure, no child of the prairies will ever go about with a hand organ and a monkey. Our friend, Honest Abe, is one of the few rich men in this neighborhood. Among his assets are Kirkham's Grammar, *The Pilgrim's Progress,* the Lives of Washington and Henry Clay, Hamlet's Soliloquy, Othello's Speech to the Senate, Marc Antony's address and a part of Webster's reply to Hayne. A man came along the other day and sold him a barrel of rubbish for two bits. In it he found a volume of Blackstone's *Commentaries.* Old Blackstone challenged him to a wrestle and Abe has grappled with him. I reckon he'll take his measure as easily as he took Jack Armstrong's. Lately he has got possession of a noble asset. It is the *Cotter's Saturday Night,* by Robert Burns. I propose to ask him to let us share his enjoyment of this treasure."

Abe, who had been sitting with his legs doubled beneath him on a buffalo skin, between Joe and Betsey Traylor, rose and said:

"Mr. Kelso's remarks, especially the part which applied to me, remind me of the story of the prosperous grocer of Joliet. One Saturday night he and his boys were busy selling sausage. Suddenly in came a man with whom he had quarreled and laid two dead cats on the counter.

" 'There,' said he, 'this makes seven to-day. I'll call Monday and get my money.'

"We were doing a good business here making fun. It seems a pity to ruin it and throw suspicion on the quality of the goods by throwing a cat on the counter. I'll only throw one cat. It is entitled:

MY SISTER SUE

"Say, boys, I guess 'at none o' you
　Has ever seen my sister Sue,
　She kin rassle an' turn han'springs kerflop,
　But Jiminy Crimps!—ye should see her hop!
　　　　Yes, sir!

"She kin h'ist one foot an' go like Ned!
　An' hop on top o' my mother's bed,
　An' back an' round the house she'll go,
　'Ith her ol' knee as limber as a hickory bow,
　　　　Yes, sir!

"She kin sing a hull song 'ithout ketchin' her breath,
　An' make up a face 'at 'ud scare ye to death!
　She kin wiggle her ears an' cross her eyes
　An' stick out her tongue till yer hair 'ud rise.
　　　　Yes, sir!

"An' play wildcat on her han's an' knees,
Honest! 'T would give ye the gibberees!
An' she sneaks along an' jumps at you
An' gives sech a yell!—my sister Sue!
          Yes, sir!

"She kin shoot off a gun an' set a trap,
An' if you don't behave she kin give you a slap!
She kin holler and scream like a flock o' geese
An' stan' on her head an' speak a piece.
          Yes, sir!

"She kin run cross legged an' ride a cow,
An' jump from the beam to the big hay mow.
I reckon yer hair 'ud stan' up to see 'er
A breakin' a colt er throwin' a steer,
          Yes, sir!

"My sister Susan has got a beau.
When he comes she sets an' acts jes' so,
An' talks so proper—it's zac'ly jes
Like the flummididles on her dress,
          Yes, sir!

"When she stan's in that darn ol' Sunday gown
Ye'd think a grasshopper could knock 'er down.
An' she laughs kind o' sick—like a kitten's mew—
Ye wouldn't think 'twas my sister Sue,
          No, sir!

"An' she says: 'Oh, dear! those horrid boys!
They act so rough an' make sech a noise!'

Good gracious! ye wouldn't think 'at she
Could talk as loud as a bumble bee—
      No, sir!

"Honest! Er lift a chip o' wood,
  She acts so puny an' nice an' good!
'Boys are awful!' she says, 'till they're grown,
  Er nelse they got to be yer own!'
      Oh, gosh!'"

This raised a storm of merriment, after which he
recited the poem of Burns, with keen appreciation of
its quality. Samson repeatedly writes of his gift for
interpretation, especially of the comic, and now and
then lays particular stress on his power of mimicry.

John Cameron sang *The Sword of Bunker Hill*
and *Forty Years Ago, Tom.* Samson played while
the older people danced until midnight. Then, after
noisy farewells, men, women and children started in
the moonlit road toward the village. Ann Rutledge
had Abe on one arm and John McNeil on the other.

CHAPTER VI

WHICH DESCRIBES THE LONELY LIFE IN A PRAIRIE
CABIN AND A STIRRING ADVENTURE ON THE UNDER-
GROUND RAILROAD ABOUT THE TIME IT BEGAN
OPERATIONS.

WHEN Samson paid Mr. Gollaher, a "detector" came
with the latter to look at the money before it was
accepted. There were many counterfeits and bills
good only at a certain discount of face value, going
about those days and the detector was in great request.
Directly after moving in, Samson dug a well and lined
it with a hollow log. He bought tools and another
team and then he and Harry began their fall plowing.
Day after day for weeks they paced with their turning furrows until a hundred acres, stretching half a
mile to the west and well to the north of the house,
were black with them. Fever and ague descended
upon the little home in the early winter.

In a letter to her brother, dated January 4th, 1832,
Sarah writes:

"We have been longing for news from home, but
not a word has come from you. It don't seem as if
we could stand it unless we hear from you or some
of the folks once in a while. We are not dead just
because we are a thousand miles away. We want to

hear from you.   Please write and let us know how
father and mother are and all the news.   Is Elizabeth
Ranney married yet, and how does the minister get
along with his new wife?   We have all been sick with
the fever and ague.   It is a beautiful country and the
soil very rich, but there is some sickness.   Samson and
I were both sick at the same time.   I never knew
Samson to give up before.   He couldn't go on, his
head ached so.   Little Joe helped me get the fire
started and brought some water and waited on us.
Then the little man put on his coat and mittens and
trudged away to the village with Betsey after the doctor.   Harry Needles had gone away to Springfield for
Mr. Offut with a drove of hogs.   Two other boys are
with him.   He is going to buy a new suit.   He is a
very proud boy.   Joe and Betsey got back with the
doctor at nine.   That night Abe Lincoln came and sat
up with us and gave us our medicine and kept the
fire going.   It was comical to see him lying beside
Joe in his trundle bed, with his long legs sticking over
the end of it and his feet standing on the floor about
a yard from the bed.   He was spread all over the
place.   He talked about religion, and his views would
shock most of our friends in the East.   He doesn't
believe in the kind of Heaven that the ministers talk
about or any eternal hell.   He says that nobody knows
anything about the hereafter, except that God is a
kind and forgiving father and that all men are His
children.   He says that we can only serve God by
serving each other.   He seems to think that every
man, good or bad, black or white, rich or poor, is his
brother.   He thinks that Henry Clay, next to Daniel
Webster, is the greatest man in the country.   He is

studying hard.   Expects to go out and make speeches for Clay next summer.   He is quite severe in his talk against General Jackson.   He and Samson agree in politics and religion.   They are a good deal alike.   He is very fond of Samson and Harry—calls them his partners.   He said to Samson the other evening.

" 'I want you for a friend always.   If you can stand it, I would like my story to be a part of yours.   If you say so, we'll stick to the same boat and pole her over the shoals and carry her across the bends and see if we can get to good going in deep water.   When the channel will permit, we can put in a steam engine.'

"We love this big awkward giant.   His feet are set in the straight way and we think that he is going to make his mark in the world.

"When I went to sleep he lay in the trundle bed, with two candles burning on the stand beside him, reading that big green book of mine entitled *The Works of William Shakespeare*.   He had brought a law book with him, but he got interested in William Shakespeare and couldn't let it alone.   He said that he was like a mired horse whenever he began to read a play of the immortal bard, and that he had to take his time in getting out.   When he went away next morning he borrowed Samson's pack basket.   I felt bad because we couldn't go and make any arrangements with Santa Claus for the children.   Joe was dreadfully worried, for Betsey had told him that Santa Claus never came to children whose father and mother were sick.   Christmas Eve Abe came with the pack basket chock-full of good things after the children were asleep.   He took out a turkey and knit caps and mittens and packages of candy and raisins for the children and some cloth for a new dress for me.   Mrs.

Kelso had come to spend the night with us, although Samson and I were so much better it really wasn't necessary. I made her go up the ladder to bed before midnight. That evening a short, fat Santa Claus came in with a loaded pack. He had a long, brown beard and a red nose and carried a new clay pipe in his mouth and was very much bundled up.

"We called the children. They stood looking at Santa Claus, and Santa Claus stood looking at them. He gave them mufflers and some candy hearts and tried to pick them up. They ran away and he chased them under our bed and got hold of Joe's foot and tried to pull him out, and Joe hollored like a painter, and Santa Claus dropped his pipe and sat down on the floor and began laughing. I saw it was Bim Kelso. Abe left with her, and I suppose they went back to the village and around in a regular Santa Claus spree.

"Mrs. Kelso said that she had been making a beard of pieces of buffalo skin and fitting up an old suit of her father's clothes that afternoon. I wonder what she'll do next. It's terrible to be so much in love and not quite seventeen. Harry is as bad as she is. I wish they had been a little older before they met.

"Joe said yesterday that he was going back to Vergennes.

" 'How are you going to get there?' I asked.

" 'Abe's going to make me a pair o' wings, and I'm going to smash right up through the sky and go awa-a-y off to Vergennes and play with Ben and Lizzie Tyler. Abe says there ain't no bad roads up there.'

"I asked him what I should do if he went away and left me like that.

" 'Oh, I'll come right back,' he said, 'and maybe I'll see Heaven way up in the clouds. If I do I'll stop there in a tavern over night and buy something for you.'

"In a minute a new idea came to him, and he said:

" 'I guess Abe would make a pair of wings for you if you'd ask him.'

"Often I wish for wings, and always when I think of those who are dear to me and so far away. You said you would come out next spring to look about. Please don't disappoint us. I think it would almost break my heart. I am counting the days. Some time ago I put down 142 straight marks on my old slate, that being the number of days before May 1. Every night I rub off one of them and thank God that you are one day nearer. Don't be afraid of fever and ague. Sapington's pills cure it in three or four days. I would take the steamboat at Pittsburg, the roads in Ohio and Indiana are so bad. You can get a steamer up the Illinois River at Alton and get off at Beardstown and drive across country. If we knew when you were coming Samson or Abe would meet you. Give our love to all the folks and friends.

                    "Yours affectionately,
                         "Sarah and Samson."

It had been a cold winter and not easy to keep comfortable in the little house. In the worst weather Samson used to get up at night to keep the fire going. Late in January a wind from the southeast melted the snow and warmed the air of the midlands so that, for a week or so, it seemed as if spring were come. One night of this week Sambo awoke the family with his barking. A strong wind was rushing across the plains and roaring over the cabin and wailing in its chimney. Suddenly there was a rap on its door. When Samson opened it he saw in the moonlight a young colored man and woman standing near the door-step.

"Is dis Mistah Traylor?" the young man asked.

"It is," said Samson. "What can I do for you?"

"Mas'r, de good Lord done fotched us here to ask you fo' help," said the negro. "We be nigh wone out with cold an' hungah, suh, 'deed we be."

Samson asked them in and put wood on the fire, and Sarah got up and made some hot tea and brought food from the cupboard and gave it to the strangers, who sat shivering in the firelight. They were a good-looking pair, the young woman being almost white. They were man and wife. The latter stopped eating and moaned and shook with emotion as her husband told their story. Their master had died the year before and they had been brought to St. Louis to be sold in the slave market. There they had escaped by night and gone to the house of an old friend of their former owner who lived north of the city on the river shore. He had taken pity on them and brought them across the Mississippi and started them on the north road with a letter to Elijah Lovejoy of Alton and a supply of food. Since then they had been hiding days in the swamps and thickets and had traveled by night. Mr. Lovejoy had sent them to Erastus Wright of Springfield, and Mr. Wright had given them the name of Samson Traylor and the location of his cabin. From there they were bound for the house of John Peasley, in Hopedale, Tazewell County.

Lovejoy had asked them to keep the letter with which they had begun their travels. Under its signature he had written: "I know the writer and know that the above was written with his own hand. His word can be relied upon. To all who follow or respect the example of Jesus Christ I commend this man and woman."

The letter stated that their late master had often expressed his purpose of leaving them their freedom when he should pass away. He had left no will and since his death the two had fallen into the hands of his nephew, a despotic, violent young drunkard of the name of Biggs, who had ruled his servants with club and bull whip and who in a temper had killed a young negro a few months before. The fugitives said that they would rather die than go back to him.

Samson was so moved by their story that he hitched up his horses and put some hay in the wagon box and made off with the fugitives up the road to the north in the night. When daylight came he covered them with the hay. About eight o'clock he came to a frame house and barn, the latter being of unusual size for that time and country. Above the door of the barn was a board which bore the stenciled legend: "John Peasley, Orwell Farm."

As Samson drew near the house he observed a man working on the roof of a woodshed. Something familiar in his look held the eye of the New Salem man. In half a moment he recognized the face of Henry Brimstead. It was now a cheerful face. Brimstead came down the ladder and they shook hands.

"Good land o' Goshen! How did you get here?" Samson asked. Brimstead answered:

"Through the help of a feller that looks like you an' the grit of a pair o' hosses. Come down this road early in September on my way to the land o' plenty. Found Peasley here. Couldn't help it. Saw his name on the barn. Used to go to school with him in Orwell. He offered to sell me some land with a house on it an' trust me for his pay. I liked the looks o' the country and so I didn't go no further. I was goin' to write you a letter, but I hain't got around to it yet. Ain't forgot what you done for us, I can tell ye that."

"Well, this looks better than the sand plains—a lot better—and you look better than that flea farmer back in York State. How are the children?"

"Fat an' happy an' well dressed. Mrs. Peasley has been a mother to 'em an' her sister is goin' to be a wife to me." He came close to Samson and added in a confidential tone: "Say, if I was any happier I'd be scairt. I'm like I was when I got over the tooth-ache—so scairt for fear it would come back I was kind o' miserable."

Mr. Peasley came out of the door. He was a big, full bearded, jovial man.

"I've got a small load o' hay for you," said Samson.

"I was expecting it, though I supposed 'twould be walkin'—in the dark o' the night," Peasley answered. "Drive in on the barn floor."

When Samson had driven into the barn its doors were closed and the negroes were called from their place of hiding. Samson writes:

"I never realized what a blessing it is to be free until I saw that scared man and woman crawling out from under the dusty hay and shaking themselves like a pair of dogs. The weather was not cold or I guess they would have been frozen. They knelt together on the barn floor and the woman prayed for God's protection through the day. I knew what slavery must mean when I saw what they were suffering to get away from it. When they came in the night I felt the call of God to help them. Now I knew that I was among the chosen to lead in a great struggle. Peasley brought food for them and stowed them away on the top of his hay mow with a pair of buffalo skins. I suppose they got some sleep there. I went into the house to breakfast and while I ate Brimstead told me about his trip. His children were there. They looked clean and decent. He lived in a log cabin a little further up the road. Mrs. Peasley's sister waited on me. She is a fat and cheerful looking lady, very light complected. Her hair is red—like tomato ketchup. Looks to me a likely, stout armed, good hearted woman who can do a lot of hard work. She can see a joke and has an answer handy every time."

For details of the remainder of the historic visit

of Samson Traylor to the home of John Peasley we
are indebted to a letter from John to his brother
Charles, dated February 21, 1832.   In this he says:

"We had gone out to the barn and Brimstead and I
were helping Mr. Traylor hitch up his horses.   All of
a sudden two men came riding up the road at a fast
trot and turned in and come straight toward us and
pulled up by the wagon.   One of them was a slim, red
cheeked young feller about twenty-three years old.
He wore top boots and spurs and a broad brimmed
black hat and gloves and a fur waistcoat and purty
linen.   He looked at the tires of the wagon and said:
'That's the one we've followed.'
    " 'Which o' you is Samson Traylor?' he asked.
    " 'I am,' said Traylor.
    "The young feller jumped off his horse and tied him
to the fence.   Then he went up to Traylor and said:
    " 'What did you do with my niggers, you dirty
sucker?'
    "Men from Missouri hated the Illinois folks them
days and called 'em Suckers.   We always call a Missouri man a name too dirty to be put in a letter.   He
acted like one o' the Roman emperors ye read of.
    " 'Hain't you a little reckless, young feller?' Traylor
says, as cool as a cucumber.
    "I didn't know Traylor them days.   If I had, I'd 'a'
been prepared for what was comin'.
    "Traylor stood up nigh the barn door, which Brim-
stead had closed after we backed the wagon out.
    "The young feller stepped close to the New Salem
man and raised his whip for a blow. Quick as lightnin'
Traylor grabbed him and threw him ag'in' the barn

door, keewhack! He hit so hard the boards bent and the whole barn roared and trembled. The other feller tried to get his pistol out of its holster, but Brimstead, who stood beside him, grabbed it, and I got his hoss by the bits and we both held on. The young feller lay on the ground shakin' as if he had the ague. Ye never see a man so spylt in a second. Traylor picked him up. His right arm was broke and his face and shoulder bruised some. Ye'd a thought a steam engyne had blowed up while he was puttin' wood in it. He was kind o' limp and the mad had leaked out o' him.

" 'I reckon I better find a doctor,' he says.

" 'You get into my wagon and I'll take ye to a good one,' says Traylor.

"Just then Stephen Nuckles, the circuit minister, rode in with the big bloodhound that follers him around.

"The other slaver had got off his hoss in the scrimmage. Traylor started for him. The slaver began to back away and suddenly broke into a run. The big dog took after him with a kind of a lion roar. We all began yelling at the dog. We made more noise than you'd hear at the end of a hoss race. It scairt the young feller. He put on more steam and went up the ladder to the roof of the woodshed like a chased weasel. The dog stood barkin' as if he had treed a bear. Traylor grabbed the ladder and pulled it down.

" 'You stay there till I get away an' you'll be safe,' said he.

"The man looked down and swore and shook his fist and threatened us with the law.

"Mr. Nuckles rode close to the woodshed and looked up at him.

" 'My brother, I fear you be not a Christian,' he said.

"He swore at the minister. That settled him.

" 'What's all this erbout?' Mr. Nuckles asked me.

" 'He and his friend are from Missouri,' I says. 'They're lookin' for some runaway slaves an' they come here and pitched into us, and one got throwed ag'in' the barn an' the other clum to the roof.'

" 'I reckon he better stay thar till he gits a little o' God's grace in his soul,' says the minister.

"Then he says to the dog: 'Ponto, you keep 'im right thar.'

"The dog appeared to understand what was expected of him.

"The minister got off his hoss and hitehed him and took off his coat and put it on the ground.

" 'What you goin' to do?' I says.

" 'Me?' says the minister. 'I be goin' to rassle with Satan for the soul o' that 'ar man, an' if you keep watch I reckon you'll see 'at the ground'll be scratched up some 'fore I git through.'

"He loosened his collar an' knelt on his coat and began to pray that the man's soul would see its wickedness and repent. You could have heard him half a mile away.

"Mr. Traylor drove off with the damaged slaver settin' beside him and the saddle hoss hitched to the rear axle. I see my chance an' before that prayer ended I had got the fugitives under some hay in my wagon and started off with them on my way to Livingston County. I could hear the prayin' until I got over the hill into Canaan barrens. At sundown I left them in good hands thirty miles up the road."

In a frontier newspaper of that time it is recorded that the minister and his dog kept the slaver on the roof all day, vainly trying with prayer and exhortation to convert his soul. The man stopped swearing before dinner and on his promise not again to violate the commandment a good meal was handed up to him. He was liberated at sundown and spent the night with Brimstead.

"Who is that big sucker who grabbed my friend?" the stranger asked Brimstead.

"His name is Samson Traylor. Comes from Vermont," was the answer.

"He's the dog-gonedest steam engyne of a man I ever see, 'pon my word," said the stranger.

"An' he's about the gentlest, womern hearted critter that ever drawed the breath o' life," said Brimstead.

"If he don't look out 'Liph Biggs'll kill him—certain."

Samson spoke not more than a dozen words on his way back to New Salem. Amazed and a little shocked by his own conduct, he sat thinking. After all he had heard and seen, the threat of the young upstart had provoked him beyond his power of endurance. Trained to the love of liberty and justice, the sensitive mind of the New Englander had been hurt by the story of the fugitives. Upon this hurt the young man had poured the turpentine of haughty, imperial manners. In all the strange adventure it seemed to him that he had felt the urge of God—in the letter of Lovejoy, in the prayers of the negro woman and the minister, in his own wrath. The more he thought of it the less inclined he was to reproach himself for his violence. Slavery was a relic of ancient imperialism. It had no right in free America. There could be no peace with it save for a little time. He would write to his friends of what he had learned of the brutalities of slavery. The Missourians would tell their friends of the lawless and violent men of the North, who cared not a fig for the property rights of a southerner. The stories would travel like fire in dry grass.

So, swiftly, the thoughts of men were being prepared for the great battle lines of the future. Samson saw the peril of it.

As they rode along young Mr. Biggs took a flask half full of whisky from his pocket and offered it to Samson. The latter refused this tender of courtesy and the young man drank alone. He complained of pain and Samson made a sling of his muffler and put it over the neck and arm of the injured Biggs and drove with care to avoid jolting. For the first time Samson took a careful and sympathetic look at him. He was a handsome youth, about six feet tall, with dark eyes and hair and a small black mustache and teeth very white and even.

In New Salem Samson took him to Dr. Allen's office and helped the doctor in setting the broken bone. Then he went to Offut's store and found Abe reading his law book and gave him an account of his adventure.

"I'm both glad and sorry," said Abe. "I'm glad that you licked the slaver and got the negroes out of his reach. I reckon I'd have done the same if I could. I'm sorry because it looks to me like the beginning of many troubles. The whole subject of slavery is full of danger. Naturally southern men will fight for their property, and there is a growing number in the North who will fight for their principles. If we all get to fighting, I wonder what will become of the country. It reminds me of the man who found a skunk in his house. His boy was going after the critter with a club.

" 'Look here, boy,' he said, 'when you've got a skunk in the house, it's a good time to be careful. You might spyle the skunk with that club, but the skunk would be right certain to spyle the house. While he's our guest, I reckon we'll have to be polite, whether we want to or not.' "

"Looks to me as if that skunk had come to stay until he's put out," said Samson.

"That may be," Abe answered. "But I keep hopin'

that we can swap a hen for the house and get rid of him. Anyhow, it's a good time to be careful."

"He may be glad to live with me, but I ain't willin' to live with him," Samson rejoined. "I ain't awful proud, but his station in life is a leetle too far below mine. If I tried to live with him, I would get the smell on my soul so that St. Peter would wonder what to do with me."

Abe laughed.

"That touches the core of the trouble," said he. "In the North most men have begun to think of the effect of slavery on the soul; in the South a vast majority are thinking of its effect on the pocket. One stands for a moral and the other for a legal right."

"But one is righter than the other," Samson insisted.

That evening Samson set down the events of the day in his book and quoted the dialogue in Offut's store in which he had had a part. On the first of February, 1840, he put these words under the entry:

"I wouldn't wonder if this was the first trip on the Underground Railroad."

CHAPTER VII

IN WHICH MR. ELIPHALET BIGGS GETS ACQUAINTED
WITH BIM KELSO AND HER FATHER.

IN a musty old ledger kept by James Rutledge, the
owner of Rutledge's Tavern, in the year 1832, is an
entry under the date of January 31st which reads as
follows:

"Arrived this day Eliphalet Biggs of 26 Olive Street,
St. Louis, with one horse."

Young Mr. Biggs remained at Rutledge's Tavern
for three weeks with his arm in a sling under the eye
of the good doctor. The Rutledges were Kentucky
folk and there the young man had found a sympathetic
hearing and tender care. Dr. Allen had forbidden him
the use of ardent spirits while the bone was knitting
and so these three weeks were a high point in his life
so to speak.

It had done him good to be hurled against a barn
door and to fall trembling and confused at the feet
of his master. He had never met his master until he
had reached Hopedale that morning. The event had
been too long delayed. Encouraged by idleness and
conceit and alcohol, evil passions had grown rank in
the soil of his spirit. Restraint had been a thing un-

known to him. He had ruled the little world in which
he had lived by a sense of divine right. He was a
prince of Egoland—that province of America which
had only half yielded itself to the principles of Democracy.

Sobriety and the barn door had been a help to his
soul. More of these heroic remedies might have saved
him. He was like one exiled, for a term, from his
native heath. After the ancient fashion of princes,
he had at first meditated the assassination of the man
who had blocked his way. Deprived of the heat of
alcohol, his purpose sickened and died.

It must be said that he served his term as a sober
human being quite gracefully, being a well born youth
of some education. A few days he spent mostly in
bed, while his friend, who had come on from Hopedale, took care of him. Soon he began to walk about
and his friend returned to St. Louis.

His fine manners and handsome form and face captured the little village, most of whose inhabitants had
come from Kentucky. They knew a gentleman when
they saw him. They felt a touch of awe in his presence. Mr. Biggs claimed to have got his hurt by a
fall from his horse, pride leading him to clothe the
facts in prevarication. If the truth had been known
Samson would have suffered a heavy loss of popularity
in New Salem.

A week after his arrival Ann Rutledge walked over

to Jack Kelso's with him. Bim fled up the stick ladder as soon as they entered the door. Mr. Kelso was away on a fox hunt. Ann went to the ladder and called:

"Bim, I saw you fly up that ladder. Come back down. Here's a right nice young man come to see you."

"Is he good-looking?" Bim called.

"Oh, purty as a picture, black eyes and hair and teeth like pearls, and tall and straight, and he's got a be-e-autiful little mustache."

"That's enough!" Bim exclaimed. "I just wish there was a knot hole in this floor."

"Come on down here," Ann urged.

"I'm scared," was the answer.

"His cheeks are as red as roses and he's got a lovely ring and big watch chain—pure gold and yaller as a dandelion. You come down here."

"Stop," Bim answered. "I'll be down as soon as I can get on my best bib and tucker."

She was singing *Sweet Nightingale* as she began "to fix up," while Ann and Mr. Biggs were talking with Mrs. Kelso.

"Ann," Bim called in a moment, "had I better put on my red dress or my blue?"

"Yer blue, and be quick about it."

"Don't you let him get away after all this trouble."

"I won't."

In a few minutes Bim called from the top of the ladder to Ann. The latter went and looked up at her. Both girls burst into peals of merry laughter. Bim had put on a suit of her father's old clothes and her buffalo skin whiskers and was a wild sight.

"Don't you come down looking like that," said Ann. "I'll go up there and 'tend to you."

Ann climbed the ladder and for a time there was much laughing and chattering in the little loft. By and by Ann came down. Bim hesitated, laughing, above the ladder for a moment, and presently followed in her best blue dress, against which the golden curls of her hair fell gracefully. With red cheeks and bright eyes, she was a glowing picture. Very timidly she gave her hand to Mr. Biggs.

"It's just the right dress," he said. "It goes so well with your hair. I'm glad to see you. I have never seen a girl like you in my life."

"If I knew how, I'd look different," said Bim. "I reckon I look cross. Cows have done it. Do you like cows?"

"I hate cows—I've got a thousand cows and I see as little of them as possible," said he.

"It is such a pleasure to hate cows!" Bim exclaimed. "There's nothing I enjoy so much."

"Why?" Ann asked.

"I am not sure, but I think it is because they give milk—such quantities of milk! Sometimes I lie awake at night hating cows. There are so many cows here it keeps me busy."

"Bim has to milk a cow—that's the reason," said Ann.

"I'd like to come over and see her do it," said Mr. Biggs.

"If you do I'll milk in your face—honest I will," said Bim.

"I wouldn't care if it rained milk. I'm going to come and see you often, if your mother will let me."

A blush spread over the girl's cheeks to the pretty dimple at the point of her chin.

"You'll see her scampering up the ladder like a squirrel," said Mrs. Kelso. "She isn't real tame yet."

"Perhaps we could hide the ladder," he suggested, with a smile.

"Do you play on the flute?" Bim asked.

"No," said Mr. Biggs.

"I was afraid," Bim exclaimed. "My Uncle Henry does." She looked into Mr. Biggs' eyes.

"You like fun—don't you?" he said.

"Have you got a snare drum?" Bim queried.

"No. What put that into your head?" Mr. Biggs asked, a little mystified.

"I don't know. I thought I'd ask. My Uncle Henry has a snare drum. That's one reason we came to Illinois."

Mr. Biggs laughed. "That smile of yours is very becoming," he said.

"Did you ever dream of a long legged, brindle cat with yellow eyes and a blue tail?" she asked, as if to change the subject.

"Never!"

"I wisht you had. Maybe you'd know how to scare it away. It carries on so."

"I know what would fix that cat," said Mrs. Kelso. "Give him the hot biscuits which you sometimes eat for supper. He'll never come again."

At this point Mr. Kelso returned with his gun on his shoulder and was introduced to Mr. Biggs.

"I welcome you to the hazards of my fireside," said Kelso. "So you're from St. Louis and stopped for repairs in this land of the ladder climbers. Sit down and I'll put a log on the fire."

"Thank you, I must go," said Biggs. "The doctor will be looking for me now."

"Can I not stay you with flagons?" Kelso asked.

"The doctor has forbidden me all drink but milk and water."

"A wise man is Dr. Allen!" Kelso exclaimed. "Cervantes was right in saying that too much wine will neither keep a secret nor fulfill a promise."

"Will you make me a promise?" Bim asked of Mr. Biggs, as he was leaving the door with Ann.

"Anything you will ask," he answered.

"Please don't ever look at the new moon through a knot hole," she said in a half whisper.

The young man laughed. "Why not?"

"If you do, you'll never get married."

"I mustn't look at the new moon through a knot hole and I must beware of the flute and the snare drum," said Mr. Biggs.

"Don't be alarmed by my daughter's fancies," Kelso advised. "They are often rather astonishing. She has a hearty prejudice against the flute. It is well founded. An ill played flute is one of the worst enemies of law and order. Goldsmith estranged half his friends with a grim determination to play the flute. It was the skeleton in his closet."

So Mr. Eliphalet Biggs met the pretty daughter of Jack Kelso. On his way back to the tavern he told Ann that he had fallen in love with the sweetest and prettiest girl in all the world—Bim Kelso. That very evening Ann went over to Kelso's cabin to take the news to Bim and her mother and to tell them that her father reckoned he belonged to a very rich and a very grand family. Naturally, they felt a sense of elation, although Mrs. Kelso, being a woman of shrewdness, was not carried away. Mr. Kelso had gone to Offut's store and the three had the cabin to themselves.

"I think he's just a wonderful man!" Bim exclaimed. "But I'm sorry his name is so much like figs and pigs. I'm plum sure I'm going to love him."

"I thought you were in love with Harry Needles," Bim's mother said to her.

"I am. But he keeps me so busy. I have to dress

him up every day and put a mustache on him and think up ever so many nice things for him to say, and when he comes he doesn't say them. He's terribly young."

"The same age as you. I think he is a splendid boy —so does everybody."

"I have to make all his courage for him, and then he never will use it," Bim went on. "He has never said whether he likes my looks or not."

"But there's time enough for that—you are only a child," said her mother. "You told me that he said once you were beautiful."

"But he has never said it twice, and when he did say it, I didn't believe my ears, he spoke so low. Acted kind o' like he was scared of it. I don't want to wait forever to be really and truly loved, do I?"

Mrs. Kelso laughed. "It's funny to hear a baby talking like that," she said. "We don't know this young man. He's probably only fooling anyway."

Bim rose and stood very erect.

"Mother, do you think I look like a baby?" she asked. "I tell you I'm every inch a woman," she added, mimicking her father in the speech of Lear.

"But there are not many inches in you yet."

"How discouraging you are!" said Bim, sinking into her chair with a sigh.

Bim went often to the little tavern after that. Of those meetings little is known, save that, with all the pretty arts of the cavalier, unknown to Harry Needles, the handsome youth flattered and delighted the girl. This went on day by day for a fortnight. The evening before Biggs was to leave for his home, Bim went over to eat supper with Ann at the tavern.

It happened that Jack Kelso had found Abe sitting alone with his Blackstone in Offut's store that afternoon.

"Mr. Kelso, did you ever hear what Eb Zane said about the general subject of sons-in-law?" Abe asked.

"Never—but I reckon it would be wise and possibly apropos," said Kelso.

"He said that a son-in-law was a curious kind o' property," Abe began. " 'Ye know,' says Eb, 'if ye have a hoss that's tricky an' dangerous an' wuth less than nothin', ye can give him away er kill him, but if ye have a son-in-law that's wuthless, nobody else will have him an' it's ag'in' the law to kill him. Fust ye know ye've got a critter on yer hands that kicks an' won't work an' has to be fed an' liquored three times a day an' is wuth a million dollars less than nothin'.' "

There was a moment of silence.

"When a man is figurin' his assets, it's better to add ten dollars than to subtract a million," said Abe. "That's about as simple as adding up the weight o' three small hogs."

"What a well of wisdom you are, Abe!" said Kelso. "Do you know anything about this young Missourian who is shining up to Bim?"

"I only know that he was a drinking man up to the time he landed here and that he threatened Traylor with his whip and got thrown against the side of a barn—plenty hard. He's a kind of American king, and I don't like kings. They're nice to look at, but generally those that have married 'em have had one h—l of a time."

Kelso rose and went home to supper.

Soon after the supper dishes had been laid away in the Kelso cabin, young Mr. Biggs rapped on its door and pulled the latch-string and entered and sat down with Mr. and Mrs. Kelso at the fireside.

"I have come to ask for your daughter's hand," he said, as soon as they were seated. "I know it will seem sudden, but she happens to be the girl I want. I've had her picture in my heart always. I love your daughter. I can give her a handsome 'home and everything she could desire."

Kelso answered promptly: "We are glad to welcome you here, but we can not entertain such a proposal, flattering as it is. Our daughter is too young to think of marriage. Then, sir, we know very little about you, and may I be pardoned if I add that it does not recommend you?"

The young man was surprised. He had not expected such talk from a ladder climber. He looked at Kelso, groping for an answer. Then—

"Perhaps not," said he. "I have been a little wild, but that is all in the past. You can learn about me and my family from any one in St. Louis. I am not ashamed of anything I have done."

"Nevertheless, I must ask you to back away from this subject. I can not even discuss it with you."

"May I not hope that you will change your mind?"

"Not at present. Let the future take care of itself."

"I generally get what I want," said the young man.

"And now and then something that you don't want," said Kelso, a bit nettled by his persistence.

"You ought to think of her happiness. She is too sweet and beautiful for a home like this."

There was an awkward moment of silence. The young man said good night and opened the door.

"I'll go with you," said Kelso.

He went with Mr. Biggs to the tavern and got his daughter and returned home with her.

Mrs. Kelso chided her husband for being hard on Mr. Biggs.

"He has had his lesson, perhaps he will turn over a new leaf," she said.

"I fear there isn't a new leaf in his book," said Kelso. "They're all dirty."

He told his wife what Abe had said in the store.

"The wisdom of the common folk is in that beardless young giant," he said. "It is the wisdom of many generations gathered in the hard school of bitter experience. I wonder where it is going to lead him."

As Eliphalet Biggs was going down the south road

next morning he met Bim on her pony near the school-house, returning from the field with her cow. They stopped.

"I'm coming back, little girl," he said.

"What for?" she asked.

"To tell you a secret and ask you a question. No-body but you has the right to say I can not. May I come?"

"I suppose you can—if you want to," she answered.

"I'll come and I'll write to you and send the letters to Ann."

Mentor Graham, who lived in the schoolhouse, had come out of its door.

"Good-by!" said young Mr. Biggs, as his heels touched the flanks of his horse. Then he went flying down the road.

CHAPTER VIII

HARRY NEEDLES met Bim Kelso on the road next
day, when he was going down to see if there was any
mail. She was on her pony. He was in his new suit
of clothes—a butternut background striped into large
checks.

"You look like a walking checkerboard," said she,
stopping her pony.

"This—this is my new suit," Harry answered, looking down at it.

"It's a tiresome suit," said she impatiently. "I've
been playing checkers on it since I caught sight o' you,
and I've got a man crowned in the king row."

"I thought you'd like it," he answered, quite
seriously, and with a look of disappointment. "Say,
I've got that razor and I've shaved three times already."

He took the razor from his pocket and drew it from
its case and proudly held it up before her.

134

"Don't tell anybody," he warned her. "They'd laugh at me. They wouldn't know how I feel."

"I won't say anything," she answered. "I reckon I ought to tell you that I don't love you—not so much as I did anyway—not near so much. I only love you just a wee little bit now."

It is curious that she should have said just that. Her former confession had only been conveyed by the look in her eyes at sundry times and by unpremeditated acts in the hour of his peril.

Harry's face fell.

"Do you—love—some other man?" he asked.

"Yes—a regular man—mustache, six feet tall and everything. I just tell you he's purty!"

"Is it that rich feller from St. Louis?" he asked.

She nodded and then whispered: "Don't you tell."

The boy's lips trembled when he answered. "I won't tell. But I don't see how you can do it."

"Why?"

"He drinks and he keeps slaves and beats them with a bull whip. He isn't respectable."

"That's a lie," she answered quickly. "I don't care what you say."

Bim touched her pony with the whip and rode away.

Harry staggered for a moment as he went on. His eyes filled with tears. It seemed to him that the world had been ruined. On his way to the village he tried

and convicted it of being no fit place for a boy to live
in. Down by the tavern he met Abe, who stopped him.

"Howdy, Harry!" said Abe. "You look kind o'
sick. Come into the store and sit down. I want to
talk to you."

Harry followed the big man into Offut's store, flattered by his attention. There had been something
very grateful in the sound of Abe's voice and the feel
of his hand. The store was empty.

"You and I mustn't let ourselves be worried by
little matters," said Abe, as they sat down together
by the fire. "Things that seem to you to be as big as
a mountain now will look like a mole hill in six
months. You and I have got things to do, partner.
We mustn't let ourselves be fooled. I was once in a
boat with old Cap'n Chase on the Illinois River. We
had got into the rapids. It was a narrow channel in
dangerous water. They had to keep her headed just
so or we'd have gone on the rocks. Suddenly a boy
dropped his apple overboard and began to holler. He
wanted to have the boat stopped. For a minute that
boy thought his apple was the biggest thing in the
world. We're all a good deal like him. We keep
dropping our apples and calling for the boat to stop.
Soon we find out that there are many apples in the
world as good as that one. You have all come to a
stretch of bad water up at your house. The folks
have been sick. They're a little lonesome and dis-

John Wolcott Adams

couraged. Don't you make it any harder by crying over a lost apple. Ye know it's possible that the apple will float along down into the still water where you can pick it up by and by. The important thing is to keep going ahead."

This bit of fatherly counsel was a help to the boy.

"I've got a book here that I want you to read," Abe went on. "It is the *Life of Henry Clay*. Take it home and read it carefully and then bring it back and tell me what you think of it. You may be a Henry Clay yourself by and by. The world has something big in it for every one if he can only find it. We're all searching—some for gold and some for fame. I pray God every day that He will help me to find my work—the thing I can do better than anything else —and when it is found help me to do it. I expect it will be a hard and dangerous search and that I shall make mistakes. I expect to drop some apples on my way. They'll look like gold to me, but I'm not going to lose sight of the main purpose."

When Harry got home he found Sarah sewing by the fireside, with Joe and Betsey playing by the bed. Samson had gone to the woods to split rails.

"Any mail?" Sarah asked.

"No mail," he answered.

Sarah went to the window and stood for some minutes looking out at the plain. Its sere grasses, protruding out of the snow, hissed and bent in the wind. In its cheerless winter colors it was a dreary thing to see.

"How I long for home!" she exclaimed, as she resumed her sewing by the fire.

Little Joe came and stood by her knee and gave her his oft repeated blessing:

"God help us and make His face to shine upon us."

She kissed him and said: "Dear comforter! It shines upon me every time I hear you say those words."

The little lad had observed the effect of the blessing on his mother in her moments of depression and many times his parroting had been the word in season. Now he returned to his play again, satisfied.

"Would you mind if I called you mother?" Harry asked.

"I shall be glad to have you do it if it gives you any comfort, Harry," she answered.

She observed that there were tears in his eyes.

"We are all very fond of you," she said, as she bent to her task.

Then the boy told her the history of his morning— the talk with Bim, with the razor omitted from it; how he had met Abe and all that Abe had said to him as they sat together in the store.

"Well, Harry, if she's such a fool, you're lucky to have found it out so soon," said Sarah. "She does little but ride the pony and play around with a gun.

I don't believe she ever spun a hank o' yarn in her life.
She'll get her teeth cut by and by. Abe is right.
We're always dropping our apples and feeling very
bad about it, until we find out that there are lots of
apples just as good. I'm that way myself. I guess
I've made it harder for Samson crying over lost apples. I'm going to try to stop it."

Then fell a moment of silence. Soon she said:

"There's a bitter wind blowing and there's no great
hurry about the rails, I guess. You sit here by the
fire and read your book this forenoon. Maybe it will
help you to find your work."

So it happened that the events of Harry's morning
found their place in the diary which Sarah and Samson kept. Long afterward Harry added the sentences
about the razor.

That evening Harry read aloud from the *Life of
Henry Clay,* while Sarah and Samson sat listening by
the fireside. It was the first of many evenings which
they spent in a like fashion that winter. When the
book was finished they read, on Abe's recommenda-
tion, Weem's *Life of Washington.*

Every other Sunday they went down to the schoolhouse to hear John Cameron preach. He was a working man, noted for good common sense, who talked
simply and often effectively of the temptations of the
frontier, notably those of drinking, gaming and swearing. One evening they went to a debate in the tavern

on the issues of the day, in which Abe won the praise of all for an able presentation of the claim of Internal Improvements. During that evening Alexander Ferguson declared that he would not cut his hair until Henry Clay became president, the news of which resolution led to a like insanity in others and an age of unexampled hairiness on that part of the border.

For Samson and Sarah the most notable social event of the winter was a chicken dinner at which they and Mr. and Mrs. James Rutledge and Ann and Abe Lincoln and Dr. Allen were the guests of the Kelsos. That night Harry stayed at home with the children.

Kelso was in his best mood.

"Come," he said, when dinner was ready. "Life is more than friendship. It is partly meat."

"And mostly Kelso," said Dr. Allen.

"Ah, Doctor! Long life has made you as smooth as an old shilling and nimbler than a sixpence," Kelso declared. "And, speaking of life, Aristotle said that the learned and the unlearned were as the living and the dead."

"It is true," Abe interposed. "I say it, in spite of the fact that it slays me."

"You? No! You are alive to your finger tips," Kelso answered.

"But I have mastered only eight books," said Abe.

"And one—the book of common sense, and that has wised you," Kelso went on. "Since I came to this country I have learned to beware of the one-book man. There are more living men in America than in any land I have seen. The man who reads one good book thoughtfully is alive and often my master in wit or wisdom. Reading is the gate and thought is the pathway of real life."

"I think that most of the men I know have read the Bible," said Abe.

"A wonderful and a saving fact! It is a sure foundation to build your life upon."

Kelso paused to pour whisky from a jug at his side for those who would take it.

"Let us drink to our friend Abe and his new ambition," he proposed.

"What is it?" Samson asked.

"I am going to try for a seat in the Legislature," said Abe. "I reckon it's rather bold. Old Samuel Legg was a good deal of a nuisance down in Hardin County. He was always talking about going to Lexington, but never went.

" 'You'll never get thar without startin',' said his neighbor.

" 'But I'm powerful skeered fer fear I'd never git back,' said Samuel. 'There's a big passel o' folks that gits killed in the city.'

" 'You always was a selfish cuss. You ought to think o' yer neighbors,' said the other man.

"So I've concluded that if I don't start I'll never get

there, and if I die on the way it will be a good thing for my neighbors," Abe added.

The toast was drunk, and by some in water, after which Abe said:

"If you have the patience to listen to it, I'd like to read my declaration to the voters of Sangamon County."

Samson's diary briefly describes this appeal as follows:

"He said that he wanted to win the confidence and esteem of his fellow citizens. This he hoped to accomplish by doing something which would make him worthy of it.   He had been thinking of the county.   A railroad would do more for it than anything else, but a railroad would be too costly.   The improvement of the Sangamon River was the next best thing.   Its channel could be straightened and cleared of driftwood and made navigable for small vessels under thirty tons' burden. He favored a usury law and said, in view of the talk he had just heard, he was going to favor the improvement and building of schools, so that every one could learn how to read, at least, and learn for himself what is in the Bible and other great books.   It was a modest statement and we all liked it."

"Whatever happens to the Sangamon, one statement in that platform couldn't be improved," said Kelso.

"What is that?" Abe asked.

"It's the one that says you wish to win the regard of your fellows by serving them."

"It's a lot better than saying that he wishes to serve Abe," said Dr. Allen, a remark which referred to a former conversation with Abe, in which Kelso had had a part.

"You can trust Abe to take the right turn at every fork in the road," Kelso went on. "If you stick to that, my boy, and continue to study, you'll get there and away beyond any goal you may now see. A passion for service is more than half the battle. Since the other night at the tavern I've been thinking about Abe and the life we live here. I've concluded that we're all very lucky, if we are a bit lonesome."

"I'd like to know about that," said Sarah. "I'm a little in need of encouragement."

"Well, you may have observed that Abe has a good memory," he continued. "While I try to be modest about it, my own memory is a fairly faithful servant. It is due to the fact that since I left the university I have lived, mostly, in lonely places. It is a great thing to be where the register of your mind is not over-burdened by the flow of facts. Abe's candidacy is the only thing that has happened here since Samson's raising, except the arrival and departure of Eliphalet Biggs. Our memories are not weakened by overwork. They have time for big undertakings—like Burns and Shakespeare and Blackstone."

"I've noticed that facts get kind o' slippery when they come in a bunch, as they did on our journey," said Samson. "Seems so they wore each other smooth and got hard to hold."

"Ransom Prigg used to say it was easy enough to ketch eels, but it was powerful hard to hold 'em," Abe remarked. "He caught three eels in a trap one day and the trap busted and let 'em loose in the boat. He kept grabbin' and tusslin' around the boat till the last eel got away. 'I never had such a slippery time in all the days o' my life,' said Rans. 'One eel is a dinner, but three eels is jest a lot o' slippin' an' disapp'intment.'"

"That's exactly the point I make," said Kelso. "A man with too many eels in the boat will have none for dinner. The city man is at a great disadvantage. Events slip away from him and leave nothing. His intellect gets the habit of letting go. It loses its power to seize and hold. His impressions are like footprints on a beach. They are washed away by the next tide."

There was much talk at the fireside after dinner, all of which doubtless had an effect on the fortunes of the good people who sat around it, and the historian must sort the straws, and with some regret, for bigger things are drawing near in the current. Samson and Sarah had been telling of their adventures on the long road.

"We are all movers," said Kelso. "We can not stay where we are for a single day—not if we are alive. Most of us never reach that eminence from which we discover the littleness of ourselves and our troubles and achievements and the immensities of power and wisdom by which we are surrounded."

At least one of that company was to remember the words in days of adversity and triumph. Soon after that dinner the memories of the little community began to register an unusual procession of thrilling facts.

Early in April an Indian scare spread from the capital to the remotest corners of the state. Black Hawk, with many warriors, had crossed the Mississippi and was moving toward the Rock River country. Governor Reynolds called for volunteers to check the invasion.

Abe, whose address to the voters had been printed in the *Sangamon Journal,* joined a volunteer company and soon became its captain. On the tenth of April he and Harry Needles left for Richland to go into training. Samson was eager to go, but could not leave his family.

Bim Kelso rode out into the fields where Harry was at work the day before he went away.

"This is a great surprise," said Harry. "I don't see you any more except at a distance."

"I don't see you either."

"I didn't think you wanted to see me."

"You're easily discouraged," she said, looking down with a serious face.

"You made me feel as if I didn't want to live any longer."

"I reckon I'm mean. I made myself feel a million times worse. It's awful to be such a human as I am. Some days I'm plum scared o' myself."

"I'm going away," the boy said, in a rather mournful tone.

"I hate to have you go. I just love to know you're here, if I don't see you. Only I wish you was older and knew more."

"Maybe I know more'n you think I do," he answered.

"But you don't know anything about my troubles," said she, with a sigh.

"I don't get the chance."

There was half a moment of silence. She ended it by saying:

"Ann and I are going to the spelling school to-night."

"Can I go with you?"

"Could you stand it to be talked to and scolded by a couple of girls till you didn't care what happened to you?"

"Yes; I've got to be awful careless."

"We'll be all dressed up and ready at quarter of eight. Come to the tavern. I'm going to have supper with Ann. She is just terribly happy. John McNeil has told her that he loves her. It's a secret. Don't you tell."

"I won't. Does she love him?"

"Devotedly; but she wouldn't let him know it—not yet."

"No?"

"Course not. She pretends she's in love with somebody else. It's the best way. I reckon he'll be plum anxious before she owns up. But she truly loves him. She'd die for him."

"Girls are awful curious—nobody can tell what they mean," said Harry.

"Sometimes they don't know what they mean themselves. Often I say something or do something and wonder and wonder what it means."

She was looking off at the distant plain as she spoke.

"Sometimes I'm surprised to find out how much it means," she added. "I reckon every girl is a kind of a puzzle and some are very easy and some would give ye the headache."

"Or the heartache."

"Did you ever ride a horse sitting backwards— when you're going one way and looking another and you don't know what's coming?" she asked.

"What's behind you is before you and the faster you go the more danger you're in?" Harry laughed.

"Isn't that the way we have to travel in this world, whether we're going to love or to mill?" the girl asked, with a sigh. "We can not tell what is ahead. We see only what is behind us. It is very sad."

Harry looked at Bim. He saw the tragic truth of

the words and suddenly her face was like them. Un-consciously in the midst of her playful talk this thing had fallen. He did not know quite what to make of it.

"I feel sad when I think of Abe," said Harry. "He don't know what is ahead of him, I guess. I heard Mrs. Traylor say that he was in love with Ann."

"I reckon he is, but he don't know how to show it. You might as well ask me to play on a flute. He's never told her. He just walks beside her to a party and talks about politics and poetry and tells funny stories. I reckon he's mighty good, but he don't know how to love a girl. Ann is afraid he'll step on her, he's so tall and awkward and wanderin'. Did you ever see an elephant talking with a cricket?"

"Not as I remember," said Harry.

"I never did myself, but if I did, I'm sure they'd both look very tired. It would be still harder for an elephant to be engaged to a cricket. I don't reckon the elephant's love would fit the cricket or that they'd ever be able to agree on what they'd talk about. It's some that way with Abe and Ann. She is small and spry; he is slow and high. She'd need a ladder to get up to his face, and I just tell you it ain't purty when ye get there. She ain't got a chance to love him."

"I love him," said Harry. "I think he's a wonder-ful man. I'd fight for him till I died. John McNeil is nothing but a grasshopper compared to him."

"That's about what my father says," Bim answered. "I love Abe, too, and so does Ann, but it ain't the hope to die, marryin' love. It's like a man's love for a man or a woman's love for a woman. John McNeil is handsome—he's just plum handsome, and smart, too. He's bought a big farm and is going into the grocery business. Mr. Rutledge says he'll be a rich man."

"I wouldn't wonder. Is he going to the spelling school?"

"No, he went off to Richland to-day with my father to join the company. They're going to fight the Injuns, too."

Harry stood smoothing the new coat of Colonel with his hand, while Bim was thinking how she would best express what was on her mind. She did not try to say it, but there was something in the look of her eyes which the boy remembered.

He was near telling her that he loved her, but he looked down at his muddy boots and soiled overalls. They were like dirt thrown on a flame. How could one speak of a sweet and noble passion in such attire? Clean clothes and white linen for that! The shell sounded for dinner. Bim started for the road at a gallop, waving her hand. He unhitched his team and followed it slowly across the black furrows toward the barn.

He did not go to the spelling school. Abe came

at seven and said that he and Harry would have to walk to Springfield that night and get their equipment and take the stage in the morning. Abe said if they started right away they could get to the Globe tavern by midnight. In the hurry and excitement Harry forgot the spelling school. To Bim it was a tragic thing. Before he went to bed that night he wrote a letter to her.

CHAPTER IX

MANY things came with the full tide of the spring-time—innumerable flowers and voices, the flowers filled with glowing color, the voices with music and delight. Waves of song swept over the limitless meadows. They went on and on as if they traveled a shoreless sea in a steady wind. Bob-whites, meadow-larks, bobolinks, song sparrows, bluebirds, competed with the crowing of the meadow cocks. This joyous tumult around the Traylor cabin sped the day and emphasized the silence of the night.

In the midst of this springtime carnival there came also cheering news from the old home in Vermont—a letter to Sarah from her brother, which contained the welcome promise that he was coming to visit them and expected to be in Beardstown about the fourth of May. Samson drove across country to meet the steamer. He was at the landing when *The Star of the North* arrived. He saw every passenger that came ashore, and Eliphalet Biggs, leading his big bay mare,

151

was one of them, but the expected visitor did not arrive. There would be no other steamer bringing passengers from the East for a number of days.

Samson went to a store and bought a new dress and sundry bits of finery for Sarah. He returned to New Salem with a heavy heart. He dreaded to meet his faithful partner and bring her little but disappointment. The windows were lighted when he got back, long after midnight. Sarah stood in the open door as he drove up.

"Didn't come," he said mournfully.

Without a word, Sarah followed him to the barn, with the tin lantern in her hand. He gave her a hug as he got down from the wagon. He was little given to like displays of emotion.

"Don't feel bad," he said.

She tried bravely to put a good face on her disappointment, but, while he was unharnessing and leading the weary horses into their stalls, it was a wet face and a silent one.

"Come," he said, after he had thrown some hay into the mangers. "Let's go into the house. I've got something for ye."

"I've given them up—I don't believe we shall ever see them again," said Sarah, as they were walking toward the door. "I think I know how the dead feel who are so soon forgotten."

"Ye can't blame 'em," said Samson. "They've

probably heard about the Injun scare and would expect to be massacreed if they came."

Indeed the scare, now abating, had spread through the border settlements and kept the people awake o' nights. Samson and other men, left in New Salem, had met to consider plans for a stockade.

"And then there's the fever an' ague," Samson added.

"Sometimes I feel sorry I told 'em about it because they'll think it worse than it is. But we've got to tell the truth if it kills us."

"Yes: we've got to tell the truth," Samson rejoined. "There'll be a railroad coming through here one of these days and then we can all get back and forth easy. If it comes it's going to make us rich. Abe says he expects it within three or four years."

Sarah had a hot supper ready for him. As he stood warming himself by the fire she put her arms around him and gave him a little hug.

"You poor tired man!" she said. "How patient and how good you are!"

There was a kind of apology for this moment of weakness in her look and manner. Her face seemed to say: "It's silly but I can't help it."

"I've been happy all the time for I knew you was waiting for me," Samson remarked. "I feel rich every time I think of you and the children. Say, look here."

He untied the bundle and put the dress and finery in her lap.

"Well, I want to know!" she exclaimed, as she held it up to the candlelight. "That must have cost a pretty penny."

"I don't care what it cost—it ain't half good enough —not half," said Samson.

As he sat down to his supper he said:

"I saw that miserable slaver, Biggs, get off the boat with his big bay mare. There was a darky following him with another horse."

"Good land!" said Sarah. "I hope he isn't coming here. Mrs. Onstott told me to-day that Bim Kelso has been getting letters from him."

"She's such an odd little critter and she's got a mind of her own—anybody could see that," Samson reflected. "She ought to be looked after purty careful. Her parents are so taken up with shooting and fishing and books they kind o' forget the girl. I wish you'd go down there to-morrow and see what's up. Jack is away you know."

"I will," said Sarah.

It was nearly two o'clock when Samson, having fed and watered his horses, got into bed. Yet he was up before daylight, next morning, and singing a hymn of praise as he kindled the fire and filled the tea kettle and lighted his candle lantern and went out to do his chores while Sarah, partly reconciled to her new disappointment, dressed and began the work of another day. So they and Abe and Harry and others like them, each under the urge of his own ambition, spent their great strength in the building and defense of the republic and grew prematurely old. Their work began and ended in darkness and often their days were doubled by the burdens of the night. So in the reckoning of their time each year was more than one.

Sarah went down to the village in the afternoon of the next day. When Samson came in from the fields to his supper she said:

"Mr. Biggs is stopping at the tavern. He brought a new silk dress and some beautiful linen to Mrs. Kelso. He tells her that Bim has made a new man of him. Claims he has quit drinking and gone to work. He looks like a lord—silver spurs and velvet riding coat and ruffled shirt and silk waistcoat. A colored servant rode into the village with him on a beautiful brown horse, carrying big saddle-bags. Bim and her mother are terribly excited. He wants them to move to St. Louis and live on his big plantation in a house next to his—rent free."

Samson knew that Biggs was the type of man who weds Virtue for her dowry.

"A man's judgment is needed there," said he. "It's a pity Jack is gone. Biggs will take that girl away with him sure as shooting if we don't look out."

"Oh, I don't believe he'd do that," said Sarah. "I hope he has turned over a new leaf and become a gentleman."

"We'll see," said Samson.

They saw and without much delay the background of his pretensions, for one day within the week he and Bim, the latter mounted on the beautiful brown horse, rode away and did not return. Soon a letter came from Bim to her mother, mailed at Beardstown. It told of their marriage in that place and said that they would be starting for St. Louis in a few hours on *The Star of the North*. She begged the forgiveness of her parents and declared that she was very happy.

"Too bad! Isn't it?" said Sarah when Mrs. Waddell, who had come out with her husband one evening to bring this news, had finished the story.

"Yes, it kind o' spyles the place," said Samson. "Bim was a wonderful girl—spite of all her foolishness—like the birds that sing among the flowers on the prairie—kind o'—yes, sir—she was. I'm afraid for Jack Kelso—'fraid it'll bust his fiddle if it don't break his heart. His wife is alone now. We must ask her to come and stay with us."

"The Allens have taken her in," said Mrs. Waddell.

"That's good," said Sarah. "I'll go down there to-morrow and offer to do anything we can."

When Mr. and Mrs. Waddell had gone Sarah said:

"I can't help thinking of poor Harry. He was terribly in love with her."

"Well, he'll have to get over it—that's all," said Samson. "He's young and the wound will heal."

It was well for Harry that he was out of the way of all this, and entered upon adventures which absorbed his thought. As to what was passing with him we have conclusive evidence in two letters, one from Colonel Zachary Taylor in which he says:

"Harry Needles is also recommended for the most intrepid conduct as a scout and for securing information of great value. Compelled to abandon his wounded horse he swam a river under fire and under the observation of three of our officers, through whose help he got back to his command, bringing a bullet in his thigh."

With no knowledge of military service and a company of untrained men, Abe had no chance to win laurels in the campaign. His command did not get in touch with the enemy. He had his hands full maintaining a decent regard for discipline among the raw frontiersmen of his company.

He saved the life of an innocent old Indian, with a passport from General Cass, who had fallen into their hands and whom, in their excitement and lust for action, they desired to hang. This was the only incident of his term of service which gave him the least satisfaction.

Early in the campaign Harry had been sent with a message to headquarters, where he won the regard of Colonel Taylor and was ordered to the front with a company of scouts. No member of the command had been so daring. He had the recklessness of youth and its wayward indifferences to peril. William Boone, a son of Daniel, used to speak of "the luck of that daredevil farmer boy."

One day in passing mounted through a thick woods on the river, near the enemy, he suddenly discovered Indians all around him. They sprang out of the bushes ahead and one of them opened fire. He turned and spurred his horse and saw the painted warriors on every side. He rode through them under a hot fire. His horse fell wounded near the river shore and Harry took to the water and swam beneath it as far as he could. When he came up for breath bullets began splashing and whizzing around him. It was then that he got his wound. He dove and reached the swift current which greatly aided his efforts. Some white men in a boat about three hundred yards away witnessed his escape and said that the bullets "tore the river surface into rags" around him as he came up. Courage and his skill as a diver and swimmer saved his life. Far below, the boat, in which were a number of his fellow scouts overtook him and helped him back to camp. So it happened that a boy won a reputation in the "Black Hawk War" which was not lavish in its bestowal of honors.

When the dissatisfied volunteers were mustered out late in May, Kelso and McNeil, being sick with a stubborn fever, were declared unfit for service and sent back to New Salem as soon as they were able to ride. Abe and Harry joined Captain Iles' Company of Independent Rangers and a month or so later Abe reenlisted to serve with Captain Early, Harry being under a surgeon's care. The latter's wound was not serious and on July third he too joined Early's command.

This company was chiefly occupied in the moving of supplies and the burying of a few men who had been killed in small engagements with the enemy. It was a band of rough-looking fellows in the costume of the frontier farm and workshop—ragged, dirty and unshorn. The company was disbanded July tenth at Whitewater, Wisconsin, where, that night, the horses of Harry and Abe were stolen. From that point they started on their long homeward tramp with a wounded sense of decency and justice. They felt that the Indians had been wronged: that the greed of land grabbers had brutally violated their rights. This feeling had been deepened by the massacre of the red women and children at Bad Ax.

A number of mounted men went with them and gave them a ride now and then. Some of the travel-

ers had little to eat on the journey. Both Abe and
Harry suffered from hunger and sore feet before
they reached Peoria where they bought a canoe and
in the morning of a bright day started down the Illinois River.

They had a long day of comfort in its current with
a good store of bread and butter and cold meat and
pie. The prospect of being fifty miles nearer home before nightfall lightened their hearts and they laughed
freely while Abe told of his adventures in the campaign. To him it was all a wild comedy with tragic
scenes dragged into it and woefully out of place. Indeed he thought it no more like war than a pig sticking and that was the kind of thing he hated.

At noon they put ashore and sat on a grassy bank
in the shade of a great oak, to escape the withering
sunlight of that day late in July, while they ate their
luncheon.

"I reckon that the Black Hawk peril was largely
manufactured," said Abe as they sat in the cool shade.

"If they had been let alone I don't believe the Indians would have done any harm. It reminds me a
little of the story of a rich man down in Lexington
who put a cast iron buck in his dooryard. Next morning all the dogs in the neighborhood got together and
looked him over from a distance. He had invaded
their territory and they reckoned that he was theirs.
They saw a chance for war. One o' their number vol-

unteered to go and scare up the buck. So he raised
the hair on his back and sneaked up from behind and
when he was about forty feet away made hell bent
for the buck's heels. The buck didn't move and the
dog nearly broke his neck on that pair o' cast iron
legs. He went limping back to his comrades.

" 'What's the trouble?' they asked.

" 'It's nary buck,' said the dog.

" 'What is it then?'

" 'Darned if I know. It kicks like a mule an' smells
like a gate post.'

" 'Come on, you fellers. It looks to me like a good
time to go home,' said a wise old dog. 'I've learned
that ye can't always believe yerself.'

"It's a good thing for a man or a government to
learn," Abe went on as they resumed their journey.
"I've learned not to believe everything I hear. The
first command I gave, one o' the company hollered
'Go to h—l.' Every one before me laughed. It was
a chance to get mad. I didn't for I knew what it
meant. I just looked sober and said:

" 'Well, boys, I haven't far to go and I reckon we'll
all get there if we don't quit fooling an' 'tend to business.'

"They agreed with me."

Harry had not heard from home since he left it.
Abe had had a letter from Rutledge which gave him
the news of Bim's elopement. The letter had said:

"I was over to Beardstown the day Kelso and Mc-Neil got off the steamer.   I brought them home with me.   Kelso was bigger than his trouble.   Said that the ways of youth were a part of the great plan. 'Thorns!   Thorns!' he said.   'They are the teachers of wisdom and who am I that I should think myself or my daughter too good for the like since it is written that Jesus Christ did not complain of them.' "

"Have you heard from home?"   Abe asked as they paddled on.

"Not a word," said Harry.

"You're not expecting to meet Bim Kelso?"

"That's the best part of getting home for me," said Harry, turning with a smile.

"Let her drift for a minute," said Abe.   "I've got a letter from James Rutledge that I want to read to you.   There's a big lesson in it for both of us—something to remember as long as we live."

Abe read the letter.   Harry sat motionless.   Slowly his head bent forward until his chin touched his breast.

Abe said with a tender note in his voice as he folded the letter:

"This man is well along in life.   He hasn't youth to help him as you have.   See how he takes it and she's the only child he has.   There are millions of pretty girls in the world for you to choose from."

"I know it but there's only one Bim Kelso in the

world," Harry answered mournfully. "She was the one I loved."

"Yes, but you'll find another. It looks serious but it isn't—you're so young. Hold up your head and keep going. You'll be happy again soon."

"Maybe, but I don't see how," said the boy.

"There are lots of things you can't see from where you are at this present moment. There are a good many miles ahead o' you I reckon and one thing you'll see plainly, by and by, that it's all for the best. I've suffered a lot myself but I can see now it has been a help to me. There isn't an hour of it I'd be willing to give up."

They paddled along in silence for a time.

"It was my fault," said Harry presently. "I never could say the half I wanted to when she was with me. My tongue is too slow. She gave me a chance and I wasn't man enough to take it. That's all I've got to say on that subject."

He seemed to find it hard to keep his word for in a moment he added:

"I wouldn't have been so good a scout if it hadn't been for her. I guess the Injuns would have got me but when I thought of her I just kept going."

"I think you did it just because you were a brave man and had a duty to perform," said Abe.

Some time afterward in a letter to his father the boy wrote:

"I often think of that ride down the river and the way he talked to me. It was so gentle. He was a big, powerful giant of a man who weighed over two hundred pounds, all of it bone and muscle. But under his great strength was a woman's gentleness; under the dirty, ragged clothes and the rough, brown skin grimy with dust and perspiration, was one of the cleanest souls that ever came to this world. I don't mean that he was like a minister. He could tell a story with pretty rough talk in it but always for a purpose. He hated dirt on the hands or on the tongue. If another man had a trouble Abe took hold of it with him. He would put a lame man's pack on top of his own and carry it. He loved flowers like a woman. He loved to look at the stars at night and the colors of the sunset and the morning dew on the meadows. I never saw a man so much in love with fun and beauty."

They reached Havana that evening and sold their canoe to a man who kept boats to rent on the river shore. They ate a hot supper at the tavern and got a ride with a farmer who was going ten miles in their direction. From his cabin some two hours later they set out afoot in the darkness.

"I reckon it will be easier under the stars than under the hot sun," said Abe. "Our legs have had a long rest anyhow."

They enjoyed the coolness and beauty of the summer night.

"Going home is the end of all journeys," said Abe as they tramped along. "Did it ever occur to you that every living creature has its home? The fish of the sea, the birds of the air, the beasts of the field and forest, the creepers in the grass, all go home. Most of them turn toward it when the day wanes. The call of home is the one voice heard and respected all the way down the line of life. And, ye know, the most wonderful and mysterious thing in nature is the power that fool animals have to go home through great distances, like the turtle that swam from the Bay of Biscay to his home off Van Dieman's Land. Somehow coming over in a ship he had blazed a trail through the pathless deep more than ten thousand miles long. It's the one miraculous gift—the one call that's irresistible. Don't you hear it now? I never lie down in the darkness without thinking of home when I am away."

"And it's hard to change your home when you're wonted to it," said Harry.

"Yes, it's a little like dying when you pull up the roots and move. It's been hard on your folks."

This remark brought them up to the greatest of mysteries. They tramped in silence for a moment. Abe broke in upon it with these words:

"I reckon there must be another home somewhere to go to after we have broke the last camp here and a kind of a bird's compass to help us find it. I reckon we'll hear the call of it as we grow older."

He stopped and took off his hat and looked up at the stars and added:

"If it isn't so I don't see why the long procession of life keeps harping on this subject of home. I think I see the point of the whole thing. It isn't the place or the furniture that makes it home, but the love and peace that's in it. By and by our home isn't here any more. It has moved. Our minds begin to beat about in the undiscovered countries looking for it. Somehow we get it located—each man for himself."

For another space they hurried along without speaking.

"I tell you, Harry, whatever a large number of intelligent folks have agreed upon for some generations is so—if they have been allowed to do their own thinking," said Abe. "It's about the only wisdom there is."

He had sounded the keynote of the new Democracy.

"There are some who think that Reason is the only guide but in the one problem of going home it don't compare with the turtle's wisdom," Abe added. "His head isn't bigger than a small apple. But I reckon the scientist can't teach him anything about navigation. Reminds me o' Steve Nuckles. His head is full of ignorance but he'll know how to get home when the time comes."

"My stars! How we're hurrying!" Harry exclaimed at length.

"I didn't realize it—I'm so taken up with the thought of getting back," said Abe. "It's as if my friends had a rope around me and were pulling it."

So under the lights of heaven, speaking in the silence of the night, of impenetrable mysteries, they journeyed on toward the land of plenty.

"It's as still as a graveyard," Harry whispered when they had climbed the bluff by the mill long after midnight and were near the little village.

"They're all buried in sleep," said Abe. "We'll get Rutledge out of bed. He'll give us a shake-down somewhere."

His loud rap on the door of the tavern signalized more than a desire for rest in the weary travelers, for just then a cycle of their lives had ended.

BOOK TWO

CHAPTER X

WITHIN a week after their return the election came
off and Abe was defeated, although in his precinct two
hundred and twenty-seven out of a total of three hundred votes had been cast for him. He began to consider which way to turn. He thought seriously of the
trade of the blacksmith which many advised. Burns
and Shakespeare, who had been with him in recent
vicissitudes seemed to disagree with him. Jack Kelso,
who had welcomed the returning warriors in the
cheery fashion of old, vigorously opposed his trying
"to force the gates of fortune with the strong arm."
They were far more likely to yield, he said, to a well
trained intellect of which mighty sinews were a poor
tool but a good setting. Moreover, Major John T.
Stuart—a lawyer of Springfield—who had been his
comrade in the "war" had encouraged him to study
law and, further, had offered to lend him books. So
he looked for an occupation which would give him
leisure for study. Offut, his former employer, had

168

failed and cleared out. The young giant regarded thoughtfully the scanty opportunities of the village. He could hurl his great strength into the axhead and make a good living but he had learned that such a use of it gave him a better appetite for sleep than study.

John McNeil, who for a short time had shared his military adventures, had become a partner of Samuel Hill in a store larger and better stocked than any the village had known. But Hill and McNeil had no need of a clerk. Rowan Herndon and William Berry— he of the morning-glory shirt—had opened a general store. Mr. Herndon offered to sell his interest to Abe and take notes for his pay. It was not a proposition that promised anything but loss. The community was small and there were three other stores and there was no other "Bill" Berry, who was given to drink and dreams as Abe knew. He was never offensive. Drink begat in Bill Berry a benevolent form of intemperance. It imparted to him a feeling of pity for the human race and a deep sense of obligation to it. In his cups he acquired a notable generosity and politeness. In the words of Jack Kelso he was then "as placid as a mill pond and as full of reflection." He had many friends and no one had questioned his honesty.

Abe Lincoln had not been trained to weigh the consequences of a business enterprise. The store would give him leisure for study and New Salem could offer him nothing else save consuming toil with the axe or the saw. He could not think of leaving the little cabin village. There were Ann Rutledge and Jack Kelso and Samson Traylor and Harry Needles. Every ladder climber in the village and on the plain around it was his friend.

Upon these people who knew and respected him Abe Lincoln based his hopes. Among them he had found his vision and failure had not diminished or dimmed it. He would try again for a place in which he could serve them and if he could learn to serve Sangamon County he could learn to serve the state and, possibly, even the Republic. With this thought and a rather poor regard for his own interest his name fell into bad company on the sign-board of Berry and Lincoln. Before he took his place in the store he walked to Springfield and borrowed a law book from his friend Major Stuart.

The career of the firm began on a hot day late in August with Bill Berry smoking his pipe in a chair on the little veranda of the store and Abe Lincoln sprawled in the shade of a tree that partly overhung its roof, reading a law book. The latter was collarless and without coat or waistcoat. His feet were in yarn socks and heavy cloth slippers. Mr. Berry was looking intently at nothing. He was also thinking of nothing with a devotion worthy of the noblest cause. No breeze touched the mill pond of his consciousness. He would have said that he "had his traps set for an idea and was watching them." Generally he was watching his traps with a look of dreamy contemplation. He, too, wore no coat or waistcoat. His calico shirt was decorated with diminutive roses in pink ink. His ready tied necktie was very red and fastened on his collar button with an elastic loop. A nugget of free gold which, he loved to explain, had come from the Rocky Mountains and had ten dollars' worth of the root of evil in it, adorned his shirt-front—dangling from a pin bar on a tiny chain.

The face of Mr. Berry suddenly assumed a look of animation. A small, yellow dog which had been lying in repose beside him rose and growled, his hair rising, and with a little cry of alarm and astonishment fled under the store.

"Here comes Steve Nuckles on his old mare with a lion following him," said Berry.

Abe closed his book and rose and looked at the approaching minister and his big dog.

"If we ain't careful we'll git prayed for plenty," said Berry.

"If the customers don't come faster I reckon we'll need it," said Abe.

"Howdy," said the minister as he stopped at the hitching bar, dismounted and tied his mare. "Don't be skeered o' this 'ere dog. He were tied when I left home but he chawed his rope an' come a'ter me. I reckon if nobody feeds him he'll patter back to-night."

"He's a whopper!" said Abe.

"He's the masteris' dog I ever did see," said the minister, a tall, lank, brawny, dark-skinned man with gray eyes, sandy whiskers on the point of his chin, and clothes worn and faded. "Any plug tobaccer?"

"A back load of it," said Berry, going into the store to wait on the minister.

When they came out the latter carved off a corner of the plug with his jack-knife, put it into his mouth and sat down on the door-step.

"Mr. Nuckles, how did you happen to become a minister?" Abe asked.

"Well, sur, I done had a dream," said the Reverend Mr. Nuckles, as he clasped his hands over a knee and chewed vigorously. "I done dreamt that I had swallered a double wagon and that the tongue o' the wagon were stickin' out o' my mouth. It were a cur'ous dream an' I cain't tell what you'd make of it, but I done tuk it for a sign that my tongue were to be used on the gospel."

"It shows that a man who can swaller a wagon can swaller anything," said Abe. "But I'm glad you took it for a sign. You've done a lot of good in this country. I've seen you out in all weather and you've made over many a man and broke and bitted some of the wildest colts on the prairie."

"I jes' keep watch an' when ol' Satan comes snoopin' eround I'm right thar to ketch holt an' flop him. It done come to pass frequent I've laid it on till he were jest a hollerin' fer mercy. Where do Samson Traylor live?"

Abe took him to the road and pointed the way.

"There be goin' to be a raid," said Nuckles. "I reckon, by all I've heard, it'll come on to-night."

"A raid! Who's going to be raided?" Abe asked.

"Them Traylor folks. A lady done tol' me yesterday. Soon as ever I got her soul saved she blabbed it. Thar be a St. Louis man name o' Biggs, done stirred up the folks from Missourey and Tennessee on the south road 'bout the Yankee who holps the niggers out o' bondage. Them folks'd have slavery in this here county if they could. They be right hot I reckon. A stranger done been goin' eround with whisky in his bags startin' a band o' regulators. Held a meetin' las' Sunday. They be goin' to do some regulatin' to-night. Ol' Satan'll break loose. Ef you don't wa'ch out they'll come over an' burn his house sartin."

"We'll watch out," said Abe. "They don't know Traylor. He's one of the best men in this county."

"I've heered he were a he man an' a right powerful, God-fearin' man," said the minister.

"He's one of the best men that ever came to this country and any one that wants to try his strength is welcome to; I don't," said 'Abe. "Are you going over there?"

"I were goin' to warn 'em an' holp 'em ef I cain.'"

"Well, go on, but don't stir 'em up," Abe cautioned him. "Don't say a word about the raid. I'll be over there with some other fellers soon after sundown. We'll just tell 'em it's a he party come over for a story-tellin' an' a rassle. I reckon we'll have some fun. Ride on over and take supper with 'em. They're worth knowing."

In a few minutes the minister mounted his horse and rode away followed by his big dog.

"If I was you I wouldn't go," said Berry.

"Why not?"

"It'll hurt trade. Let the rest of Traylor's friends go over. There's enough of 'em."

"We must all stand as one man for law and order," said Abe. "If we don't there won't be any."

As soon as Abe had had his supper he went from house to house and asked the men to come to his store for a piece of important business. When they had come he told them what was in the wind. Soon after that hour Abe and Philemon Morris, and Alexander Ferguson, and Martin Waddell and Robert Johnson and Joshua Miller and Jack Kelso and Samuel Hill and John McNeil set out for the Traylor cabin. Doctors Allen and Regnier and James Rutledge and John Cameron and Isaac Gollaher, being older men, were requested to remain in the village and to use their guns, if necessary, to prevent a demonstration there. Samson greeted the party with a look of surprise.

"Have you come out to hang me?" he asked.

"No just to hang around ye," said Abe.

"This time it's a heart warmin'," Jack Kelso averred. "We left our wives at home so that we could pay our compliments to Mrs. Traylor without reserve knowing you to be a man above jealousy."

"It's what we call a he party on the prairies," said Ferguson. "For one thing I wanted to see Abe and the minister have a rassle."

The Reverend Stephen Nuckles stood in front of the door with Sarah and Harry and the children. He was a famous wrestler. Forthwith he playfully jumped into the air clapping his heels together three times before he touched the ground.

"I cain't rassle like I used to could but I be willin' to give ye a try, Abe," said the minister.

"You'd better save your strength for ol' Satan," said Abe.

"Go on, Abe," the others urged. "Give him a try."

Abe modestly stepped forward. In the last year he had grown less inclined to that kind of fun. The men took hold of each other, collar and elbow. They parried with their feet for an instant. Suddenly Abe's long right leg caught itself behind the left knee of the minister. It was the hip lock as they called it those days. Once secured the stronger man was almost sure to prevail and quickly. The sturdy circuit rider stood against it for a second until Abe sprang his bow. Then the heels of the former flew upward and his body came down to the grass, back first.

"That ar done popped my wind bag," said the minister as he got up.

"Call in," said John McNeil and the others echoed it.

"I call you," said the minister turning to McNeil.

"McNeil!" the onlookers called.

The stalwart young Irishman stepped forward and said:

"I don't mind measuring my length on the grass."

This he did in less than half a moment. As the young man rose from the grass he said:

"I call in Samson Traylor."

At last the thing which had long been a subject of talk and argument in the stores and houses of New Salem was about to come to pass—a trial of strength and agility between the two great lions of Sangamon County. Either of them would have given a month's work to avoid it.

"I reckon we better begin our **story-tellin'**," said Abe.

"I think so too," Samson declared. "It's purty dusk now."

"A rassle—a rassle," their neighbors shouted.

"I'd rather give ten bushel o' wheat than miss seein' you fellers take hold o' each other," said Alexander Ferguson.

"I would too," said Martin Waddell.

So it happened that these friendly giants, each dreading the ordeal, faced each other for a contest.

"Now we shall see which is the son of Peleus and which the son of Telemon," Kelso shouted.

"How shall we rassle?" Samson asked.

"I don't care," said Abe.

"Rough and tumble," Ferguson proposed.

Both men agreed. They bent low intently watching each other, their great hands outreaching. They stood braced for a second and suddenly both sprang forward. Their shoulders came together with a thud. It was like two big bison bulls hurling their weight in the first shock of battle. For a breath each bore with all his strength and then closed with his adversary. Each had an under hold with one arm, the other hooked around a shoulder. Samson lifted Abe from his feet but the latter with tremendous efforts loosened the hold of the Vermonter, and regained the turf. They struggled across the dooryard, the ground trembling beneath their feet. They went against the side of the house shaking it with the force of their impact. Samson had broken the grip of one of Abe's hands and now had his feet in the air again but the young giant clung to hip and shoulder and wriggled back to his foothold. Those lesser men were thrilled and a little frightened by the mighty struggle. Knowing the strength of the wrestlers they felt a fear of broken bones. Each had torn a rent in the coat of the other. If they kept on there was danger that both would be stripped. The children had begun to cry. Sarah begged the struggling men to stop and they obeyed her.

"If any of you fellers think that's fun you can have my place," said Abe. "Samson, I declare you elected the strongest man in this county. You've got the muscle of a grizzly bear. I'm glad to be quit o' ye."

"It ain't a fair election, Abe," Samson laughed. "If you were rassling for the right you could flop me. This little brush was nothing. Your heart wasn't in it, and by thunder, Abe! when it comes to havin' fun I rather guess we'd both do better to let each other alone."

" 'Tain't exactly good amusement, not for us," Abe agreed.

It was growing dark. Ann Rutledge arrived on her pony, and called Abe aside and told him that the raiders were in the village and were breaking the windows of Radford's store because he had refused to sell them liquor.

"Have they any guns with them?" Abe asked.

"No," Ann answered.

"Don't say anything about it," Abe cautioned her.

"Just go into the house with Sarah Traylor and sit down and have a good visit. We'll look after the raiders."

Then Abe told Samson what was up. The men concealed themselves in some bushes by the roadside while the minister sat close against an end of the house with his blood hound beside him. Before they were settled in their places they heard the regulators coming. The horses of the latter were walking as they approached. Not a sound came from the men who rode them. They proceeded to the grove just beyond the cabin and hitched their horses. There were eight men in the party according to Abe's count as they passed. The men, in concealment, hurried to the cabin and surrounded it, crouched against the walls. In a moment they could see a big spot, blacker than the darkness, moving toward them. It was the massed raiders. They came on with the stealth of a cat nearing its prey. A lion-like roar broke the silence. The blood hound leaped forward. The waiting men sprang to their feet and charged. The raiders turned and ran, pell mell, in a panic toward their horses. Suddenly the darkness seemed to fill with moving figures. One of the fleeing men, whose coat tails the dog had seized, was yelling for help. The minister rescued him and the dog went on roaring after the others. When the New Salemites got to the edge of the grove they could hear a number of regulators climbing into the tree-

tops. Samson had a man in each hand; Abe had another, while Harry Needles and Alexander Ferguson
were in possession of the man whom the dog had captured. The minister was out in the grove with his
blood hound that was barking and growling under a
tree. Jack Kelso arrived with a lantern. One of Samson's captives began swearing and struggling to get
away. Samson gave him a little shake and bade him
be quiet. The man uttered a cry of fear and pain
and offered no more resistance. Stephen Nuckles came
out of the grove.

"The rest o' that ar party done gone up-stairs to
roost," said the minister. "I reckon my dog'll keep
'em thar. We better jest tote these men inter the
house an' have a prayin' bee. I've got a right smart
good chanct, now, to whop ol' Satan."

They moved the raiders' horses. Then the party—
save Harry Needles, who stayed in the grove to keep
watch—took its captives into the cabin.

"You set here with this gun and if any o' them tries
to get away you take a crack at him," said Samson,
as they were leaving, in a voice intended for the men
in the tree-tops.

The men and the four dejected raiders crowded
into the cabin.

Sarah, who had heard the disturbance and wondered what it meant, met them at the door with a
look of alarm.

"These men came to do us harm," Samson said to

Sarah. "They are good fellows but they got an idea in their heads that we are bad folks. I hear that young Mr. Biggs set them up against us. Let's give them a bite to eat the first thing we do."

They took a look at the captives. Three of them were boys from eighteen to twenty years of age. The other was a lanky, bearded Tennessean some forty years old. One of the young lads had hurt his hand in the evening's frolic. Blood was dripping from it. The four sat silent and fearful and ashamed.

Sarah made tea and put it with meat and milk and doughnuts and bread and butter on the table for them. Samson washed and bandaged the boy's wound. The captives ate as if they were hungry while the minister went out to feed his dog. When the men had finished eating Samson offered them tobacco. The oldest man filled his pipe and lighted it with a coal. Not one of the captives had said a word until this tall Tennessean remarked after his pipe was going:

"Thankee, mister. You done been right good to us."

"Who told you to come here?" Samson demanded.

" 'Twere a man from St. Louis. He done said you hated the South an' were holpin' niggers to run away."

"And he offered to pay you to come here and burn this house and run Traylor out of the county, didn't he?" Abe asked.

"He did—yes, suh—he suah did," answered the man —like a child in his ignorance and simplicity.

"I thought so," Abe rejoined. "You tackled a big

job, my friend. Did you know that every one of
you could be sent to prison for a term of years and
I've a good mind to see that you go there. You men
have got to begin right now to behave yourselves
mighty proper or you'll begin to sup sorrow."

Stephen Nuckles returned as Abe was speaking.

"You jest leave 'em to me, Mr. Lincoln," he said.
"These be good men but ol' Satan done got his hooks
on 'em. Mis' Traylor, ef you don't mind I be goin'
to do a job o' prayin' right now. Men, you jest git
down on yo' knees right hyar along o' me."

The men and the minister knelt on the puncheon
floor while the latter prayed long and loudly for the
saving of their souls. Every one who heard it felt
the simple, moving eloquence of the prayer. Kelso
said that Christ's love of men was in it. When the
prayer was ended the minister asked permission to go
with the raiders to the barn and spend the night with
them. Of this curious event Samson wrote in his
diary:

"Of what was done in the barn I have no knowledge but when Nuckles came back to the house with
them in the morning the minister said that they had
come into the fold and that he would promise for them
that they would be good citizens in the future. They
got their breakfast, fed and watered their horses and
rode away. We found five men up in the tree-tops
and the dog on watch. The minister went out and
preached to them for about half an hour and then

prayed for their souls.   When that was over he said:

"'Now, boys, be you ready to accept Christ and a good breakfast?   If not you'll have to git a new grip on yer pews an' set right thar while I preach another sermon.   Thar ain't nary one of us goin' to break our fast till you're willin' to be saved.'

"They caved in.

"'I couldn't stan' another sermon no how,' said one in a sorrowful voice.   'I feel like a wownded bird. Send up a charge o' buck shot if you keer to, but don't preach no more sermons to me.   It's jest a waste o' breath.   I reckon we're all on the monah's bench.'

"When they had come down out of the tree-tops not one of them could stand on his legs for a little while."

The gentleman of the sorrowful voice and the broken spirit said:

"'Pears like I'll have to be tuk down an' put together again."

They were meek and sore when they limped to the cabin and washed on the stand by the doorside and went in to breakfast.   After they had eaten the minister prayed some more and rode away with them.

It is recorded later in the diary that the rude Shepherd of the prairies worked with these men on their farms for weeks until he had them wonted to the fold.

CHAPTER XI

RADFORD'S grocery had been so wrecked by the raiders that its owner was disheartened. Reenforced by John Cameron and James Rutledge he had succeeded in drawing them away before they could steal whisky enough to get drunk. But they had thrown many of his goods into the street. Radford mended his windows and offered his stock for sale. After a time Berry and Lincoln bought it, giving notes in payment, and applied for a license to sell the liquors they had thus acquired.

The Traylors had harvested a handsome crop of corn and oats and wheat only to find that its value would be mostly consumed by threshing and transportation to a market. Samson was rather discouraged.

"It's the land of plenty but it's an awful ways from the land of money," he said. "We've got to hurry up and get Abe into the Legislature or this community can't last.   We've got to have some way to move things."

None of their friends had come out to them and only one letter from home had reached the cabin since April.

Late that autumn a boy baby arrived in their home. Mrs. Onstott, Mrs. Waddell and Mrs. Kelso came to help and one or the other of them did the nursing and cooking while Sarah was in bed and for a little time thereafter.   The coming of the baby was a comfort to this lonely mother of the prairies.   Joe and Betsey asked their father in whispers while Sarah was lying sick where the baby had come from.

"I don't know," he answered.

"Don't you know?" Joe asked with a look of wonder.

"No, sir, I don't—that's honest," said Samson. "But there's some that say they come on the back of a big crane and at the right home the ol' crane lights an' pecks on the door and dumps 'em off, just as gentle as he can."

Joe examined the door carefully to find where the crane had pecked on it.

That day he confided to Betsey that in his opinion the baby didn't amount to much.

"Why?" Betsey asked.

"Can't talk or play with any one or do anything but just make a noise like a squirrel.   Nobody can do anything but whisper an' go 'round on his tiptoes."

"He's our little brother and we must love him," said Betsey.

"Yes; we've got to love him," said Joe. "But it's worse 'n pickin' up potatoes. I wisht he'd gone to some other house."

That day Sarah awoke from a bad dream with tears flowing down her cheeks. She found the little lad standing by her pillow looking very troubled. He kissed her and whispered:

"God help us all and make His face to shine upon us."

There is a letter from Sarah to her brother dated May, 10, 1833, in which she sums up the effect of all this and some months of history in the words that follow:

"The Lord has given us a new son. I have lived through the ordeal—thanks to His goodness—and am strong again. The coming of the baby has reconciled us to the loss of our old friends as much as anything could. It has made this little home dear to us and proved the quality of our new friends. Nothing is too much for them to do. I don't wonder that Abe Lincoln has so much confidence in the people of this country. They are sound at heart both the northerners and the southerners 'though some of the latter that we see here are awfully ignorant and prejudiced. We have had wonderful fun with the children since the baby was born. It has been like a play or a story book to hear the talk of Joe and Betsey. She loves to play mother to this wonderful new doll and is quite a help to me. Harry Needles is getting over his disappointment. He goes down to the store often to sit with Abe and Jack Kelso and hear them talk. He and Samson are getting deeply interested in politics. Abe lets Harry read the books that he borrows from Major Stuart of Springfield. The boy is bent on being a lawyer and improving his mind. Samson found him the other day making a speech to the horses and to poor Sambo out in the barn. Bim Kelso writes to her mother that she is very happy in her new home but there is something between the lines which seems to indicate that she is trying to put a good face on a bad matter. What a peril it is to be young and pretty and a girl! Berry and Lincoln have got a license and are selling liquor in their store but nobody thinks anything of that here. Abe has been appointed Postmaster. Everytime he leaves the store he takes the letters in his hat and delivers them as he gets a chance. We have named the new baby Samuel."

The firm of Lincoln and Berry had not prospered. After they had got their license things went from bad to worse with them. Mr. Berry, who handled the liquors, kept himself in a genial stage of inebriation and sat in smiles and loud calico talking of gold mines and hidden treasure. Jack Kelso said that a little whisky converted Berry's optimism into opulence.

"It is the opulence that tends to poverty," Abe answered. "Berry gets so rich, at times, that he will have nothing to do with the vulgar details of trade."

"And he exhibits such a touching sympathy for the poor," said Kelso, "you can't help loving him. I have never beheld such easy and admirable grandeur."

The addition of liquors to its stock had attracted some rather tough characters to the store. One of them who had driven some women out of it with profanity was collared by Abe and conducted out of the door and thrown upon the grass where his face was rubbed with smart weed until he yelled for mercy. After that the rough type of drinking man chose his words with some care in the store of Berry and Lincoln.

One evening, of that summer, Abe came out to the Traylors' with a letter in his hat for Sarah.

"How's business?" Samson asked.

"Going to peter out I reckon," Abe answered with a sorrowful look. "It will leave me badly in debt. I wanted something that would give me a chance for study and I got it. By jing! It looks as if I was going to have years of study trying to get over it. I've gone and jumped into a mill pond to get out of the rain. I'd better have gone to Harvard College and walked all the way. Have you got any work to give me? You know I can split rails about as fast as the next man and I'll take my pay in wheat or corn."

"You may give me all the time you can spend outside the store," said Samson.

That evening they had a talk about the whisky

business and its relation to the character of Eliphalet Biggs and to sundry infractions of law and order in their community. Samson had declared that it was wrong to sell liquor.

"All that kind of thing can be safely left to the common sense of our people," said Abe. "The remedy is education, not revolution. Slowly the people will have to set down all the items in the ledger of common sense that passes from sire to son. By and by some generation will strike a balance. That may not come in a hundred years. Soon or late the majority of the people will reach a reckoning with John Barleycorn. If there's too much against him they will act. You might as well try to stop a glacier by building a dam in front of it. They have opened an account with Slavery too. By and by they'll decide its fate."

Such was his faith in the common folk of America whose way of learning and whose love of the right he knew as no man has known it.

In this connection the New Englander wrote in his diary:

"He has spent his boyhood in the South and his young manhood in the North. He has studied the East and lived in the West. He is the people—I sometimes think—and about as slow to make up his mind. As Isaiah says: 'He does not judge after the sight of his eyes neither reprove after the hearing of his ears.' Abe has to think about it."

Many days thereafter Abe and Harry and Samson were out in the woods together splitting rails and making firewood. Abe always took his book with him and read aloud to Harry and Samson in the noon-hour. He liked to read aloud and thought that he remembered better what he had read with both eye and ear taking it in.

One day while they were at work Pollard Simmons came out to them and said that John Calhoun the County Surveyor wanted Abe to be his assistant.

"I don't know how to survey," said Abe.

"But I reckon you can learn it," Simmons answered. "You're purty quick to learn."

Abe thought a moment. Calhoun was a Democrat.

"Would I have to sacrifice any of my principles?" he asked.

"Nary a one," said Simmons.

"Then I'll try and see if I can get the hang of it," Abe declared. "I reckon **Mentor** Graham could help me."

"Three dollars a day is not to be sneezed at," said Simmons.

"No, sir—not if you can get it honest," Abe answered. "I'm not so careless with my sneezing as some men. Once when Eb Zane was out on the Ohio in a row-boat Mike Fink the river pirate got after him. Eb had a ten dollar gold piece in his pocket. For fear that he would be captured he clapped it into his mouth.

Eb was a good oarsman and got away. He was no sooner out of danger than he fetched a sneeze and blew the gold piece into the river. After that he used to say that he had sneezed himself poor and that if he had a million dollars it wouldn't bother him to sneeze 'em away. Sneezing is a form of dissipation which has not cost me a cent so far and I don't intend to yield to it."

Immediately after that Abe got Flint and Gibson's treatise on surveying and began to study it day and night under the eye of the kindly schoolmaster. In about six weeks he had mastered the book and reported for duty.

In April Abe wrote another address to the voters announcing that he was again a candidate for a seat in the Legislature. Late that month Harry walked with him to Pappsville where a crowd had assembled to attend a public sale. When the auctioneer had finished Abe made his first stump speech. A drunken man tried to divert attention to himself by sundry interruptions. Harry asked him to be quiet, whereupon the ruffian and a friend pitched upon the boy and began to handle him roughly. Abe jumped down, rushed into the crowd, seized the chief offender and raising him off his feet flung him into the air. He hit the ground in a heap some four yards from where Abe stood. The latter resumed his place and went on with his speech. The crowd cheered him and there

was no further disturbance at that meeting. The
speech was a modest, straightforward declaration of
his principles. When he was leaving several voices
called for a story. Abe raised a great laugh with a
humorous anecdote in which he imitated the dialect
and manners of a Kentucky backwoodsman. They
kept him on the auctioneer's block for half an hour
telling the wise and curious folk tales of which he
knew so many. He had won the crowd by his principles, his humor and good nature as well as by the
brave and decisive exhibition of his great strength.

Abe and Harry went to a number of settlements in
the county with a like result save that no more violence
was needed. At one place there were men in the
crowd who knew Harry's record in the war. They
called on him for a speech. He spoke on the need of
the means of transportation in Sangamon County
with such insight and dignity and convincing candor
that both Abe and the audience hailed him as a coming man. Abe and he were often seen together those
days.

In New Salem they were called the disappointed lovers. It was known there that Abe was very fond of
Ann Rutledge although he had not, as yet, openly
confessed to any one—not even to Ann—there being
no show of hope for him. Ann was deeply in love
with John McNeil—the genial, handsome and successful young Irishman. The affair had reached the stage

of frankness, of an open discussion of plans, of fond affection expressing itself in caresses quite indifferent to ridicule.

For Ann it had been like warm sunlight on the growing rose. She was neater in dress, lovelier in form and color, more graceful in movement and sweeter-voiced than ever she had been. It is the old way that Nature has of preparing the young to come out upon the stage of real life and to act in its moving scenes. Abe manfully gave them his best wishes and when he spoke of Ann it was done very tenderly. The look of sadness, which all had noted in his moments of abstraction, deepened and often covered his face with its veil. That is another way that Nature has of preparing the young. For these the roses have fallen and only the thorns remain. They are not lured; they seem to be driven to their tasks, but for all, soon or late, her method changes.

On a beautiful morning of June, 1834, John McNeil left the village. Abe Lincoln and Harry and Samson and Sarah and Jack Kelso and his wife stood with the Rutledges in the dooryard of the tavern when he rode away. He was going back to his home in the far East to return in the autumn and make Ann his bride. The girl wept as if her heart would break when he turned far down the road and waved his hand to her.

"Oh, my pretty lass! Do you not hear the birds

singing in the meadows?" said Jack Kelso. "Think of the happiness all around you and of the greater happiness that is coming when he returns. Shame on you!"

"I'm afraid he'll never come back," Ann sobbed.

"Nonsense! Don't get a maggot in your brain and let the crows go walking over your face. Come, we'll take a ride in the meadows and if I don't bring you back laughing you may call me no prophet."

So the event passed.

Harry traveled about with Abe a good deal that summer, "electioneering," as they called it, from farm to farm. Samson and Sarah regarded the association as a good school for the boy who had a taste for politics. Abe used to go into the fields, with the men whose favor he sought, and bend his long back over a scythe or a cradle and race them playfully across the field of grain cutting a wider swath than any other and always holding the lead. Every man was out of breath at the end of his swath and needed a few minutes for recuperation. That gave Abe a chance for his statement of the county's needs and his plan of satisfying them. He had met and talked with a majority of the voters before the campaign ended in his election in August. Those travels about the county had been a source of education to the candidate and the voters.

At odd times that summer he had been surveying a

new road with Harry Needles for his helper. In September they resumed their work upon it in the vicinity of New Salem and Abe began to carry the letters in his hat again. Every day Ann was looking for him as he came by in the dim light of the early morning on his way to work.

"Anything for me?" she would ask.

"No mail in since I saw you, Ann," was the usual answer.

Often he would say: "I'm afraid not, but here—you take these letters and look through 'em and make sure."

Ann would take them in her hands, trembling with eagerness, and run indoors to the candlelight, and look them over. Always she came back with the little bundle of letters very slowly as if her disappointment were a heavy burden.

"There'll be one next mail if I have to write it myself," Abe said one morning in October as he went on.

To Harry Needles who was with him that morning he said:

"I wonder why that fellow don't write to Ann. I couldn't believe that he has been fooling her but now I don't know what to think of him. Every day I have to deliver a blow that makes her a little paler and thinner. It hurts me like smashing a finger nail. I wonder what has happened to the fellow."

The mail stage was late that evening. As it had

not come at nine Mr. Hill went home and left Abe in the store to wait for his mail. The stage arrived a few minutes later. It came as usual in a cloud of dust and a thunder of wheels and hoofs mingled with the crack of the lash, the driver saving his horses for this little display of pride and pomp on arriving at a village. Abe examined the little bundle of letters and newspapers which the driver had left with him. Then he took a paper and sat down to read in the firelight. While he was thus engaged the door opened softly and Ann Rutledge entered. The Postmaster was not aware of her presence until she touched his arm. ·

"Please give me a letter," she said.

"Sit down, Ann," said he, very gently, as he placed a chair in the fire-glow.

She took it, turning toward him with a look of fear and hope. Then he added:

"I'm sorry but the truth is it didn't come."

"Don't—don't tell me that again," she pleaded in a broken voice, as she leaned forward covering her face with her hands.

"It is terrible, Ann, that I have to help in this breaking of your heart that is going on. I seem to be the head of the hammer that hits you so hard but the handle is in other hands. Honestly, Ann, I wish I could do the suffering for you—every bit of it—and give your poor heart a rest. Hasn't he written you this summer?"

"Not since July tenth," she answered. Then she

confided to Abe the fact that her lover had told her
before he went away that his name was not McNeil
but McNamar;·that he had changed his name to keep
clear of his family until he had made a success; that
he had gone east to get his father and mother and
bring them back with him; lastly she came to the
thing that worried her most—the suspicion of her
father and mother that John was not honest.

"They say that nobody but a liar would live with a
false name," Ann told him. "They say that he probably had a wife when he came here—that that is why
he don't write to me."

Then after a little silence she pleaded: "You don't
think that, do you, Abe?"

"No," said the latter, giving her the advantage of
every doubt. "John did a foolish thing but we must
not condemn him without a knowledge of the facts.
The young often do foolish things and sickness would
account for his silence. But whatever the facts are
you mustn't let yourself be slain by disappointment.
It isn't fair to your friends. John McNamar may be
the best man in the world still the fact remains that
it would be a pretty good world even if he were not
in it and I reckon there'd be lots of men whose love
would be worth having too. You go home and go to
sleep and stop worrying, Ann. You'll get that letter
one of these days."

A day or two later Abe and Harry went to Springfield. Their reason for the trip lay in a talk between

the Postmaster and Jack Kelso the night before as they sat by the latter's fireside.

"I've been living where there was no one to find fault with my parts of speech or with the parts of my legs which were not decently covered," said Abe. "The sock district of my person has been without representation in the legislature of my intellect up to its last session. Then we got a bill through for local improvements and the Governor has approved the appropriation. Suddenly we discovered that there was no money in the treasury. But Samson Traylor has offered to buy an issue of bonds of the amount of fifteen dollars."

"I'm glad to hear you declare in favor of external improvements," said Kelso. "We've all been too much absorbed by internal improvements. You're on the right trail, Abe. You've been thinking of the public ear and too little of the public eye. We must show some respect for both."

"Sometimes I think that comely dress ought to go with comely diction," said Abe. "But that's a thing you can't learn in books. There's no grammarian of the language of dress. Then I'm so big and awkward. It's a rather hopeless problem."

"You're in good company," Kelso assured him. "Nature guards her best men with some sort of singularity not attractive to others. Often she makes them odious with conceit or deformity or dumbness or garrulity. Dante was such a poor talker that no one would ever ask him to dinner. If it had not been so I presume his muse would have been sadly crippled by indigestion. If you had been a good dancer and a lady's favorite I wonder if you would have studied Kirkham and Burns and Shakespeare and Blackstone and Greenleaf, and the science of surveying and been elected to the Legislature. I wonder if you could even have whipped Jack Armstrong."

"Or have enjoyed the friendship of Bill Berry and acquired a national debt, or have saved my imperiled country in the war with Black Hawk," Abe laughed.

In the matter of dress the Postmaster had great confidence in the taste and knowledge of his young friend, Harry Needles, whose neat appearance Abe regarded with serious admiration. So he asked Harry to go with him on this new mission and help to choose the goods and direct the tailoring, for it seemed to him a highly important enterprise.

"It's a difficult problem," said Abe. "Given a big man and a small sum and the large amount of respectability that's desired. We mustn't make a mistake."

They got a ride part of the way with a farmer going home from Rutledge's Mill.

"Our appropriation is only fifteen dollars," said Abe as they came in sight of "the big village" on a warm bright day late in October. "Of course I can't expect to make myself look like the President of the United States with such a sum but I want to look like a respectable citizen of the United States if that is possible. I'll give the old Abe and fifteen dollars to boot for a new one and we'll see what comes of it."

Springfield had been rapidly changing. It was still small and crude but some of the best standards of civilization had been set up in that community. Families of wealth and culture in the East had sent their sons and a share of their capital to this little metropolis of the land of plenty to go into business. The Edwardses in their fine top boots and ruffled shirts were there. So were certain of the Ridgleys of Maryland— well known and successful bankers. The Logans and the Conklings and the Stuarts who had won reputations at the bar before they arrived were now settled in Springfield. Handsome, well groomed horses, in silver mounted harness, drawing carriages that shone "so you could see your face in them," to quote from Abe again, were on its streets.

"My conscience! What a lot of jingling and high stepping there is here in the street and on the sidewalk," said Abe as they came into the village. "I reckon there's a mile of gold watch chains in this crowd."

A public sale was on and the walks were thronged. Women in fine silks and millinery; men in tall beaver

hats and broadcloth and fine linen touched elbows
with the hairy, rough clad men of the prairies and
their worn wives in old-fashioned bonnets and faded
coats.

The two New Salem men stopped and studied a
big sign in front of a large store on which this an-
nouncement had been lettered:

"Cloths, cassinettes, cassimeres, velvet silks, satins,
Marseilles waistcoating, fine, calf boots, seal and mo-
rocco pumps for gentlemen, crepe lisse, lace veils.
Thibet shawls, fine prunella shoes."

"Reads like a foreign language to me," said Abe.
"The pomp of the East has got here at last. I'd like
to know what seal and morocco pumps are. I reckon
they're a contrivance that goes down into a man's
pocket and sucks it dry. I wonder what a cassinette
is like, and a prunella shoe. How would you like a
little Marseilles waistcoating?"

Suddenly a man touched his shoulder with a hearty
"Howdy, Abe?"

It was Eli, "the wandering Jew," as he had been
wont to call himself in the days when he carried a pack
on the road through Peter's Bluff and Clary's Grove
and New Salem to Beardstown and back.

"Dis is my store," said Eli.

"Your store!" Abe exclaimed.

"Ya, look at de sign."

The Jew pointed to his sign-board, some fifty feet long under the cornice, on which they read the legend:

"Eli Fredenberg's Emporium."

Abe looked him over from head to foot and exclaimed:

"My conscience! You look as if you had been fixed up to be sold to the highest bidder."

The hairy, dusty, bow-legged, threadbare peddler had been touched by some miraculous hand. The lavish hand of the West had showered her favors on him. They resembled in some degree the barbaric pearl and gold of the East. He glowed with prosperity. Diamonds and ruffled linen and Scotch plaid and red silk on his neck and a blue band on his hat and a smooth-shorn face and perfumery were the glittering details that surrounded the person of Eli.

"Come in," urged the genial proprietor of the Emporium. "I vould like to show you my goots and introduce you to my brudder."

They went in and met his brother and had their curiosity satisfied as to the look and feel of cassinettes and waistcoatings and seal and morocco pumps and prunella shoes.

In the men's department after much thoughtful discussion they decided upon a suit of blue jeans—that being the only goods which, in view of the amount of cloth required, came within the appropriation. Eli advised against it.

"You are like Eli already," he said. "You haf got de pack off your back. Look at me. Don't you hear my clothes say somet'ing?"

"They are very eloquent," said Abe.

"Vell dey make a speech. Dey say 'Eli Fredenberg he is no more a poor devil. You can not sneeze at him once again. Nefer. He has climb de ladder up.' Now you let me sell you somet'ing vat makes a good speech for you."

"If you'll let me dictate the speech I'll agree," said Abe.

"Vell—vat is it?" Eli asked.

"I would like my clothes to say in a low tone of voice: 'This is humble Abraham Lincoln about the same length and breadth that I am. He don't want to scare or astonish anybody. He don't want to look like a beggar or a millionaire. Just put him down for a hard working man of good intentions who is badly in debt.'"

That ended all argument. The suit of blue jeans was ordered and the measures taken. As they were about to go Eli said:

"I forgot to tell you dot I haf seen Bim Kelso de odder day in St. Louis. I haf seen her on de street. She has been like a queen so grand! De hat and gown from Paris and she valk so proud! But she look not so happy like she usit to be. I speak to her. Oh my, she vas glad and so surprised! She tolt me dot she vould like to come home for a visit but her husband he does not vant her to go dere—nefer again. My jobber haf tolt me dot Mr. Biggs is git drunk efery day. Bim she t'ink de place no good. She haf tolt me dey treat de niggers awful. She haf cry ven she tolt me dot."

"Poor child!" said Abe. "I'm afraid she's in trouble."

"I've been thinking for some time that I'd go down there and try to see her," said Harry as they were leaving the store. "Now, I'll have to go."

"Maybe I'll go with you," said Abe.

They got a ride part of the way back and had a long tramp again under the starlight.

"I don't believe you had better go down to St. Louis," Abe remarked as they walked along. "It might make things worse. I'm inclined to think that I'd do better alone with that problem."

"I guess you're right," said Harry. "It would be like me to do something foolish."

"And do it very thoroughly," Abe suggested. "You're in love with the girl. I wouldn't trust your judgment in St. Louis."

"She hasn't let on to her parents that she's unhappy. Mother Traylor told me that they got a letter from her last week that told of the good times she was having."

"We know what that means. She can't bear to acknowledge to them that she has made a mistake and she don't want to worry them. Her mother is in part responsible for the marriage. Bim don't want her to be blamed. Eli caught her off her guard and her heart and her face spoke to him."

In a moment Abe added: "Her parents have begun to suspect that something is wrong. They have never been invited to go down there and visit the girl. I reckon we'd better say nothing to any one of what we have heard at present."

They reached New Salem in the middle of the night and went into Rutledge's barn and lay down on the haymow between two buffalo hides until morning.

CHAPTER XII

THE next day after his return, Abe received a letter
for Ann. She had come over to the store on the arrival of the stage and taken her letter and run home
with it. That Saturday's stage brought the new suit
of clothes from Springfield. Sunday morning Abe
put it on and walked over to Kelso's. Mrs. Kelso was
sweeping the cabin.

"We shall have to stand outside a moment," said
Jack. "I have an inappeasable hatred of brooms. A
lance in the hand of the Black Knight was not more
terrible than a broom in the hands of a righteous
woman. I had to flee from *The Life and Adventures
of Duncan Campbell* when I saw the broom flashing in
a cloud of dust and retreated."

He stepped to the door and said: "A truce, madam!
Here is the Honorable Abraham Lincoln in his new
suit."

Mrs. Kelso came out-of-doors and she and her
husband surveyed the tall young Postmaster.

"Well it is, at least, sufficient," said Kelso.

"The coat ought to be a little longer," Mrs. Kelso suggested.

"It will be long enough before I get another," said Abe.

"It is not what one would call an elegant suit but it's all right," Kelso added.

"The fact is, elegance and I wouldn't get along well together," Abe answered. "It would be like going into partnership with Bill Berry."

"Next month you'll be off at the capital and we shall be going to Tazewell County," said Kelso.

"To Tazewell County!"

"Aye. It's a changing world! We should always remember that things can not go on with us as they are. The Governor has given me a job."

"And me a great sadness," said Abe. "You must always let me know where to find you."

"Aye! Many a night you and I shall hear the cock crowing."

It was an Indian summer day of the first week in November. That afternoon Abe went to the tavern and asked Ann to walk out to the Traylors' with him. She seemed to be glad to go. She was not the cheerful, quick footed, rosy cheeked Ann of old. Her face was pale, her eyes dull and listless, her step slow. Neither spoke until they had passed the Waddell cabin and were come to the open fields.

"I hope your letter brought good news," said Abe.

"It was very short," Ann answered. "He took a

fever in Ohio and was sick there four weeks and then he went home. In two months he never wrote a word to me. And this one was only a little bit of a letter with no love in it. I don't believe he will ever come back. I don't think he cares for me now or, perhaps, he is married. I don't know. I'm not going to cry about it any more. I can't. I've no more tears to shed. I've given him up."

"Then I reckon the time has come for me to tell you what is on my heart," said Abe. "I love you, Ann. I have loved you for years. I would have told you long ago but I could not make myself believe that I was good enough for you. I love you so much that if you can only be happy with John McNamar I will pray to God that he may turn out to be a good and faithful man and come back and keep his promise."

She looked up at him with a kind of awe in her face.

"Oh, Abe!" she whispered. "I had made up my mind that men were all bad but my father. I was wrong. I did not think of you."

"Men are mostly good," said Abe. "But it's very easy to misunderstand them. In my view it's quite likely that John McNamar is better than you think him. I want you to be fair to John. If you conclude that you can not be happy with him give me a chance. I would do my best to bring back the joy of the old days. Sometimes I think that I am going to do some-

thing worth while. Sometimes I think that I can see
my way far ahead and it looks very pleasant, and you,
Ann, are always walking beside me in it."

They proceeded in silence for a moment. A great
flock of wild pigeons darkened the sky above them and
filled it with the whirr of their wings. The young
man and woman stopped to look up at them.

"They are going south," said Abe. "It's a sign of
bad weather."

They stood talking for a little time.

"I'm glad they halted us for we have not far to go,"
Abe remarked. "Before we take another step I wish
you could give me some hope to live on—just a little
straw of hope."

"You are a wonderful man, 'Abe," said Ann, touched
by his appeal. "My father says that you are going to
be a great man."

"I can not hold out any such hope to you," 'Abe answered. "I'm rather ignorant and badly in debt but
I reckon that I can make a good living and give you
a comfortable home. Don't you think, taking me just
as I am, you could care for me a little?"

"Yes; sometimes I think that I could love you,
Abe," she answered. "I do not love you yet but I
may—sometime. I really want to love you."

"That is all I can ask now," said Abe as they went
on. "Do you hear from Bim Kelso?"

"I have not heard from her since June."

"I wish you would write to her and tell her that I am thinking of going down to St. Louis and that I would like to go and see her."

"I'll write to her to-morrow," said Ann.

They had a pleasant visit and while Ann was playing with the baby she seemed to have forgotten her troubles. They stayed to supper, after which the whole family walked to the tavern with them, Joe and Betsey drawing the baby in their "bumble wagon," which Samson had made for them. When Ann began to show weariness, Abe gently lifted her in his arms and carried her.

That evening Mrs. Peter Lukins called upon Abe at Sam Hill's store where he sat alone, before the fire, reading with two candles burning on the end of a dry goods box at his elbow.

There was an anxious look in her one eye as she accepted his invitation to sit down in the firelight.

"I wanted to see you private 'bout Lukins," she began. "There's them that calls him Bony Lukins but I reckon he ain't no bonier than the everidge run o' men —not a bit—an' if he was I don't reckon his bones orto be throwed at him every time he's spoke to that away."

Peter Lukins was a slim, sober faced, quiet little man with a long nose who worked in the carding mill. He never spoke, save when spoken to, and then with a solemn look as if the matter in hand, however slight,

were likely to affect his eternal welfare. In his cups
he was speechless and, in a way, dumb with merriment.
He answered no questions, he expressed no opinions, he
told no stories. He only smiled and broke into roars
of laughter, even if there was no one to share his
joy, as if convinced, at last, of the hopeless absurdity
of life. Some one told of following him from Springfield to New Salem and of hearing him laugh all the
way. Many had noted another peculiarity in the man.
He seemed always to have a week's growth of beard
on his face.

"What can I do about it?" Abe asked.

"I've been hopin' an' wishin' some kind of a decent
handle could be put on to his name," said Mrs. Lukins,
with her eye upon a knot hole in the counter.
"Something with a good sound to it. You said that
anything you could do for the New Salem folks you
was goin' to do an' I thought maybe you could fix it."

Abe smiled and asked: "Do you want a title?"

"If it ain't plum owdacious I wisht he could be
made a Colonel."

"That's a title for fighting men," said Abe.

"An' that man has fit for his life ever since he was
born," said Mrs. Lukins. "He's fit the measles an' the
smallpox an' the fever an' ager an' conquered 'em."

"I reckon he deserves the title," Abe remarked.

"I ain't sayin' but what there is purtier men," she
said, reflectively, as she stuck her finger into the knot

hole and felt its edges. "I ain't sayin' but what there is smarter men but I do say that the name o' Bony ain't hardly fit to be heard in company."

"A little whitewash wouldn't hurt it any," said Abe. "I'd gladly give him my title of Captain if I could un-hitch it someway."

"Colonel is a more grander name," she insisted. "I call it plum coralapus."

She had thus expressed her notion of the limit of human grandeur.

"Do you like it better than Judge?"

"Wall, Judge has a good sound to it but I'm plum sot on Colonel. If you kin give that name to a horse, which Samson Traylor has done it, I don't see why a man shouldn't be treated just as well."

"I'll see what can be done but if he gets that title he'll have to live up to it."

"I'll make him walk a chalk line—you see," the good woman promised as she left the store.

That evening Abe wrote a playful commission as Colonel for Peter Lukins which was signed in due time by all his friends and neighbors and presented to Lukins by a committee of which Abe was chairman.

Coleman Smoot—a man of some means who had a farm on the road to Springfield—was in the village that evening. Abe showed him the commission and asked him to sign it.

"I'll sign it on one condition," said Smoot.

John Wolcott Adams

"What is that?" Abe asked.

"That you'll give me a commission."

"A man like you can't expect too much. Would you care to be a General?"

"I wouldn't give the snap of my finger for that. What I want to be is your friend."

"You are that now, aren't you?" Abe asked.

"Yes, but I haven't earned my commission. You haven't given me a chance yet. What can I do to help you along?"

Abe was much impressed by these kindly words.

"My friends do not often ask what they can do for me," he said. "I suppose they haven't thought of it. I'll think it over and let you know."

Three days later he walked out to Coleman Smoot's after supper. As they sat together by the fireside Abe said:

"I've been thinking of your friendly question. It's dangerous to talk that way to a man like me. The fact is I need two hundred dollars to pay pressing debts and give me something in my pocket when I go to Vandalia. If you can not lend it to me I shall think none the less of you."

"I can and will," said Smoot. "I've been watching you for a long time. A man who tries as hard as you do to get along deserves to be helped. I believe in you. I'll go up to Springfield and get the money and bring it to you within a week or so."

Abe Lincoln had many friends who would have done the like for him if they could, and he knew it.

"Every one has faith in you," said Smoot. "We expect much of you and we ought to be willing to do what we can to help."

"Your faith will be my strength if I have any," said Abe.

On his way home that night he thought of what Jack Kelso had said of democracy and friendship.

On the twenty-second of November a letter came to Ann from Bim Kelso which announced that she was going to New Orleans for the winter with her husband. Thereupon Abe gave up the idea of going to St. Louis and six days later took the stage for the capital, at Rutledge's door, where all the inhabitants of the village had assembled to bid him good-by. Ann Rutledge with a flash of her old playfulness kissed him when he got into the stage. Abe's long arm was waving in the air as he looked back at his cheering friends while the stage rumbled down the road toward the great task of his life upon which he was presently to begin in the little village of Vandalia.

CHAPTER XIII

WHEREIN THE ROUTE OF THE UNDERGROUND RAILROAD IS SURVEYED AND SAMSON AND HARRY SPEND A NIGHT IN THE HOME OF HENRY BRIMSTEAD AND HEAR SURPRISING REVELATIONS, CONFIDENTIALLY DISCLOSED, AND ARE CHARMED BY THE PERSONALITY OF HIS DAUGHTER ANNABEL.

EARLY in the autumn of that year the Reverend Elijah Lovejoy of Alton had spent a night with the Traylors on his way to the North. Sitting by the fireside he had told many a vivid tale of the cruelties of slavery.

"I would not have you think that all slave-holders are wicked and heartless," he said. "They are like other men the world over. Some are kind and indulgent. If all men were like them slavery could be tolerated. But they are not. Some men are brutal in the North as well as in the South. If not made so by nature they are made so by drink. To give them the power of life and death over human beings, which they seem to have in parts of the South, is a crime against God and civilization. Our country can not live and prosper with such a serpent in its bosom. No good man should rest until the serpent is slain."

"I agree with you," said Samson.

"I knew that you would," the minister went on. "We have already had some help from you but we need more. I take it as a duty which God has laid upon me to help every fugitive that reaches my door. Thousands of New Englanders have come into Illinois in the last year. They will help the good work of mercy and grace. If you hear three taps upon your window after dark or the hoot of an owl in your dooryard you will know what it means. Fix some place on your farm where these poor people who are seeking the freedom which God wills for all His children, may find rest and refreshment and security until they have strength to go on."

Within a week after the visit of Mr. Lovejoy, Samson and Harry built a hollow haystack about half-way from the house to the barn. The stack had a comfortable room inside of it about eight feet by seven and some six feet in height. Its entrance was an opening near the bottom of the stack well screened by the pendant hay. But no fugitive came to occupy it that winter.

Early in March Abe wrote a letter to Samson in which he said:

"I have not been doing much. I have been getting the hang of things. There are so many able men here that I feel like being modest for a while. It's good practice if it is a little hard on me. Here are such men as Theodore Ford, William L. D. Ewing, Stephen T. Logan, Jesse K. Dubois and Governor Duncan. You can not wonder that I feel like lying low until I can see my way a little more clearly. I have met here a young man from your state of the name of Stephen A. Douglas. He is twenty-one years old and about the least man I ever saw to look at but he is bright and very ambitious. He has taught school and studied law and been admitted to the bar and is bristling up to John J. Hardin in a contest for the office of State's Attorney. Some pumpkins for a boy of twenty-one I reckon. No chance for internal improvements this session. Money is plenty and next year I think we can begin harping on that string. More than ever I am convinced that it is no time for anti-slavery agitation much as we may feel inclined to it. There's too much fire under the pot now."

Soon after the new year of 1835 Samson and Harry moved the Kelsos to Tazewell County. Mr. Kelso had received an appointment as Land Agent and was to be stationed at the little settlement of Hopedale near the home of John Peasley.

"I hate to be taking you so far away," said Samson.

"Hush, man," said Kelso. "It's a thing to be thought about only in the still o' the night."

"I shall be lonesome."

"But we live close by the wells of wisdom and so we shall not be comfortless."

Late in the afternoon Harry and Samson left the Kelsos and their effects at a small frame house in the little village of Hopedale. The men had no sooner begun to unload than its inhabitants came to welcome the newcomers and help them in the work of getting settled. When the goods were deposited in the dooryard Samson and Harry drove to John Peasley's farm. Mr. Peasley recognized the big, broad-shouldered Vermonter at the first look.

"Do I remember you?" he said. "Well, I guess I do. So does my barn door. Let me take hold of that right hand of yours again. Yes, sir. It's the same old iron hand. Many Ann!" he called as his wife came out of the door. "Here's the big man from Vergennes who tossed the purty slaver."

"I see it is," she answered. "Ain't ye comin' in?"

"We've been moving a man to Hopedale and shall have to spend the night somewhere in this neighborhood," said Samson. "Our horses are played out."

"If you try to pass this place I'll have ye took up," said Peasley. "There's plenty of food in the house an' stable."

"Look here—that's downright selfish," said his wife. "If we tried to keep you here Henry Brimstead would never forgive us. He talks about you morning, noon and night. Any one would think that you was the Samson that slew the Philistines."

"How is Henry?" Samson asked.

"He married my sister and they're about as happy as they can be this side the river Jordan," she went on. "They've got one o' the best farms in Tazewell County and they're goin' to be rich. They've built 'em a splendid house with a big spare room in it. Henry would have a spare room because he said that maybe the Traylors would be comin' here to visit 'em some time."

"Yes, sir; I didn't think o' that," said Peasley. "Henry and his wife would holler if we didn't take ye over there. It's only a quarter of a mile. I'll show ye the way and we'll all come over this evening and have a talkin' bee."

Samson was pleased and astonished by the look of Brimstead and his home and his family and the account of his success. The man from the sand flats had built a square, two-story house with a stairway and three rooms above it and two below. He was cleanly shaved, save for a black mustache, and neatly dressed and his face glowed with health and high spirits. A handsome brown-eyed miss of seventeen came galloping up the road on her pony and stopped near them.

"Annabel, do you remember this man?" Brimstead asked.

The girl looked at Samson.

"He is the man who helped us out of Flea Valley," said the girl.

Brimstead leaned close to the ear of Samson and said in a low tone:

"Say, everything knew how to jump there. I had a garden that could hop over the fence and back ag'in. Sometimes it was there and sometimes it was off on a vacation. I jumped as soon as I got the chance."

"We call it No Santa Claus Land," said Samson. "Do ye remember how the little girl clung to the wagon?"

"That was me," said a small miss of ten who ran out of the door into the arms of the big man and kissed him.

"Would you mind if I kissed you?" Annabel asked.

"I would be sorry if you didn't," said Samson. "Here's my boy, Harry Needles. You wouldn't dare kiss him I guess."

"I would be sorry, too, if you didn't," Harry laughed as he took her hand.

"I'm afraid you'll have to stay sorry," said Annabel turning red with embarrassment. "I never saw you before."

"Better late than never," Samson assured her. "You don't often see a better fellow."

The girl laughed, with a subtle look of agreement in her eyes. Then came up from the barn the ragged little lad of No Santa Claus Land—now a sturdy, bright eyed, handsome boy of twelve.

The horses were put out and all went in to supper.

"I have always felt sorry for any kind of a slave," said Samson as they sat down. "When I saw you on the sand plains you were in bondage."

"Say, I'll tell ye," said Brimstead, as he leaned toward Samson, seeming to be determined at last to make a clean breast of it. "Say, I didn't own that farm. It owned me. I got a sandy intellect. Couldn't get anything out of it but disappointment. My farm was mortgaged to the bank and I was mortgaged to the children. I couldn't even die."

Samson wrote in his diary that night:

"When Brimstead brings his sense of humor into play he acts as if he was telling a secret. When he says anything that makes me laugh, he's terribly confidential. Seems so he was kind of ashamed of it. He never laughs himself unless he does it inside. His voice always drops, too, when he talks business."

"The man that's a fool and don't know it is a good deal worse off," said Samson.

"Say, I'll tell ye he's worse off but he's happier. If it hurts there's hope for ye."

"They tell me you've prospered," said Samson.

Brimstead spoke in a most confidential tone as he answered: "Say, I'll tell ye—no wise man is ever an idiot but once. I wouldn't care to spread it around much but we're gettin' along. I've built this house and got my land paid for. You see we are only four miles from the Illinois River on a good road. I can ship my grain to Alton or St. Louis or New Orleans without much trouble. I've invented a machine to cut it and a double plow and I expect to have them both working next year. They ought to treble my output at least."

After supper Brimstead showed models of a mowing machine with a cut bar six feet long, and a plow which would turn two furrows.

"That's what we need on these prairies," said Samson. "Something that'll turn 'em over and cut the crop quicker."

"Say, I'll tell ye," said Brimstead as if about to disclose another secret. "I found after I looked the ground over here that I needed a brain. I began to paw around an' discovered a rusty old brain among my tools. It hadn't been used for years. I cleaned an' oiled the thing an' got it workin'. On a little Vermont farm you could git along without it but here the ground yells for a brain. We don't know how to use our horses. They have power enough to do all the hard work, if we only knew how to put it into wheels and gears. We must begin to work our brains as well as our muscles on a farm miles long an' wide."

"It ain't fair to expect the land to furnish all the fertility," said Samson

Brimstead's face glowed as he outlined his vision:

"These great stretches of smooth, rich land just everlastingly ram the spurs into you and keep your brain galloping. Mine is goin' night and day. The prairies are a new thing and you've got to tackle 'em in a new way. I tell you the seeding and planting and mowing and reaping and threshing is all going to be done by machinery and horses. The wheel will be the foundation of the new era."

"You're right," said Samson.

"How are you gettin' along?"

"Rather slow," Samson answered. "It's hard to get our stuff to market down in the Sangamon country. Our river isn't navigable yet. We hope that Abe Lincoln, who has just been elected to the Legislature, will be able to get it widened and straightened and cleaned up so it will be of some use to us down there."

"I've heard of him. They call him Honest Abe, don't they?"

"Yes; and he is honest if a man ever was."

"That's the kind we need to make our laws," said Mrs. Brimstead. "There are not many men who get a reputation for honesty. It ought to be easy, but it isn't."

"Men are pretty good in the main," said Samson. "But ye know there are not so many who can exactly toe the mark. They don't know how or they're too busy or something. I guess I'm a little careless, and I don't believe I'm a bad fellow either. Abe's conscience don't ever sit down to rest. He traveled three miles one night to give back four cents that he had overcharged a customer. I'd probably have waited to have her come back, and by that time it might have slipped my mind or maybe she would have moved away. I sup-

pose that in handling dollars we're mostly as honest
as Abe, but we're apt to be a little careless with the
cents. Abe toed the penny mark, and that's how he
got his reputation. The good God has given him a
sense of justice that is like a chemist's balance. It can
weigh down to a fraction of a grain. Now he don't
care much about pennies. He can be pretty reckless
with 'em. But when they're a measure on the balance,
he counts 'em careful, I can tell ye."

"Say, I'll tell ye," said Brimstead. "Honesty is
like Sapington's pills. There's nothing that's so well
recommended. It has a great many friends. But
Honesty has to pay prompt. We don't trust it long.
It has poor credit. When we have to give a dollar's
worth of work to correct an error of four cents, we're
apt to decide that Honesty don't pay. But that's when
it pays best. We've heard the jingle o' them four
cents 'way up here in Tazewell County, an' long before you told us. They say he's a smart talker an'
that he can split ye wide open laughin'."

"He's a great story-teller, but that's a small part of
him," said Samson. "He's a kind of a four horse
team. He knows more than any man I ever saw and
can tell it and he can wrestle like old Satan and swing
a scythe or an axe all day an' mighty supple. He's
one of us common folks and don't pretend to be a bit
better. He is, though, and we know it, but I don't
think he knows it."

"Say, there ain't many of us smart enough to keep

that little piece of ignorance in our heads," said Brimstead. "It's worth a fortune, now—ain't it?"

"Is he going to marry the Rutledge girl?" was the query of Mrs. Brimstead.

"I don't think so," Samson answered, a little surprised at her knowledge of the attachment. "He's as humly as Sam Hill and dresses rough and ain't real handy with the gals. Some fellers are kind o' fenced in with humliness and awkwardness."

Brimstead expressed his private opinion in a clearly audible whisper: "Say, that kind o' protection is better'n none. A humly boy don't git tramped on an' nibbled too much."

Annabel and Harry sat in a corner playing checkers. They seemed to be much impressed by the opinion of Mr. Brimstead. For a moment their game was forgotten.

"That boy has a way with the gals," Samson laughed. "There's no such fence around either of them."

"They're both liable to be nibbled some," said Brimstead.

"I like to see 'em have a good time," said his wife. "There are not many boys to play with out here."

"The boys around here are all fenced in," said Annabel. "There's nobody here of my age but Lanky Peters, who looks like a fish, and a red-headed Irish boy with a wooden leg."

"Say, she's like a woodpecker in a country where

there ain't any trees," said Brimstead, in his confidential tone.

"No I'm not," the girl answered. "A woodpecker has wings and the right to use them."

"Cheer up. A lot of people will be moving in here this spring—more boys than you could shake a stick at," Mrs. Brimstead remarked, cheerfully.

"If I shake any stick at them, it will be a stick of candy, for fear of scaring them away," said Annabel, with a laugh.

Brimstead said to Samson: "Say, I'll tell ye, you're back in a cove. You must get out into the current."

"And give the young folks a chance to play checkers together," said Samson.

"Say, I'll tell ye," said Brimstead. "This country is mostly miles. They can be your worst enemy unless you get on the right side of 'em. Above all, don't let 'em get too thick between you an' your market. When you know about where it is, keep the miles behind ye. Great markets will be springin' up in the North. You'll see a big city growin' on the southern shore of Lake Michigan before long. I think there will be better markets to the north than there are to the south of us."

"By jingo!" Samson exclaimed. "Your brain is about as busy as a beehive on a bright summer day."

"Say, don't you mention that to a livin' soul," said Brimstead. "My brain began to chase the rainbow when I was a boy. It drove me out o' Vermont into the trail to the West and landed me in Flea Valley.

Now I'm in a country where no man's dreams are goin' to be big enough to keep up with the facts. We're right under the end o' the rainbow and there's a pot o' gold for each of us."

"The railroad will be a help in our fight with the miles," said Samson.

"All right. You get the miles behind ye and let the land do the waiting. It won't hurt the land any, but you'd be spoilt if you had to wait twenty years."

The Peasleys arrived and the men and women spent a delightful hour traveling without weariness over the long trail to beloved scenes and the days of their youth. Every day's end thousands were going east on that trail, each to find his pot of gold at the foot of the rainbow of memory.

Before they went to bed that night Brimstead paid his debt to Samson, with interest, and very confidentially.

At daylight in the morning the team was at the door ready to set out for the land of plenty. As Samson and Harry were making their farewells, Annabel asked the latter:

"May I whisper something in your ear?"

"I was afraid you wouldn't," he said.

He bent his head to her and she kissed his cheek and ran away into the house.

"That means come again," she called from the door, with a laugh.

"I guess I'll have to—to get even," he answered.

"That's a pretty likely girl," said Samson, as they were driving away.

"She's as handsome as a picture."

"She is—no mistake!" Samson declared. "She's a good-hearted girl, too. You can tell that by her face and her voice. She's as gentle as a kitten, and about as wide awake as a weasel."

"I don't care much for girls these days," Harry answered. "I guess I'll never get married."

"Nonsense! A big, strapping, handsome young feller like you, only twenty years old! Of course you'll get married."

"I don't see how I'm ever going to care much for another girl," the boy answered.

"There are a lot o' things in the world that you don't see, boy. It's a big world and things shift around a good deal and some of our opinions are apt to move with the wind like thistledown."

It was a long, wearisome ride back to the land of plenty, over frozen ground, with barely an inch of snow upon it, under a dark sky, with a chilly wind blowing.

"After all, it's home," said Samson, when late in the evening they saw the lighted windows of the cabin ahead. When they had put out their horses and come in by the glowing fire, Samson lifted Sarah in his arms again and kissed her.

"I'm kind o' silly, mother, but I can't help it—you look so temptin'," said Samson.

"She looks like an angel," said Harry, as he improved his chance to embrace and kiss the lady of the cabin.

"The wind has been peckin' at us all day," said Samson. "But it's worth it to get back home and see your face and this blazin' fire."

"And the good, hot supper," said Harry, as they sat down at the table.

They told of the Brimsteads and their visit.

"Well, I want to know!" said Sarah. "Big house and plenty o' money! If that don't beat all!"

"That oldest girl is the thing that beats all," said Samson. "She's as handsome as Bim."

"I suppose Harry fell in love with her," Sarah suggested, with a smile.

"I've lost my ability to fall in love," said the young man.

"It will come back—you see," said Sarah. "I'm going to get her to pay us a visit in the spring."

Harry went out to feed and water the horses.

"Did you get along all right?" Samson asked.

"Colonel Lukins did the chores faithfully, night and morning," Sarah answered. "His wife helped me with the sewing yesterday. She talked all day about the 'Colonel.' Mrs. Beach, that poor woman from Ohio on the west road who has sent her little girl so often to borrow tea and sugar, came to-day and wanted to borrow the baby. Her baby is sick and her breasts were paining her."

CHAPTER XIV

IN WHICH ABE RETURNS FROM VANDALIA AND IS EN-
GAGED TO ANN, AND THREE INTERESTING SLAVES
ARRIVE AT THE HOME OF SAMSON TRAYLOR, WHO,
WITH HARRY NEEDLES, HAS AN ADVENTURE OF
MUCH IMPORTANCE ON THE UNDERGROUND ROAD.

AGAIN spring had come. The great meadows were
awake and full of color. Late in April their green
floor was oversown with golden blossoms lying close
to the warming breast of the earth. Then came the
braver flowers of May lifting their heads to the sunlight in the lengthening grasses—red and white and
pink and blue—and over all the bird songs. They
seemed to voice the joy in the heart of man. Sarah
Traylor used to say that the beauty of the spring more
than paid for the loneliness of the winter.

Abe came back from the Legislature to resume his
duties as postmaster and surveyor. The evening of
his arrival he went to see Ann. The girl was in poor
health. She had had no news of McNamar since
January. Her spirit seemed to be broken. They
walked together up and down the deserted street of
the little village that evening. Abe told her of his life
in Vandalia and of his hopes and plans.

"My greatest hope is that you will feel that you can

put up with me," he said. "I would try to learn how
to make you happy. I think if you would help me a
little I could do it."

"I don't think I am worth having," the girl answered. "I feel like a little old woman these days."

"It seems to me that you are the only one in the
world worth having," said Abe.

"If you want me to, I will marry you, Abe," said
she. "I can not say that I love you, but my mother
and father say that I would learn to love you, and
sometimes I think it is true. I really want to love
you."

They were on the bluff that overlooked the river and
the deserted mill. They were quite alone looking down
at the moonlit plains. A broken sigh came from the
lips of the tall young man. He wiped his eyes with
his handkerchief. He took her hand in both of his
and pressed it against his breast and looked down into
her face and said:

"I wish I could tell you what is in my heart. There
are things this tongue of mine could say, but not that.
I shall show you, but I shall not try to tell you. Words
are good enough for politics and even for the religion
of most men, but not for this love I feel. Only in my
life shall I try to express it."

He held her hand as they walked on in silence for a
moment.

"About a year from now we can be married," he
said. "I shall be able to take care of you then, I

think.   Meanwhile we will all help you to take care of
yourself.   You don't look well."

She kissed his cheek and he kissed hers when they
parted at the door of the tavern.

"I am sure I shall love you," she whispered.

"Those are the best words that ever came to my
ears," he answered, and left her with a solemn sense
of his commitment.

Soon after that Abe went to the north line of the
county to do some surveying, and on his return, in
the last week of May, came out for a talk with the
Traylors.

"I've been up to the Kelsos' home and had a wonderful talk with him and Brimstead," said Abe. "They
have discovered each other.   Kelso lives in a glorious
past and Brimstead in a golden future.   They're both
poets.   Kelso is translating the odes of Pindar.   Brimstead is constructing the future of Illinois.   They laugh
at each other and so create a fairly agreeable present."

"Did you see Annabel?" Harry asked.

"About sixty times a minute while I was there.   So
pretty you can't help looking at her.   She's coming
down to visit Ann, I hope.   If you don't see her every
day she's here, I shall lose my good opinion of you.
It will be a sure sign that your eyes don't know how
to enjoy themselves."

"We shall all see her and fall in love with her, too,
probably," said Sarah.

"She's made on the right pattern of the best material," Abe went on. "She's full of fun and I thought
it would be a great thing for Ann. She hasn't had
any one to play with of her own age and standing
since Bim went away. I was thinking of Harry, too.
He needs somebody to play with."

"Much obliged!" the young man exclaimed. "I was
thinking that I'd have to take a trip to Hopedale,
myself."

"I knew he'd come around," Sarah laughed.

But all unknown to these good people, the divinities
were at that moment very busy.

That was the 26th of May, 1835, a date of much importance in the calendar of the Traylors. It had been
a clear, warm day, followed by a cloudless, starry
night, with a chilly breeze blowing. Between eleven
and twelve o'clock Sarah and Samson were awakened
by the hoot of an owl in the dooryard. In a moment
they heard three taps on a window-pane. They knew
what it meant. Both got out of bed and into their
clothes as quickly as possible. Samson lighted a candle
and put some wood on the fire. Then he opened the
door with the candle in his hand. A stalwart, good-
looking mulatto man, with a smooth shaven face, stood
in the doorway.

"Is the coast clear?" he whispered.

"All clear," Samson answered, in a low tone.

"I'll be back in a minute," said the negro, as he

disappeared in the darkness, returning presently with two women, both very black. They sat down in the dim light of the cabin.

"Are you hungry?" Sarah asked.

"We have had only a little bread and butter to-day, madame," said the mulatto, whose speech and manners were like those of an educated white man of the South.

"I'll get you something," said Sarah, as she opened the cupboard.

"I think we had better not stop to eat now, madame," said the negro. "We will be followed and they may reach here any minute."

Harry, who had been awakened by the arrival of the strangers, came down the ladder.

"These are fugitive slaves on their way north," said Samson. "Take them out to the stack. I'll bring some food in a few minutes."

Harry conducted them to their hiding-place, and when they had entered it, he brought a ladder and opened the top of the stack. A hooped shaft in the middle of it led to a point near its top and provided ventilation. Then he crawled in at the entrance, through which Samson passed a pail of food, a jug of water and some buffalo hides. Harry sat with them for a few moments in the black darkness of the stack room to learn whence they had come and whither they wished to go.

"We are from St. Louis, suh," the mulatto answered. "We are on our way to Canada. Our next station is the house of John Peasley, in Tazewell County."

"Do you know a man of the name of Eliphalet Biggs who lives in St. Louis?" Harry asked.

"Yes, suh; I see him often, suh," the negro answered.

"What kind of a man is he?"

"Good when he is sober, suh, but a brute when he is drunk."

"Is he cruel to his wife?"

"He beats her with a whip, suh."

"My God!" Harry exclaimed. "Why don't she leave him?"

"She has left him, suh. She is staying with a friend. It has been hard for her to get away. She has been a slave, too."

Harry's voice trembled with emotion when he answered:

"I am sure that none of her friends knew how she was being treated."

"I suppose that she was hoping an' praying, suh, that he would change."

"I think that one of us will take you to Peasley's to-morrow night," said Harry. "Meanwhile I hope you get a good rest."

With that he left them, filled the mouth of the cave with hay and went into the house. There he told his good friends of what he had heard.

"I shall go down to St. Louis," he said. "I read in the paper that there was a boat Monday."

"The first thing to do is to go to bed," said Sarah. "There's not much left of the night."

They went to bed, but the young man could not sleep. Bim had possession of his heart again. In a kind of half sleep he got the notion that she was sitting by his bedside and trying to comfort him. Then he thought that he heard her singing in the sweet voice of old:

> "Come sit yourself down
> With me on the ground
> On this bank where the primroses grow.
> We will hear the fond tale
> Of the sweet nightingale,
> As she sings in the valleys below,
> As she sings in the valleys below."

He roused himself and thought that he saw her form receding in the darkness.

Fortunately, the spring's work was finished and there was not much to be done next day. Samson went to "Colonel" Lukins' cabin and arranged with him and his wife to come and stay with Sarah and made other preparations for the journey to the north. Soon after nightfall they put their guests on a small load of hay, so that they could quickly cover themselves if necessary, and set out for Peasley's farm. As they rode along Samson had a frank talk with Harry.

"I think you ought to get over being in love with Bim," he said.

"I've told myself that a dozen times, but it don't do any good," said the boy.

"She's another man's wife and you have no right to love her."

"She's another man's slave, and I can't stand the thought of it," Harry answered. "If she was happy I could mind my business and get over thinking of her, by and by, maybe, but now she needs a friend, if she ever did, and I intend to do what I can for her."

"Of course, we'll all do what we can for her," said Samson. "But you must get over being in love with a married woman."

"If a man's sister were in such trouble, I think he'd have the right to help her, and she's more than a sister to me."

"I'll stand with you on the sister platform," said Samson.

In the middle of the night they stopped by a stream of water to feed the horses and take a bite of luncheon. The roads were heavy from recent rains and daylight came before they could make their destination. At sunrise they stopped to give their horses a moment to rest. In the distance they could see Brimstead's house and the harrowed fields around it. The women were lying covered by the hay; the man was sitting up and looking back down the road.

"They're coming," he exclaimed, suddenly, as he got under the hay.

Samson and Harry could see horsemen following at a gallop half a mile or so down the road. It looked like trouble, for at that hour men were not likely to be abroad in the saddle and riding fast on any usual errand. Our friends hurried their team and got to Brimstead's door ahead of the horsemen. A grove of trees screened the wagon from the view of the latter for a moment. Henry Brimstead stood in the open door.

"Take these slaves into the house and get them out of sight as quick as you can," said Samson. "There's going to be a quarrel here in a minute."

The slaves slid off the load and ran into the house.

This was all accomplished in a few seconds. The team started on toward Peasley's farm as if nothing had happened, with Harry and Samson standing on the load. In a moment they saw, to their astonishment, Biggs and a colored servant coming at a slow trot. Were the slaves they carried the property of Biggs?

"Stop that wagon," the latter shouted.

Samson kept on, turning out a little to let them pass.

"Stop or we'll shoot your horses," Biggs demanded.

"They'll have to pass close to the load," Harry whispered. "I'll jump on behind Biggs as he goes by."

The words were scarcely out of his mouth when Harry sprang off the load, catching Biggs's shoulders and landing squarely on the rump of his horse. It was a rough minute that followed. The horse leaped and reared and Biggs lost his seat, and he and Harry rolled to the ground and into a fence corner, while the horse ran up the road, with the pistols in their holsters on his back. They rose and fought until Harry, being quicker and stronger, got the best of it. The slaver was severely punished. The negro's horse, frightened by the first move in the fracas, had turned and run back down the road.

Biggs swore bitterly at the two Yankees.

"I'll have you dirty suckers arrested if there's any law in this state," he declared, as he stood leaning against the fence, with an eye badly swollen and blood streaming from his nose.

"I suppose you can do it," said Samson. "But first let's see if we can find your horse. I think I saw him turn in at the house above."

Samson drove the team, while Biggs and Harry walked up the road in silence. The negro followed in the saddle. Peasley had caught Biggs's horse and was standing at the roadside.

"I want to find a Justice of the Peace," said Biggs.

"There's one at the next house above. I'll send my boy for him," Peasley answered.

The Justice arrived in a few minutes and Biggs lodged a complaint founded on the allegation that his slaves were concealed in the hay on Samson's wagon. The hay was removed and no slaves were discovered.

"I suppose they left my niggers at the house below," said Biggs as he mounted his horse and, with his companion, started at a gallop in the direction of 'Brimstead's. Samson remained with Peasley and the Justice.

"You had better go down and see what happens," he said to Harry. "We'll follow you in a few minutes."

So Harry walked down to Brimstead's.

He found the square house in a condition of panic. Biggs and his helper had discovered the mulatto and his wife hiding in the barn. The negroes and the children were crying. Mrs. Brimstead met Harry outside the door.

"What are we to do?" she asked, tearfully.

"Just keep cool," said Harry. "Father Traylor and Mr. Peasley will be here soon."

Biggs and his companion came out of the door with Brimstead.

"We will take the niggers to the river and put them on a boat," Biggs was saying.

His face and shirt and bosom were smeared with

blood. He asked Mrs. Brimstead for a basin of water and a towel. The good woman took him to the washstand and supplied his needs.

In a few moments Samson and Peasley arrived, with the latter's team hitched to a Conestoga wagon.

"Well, you've found them, have you?" Peasley asked.

"They were here, as I thought," said Biggs.

"Well, the Justice says we must surrender the negroes and take them to the nearest landing for you. We've come to do it."

"It's better treatment than I expected," Biggs answered.

"You'll find that we have a good deal of respect for the law," said Peasley.

Biggs and his friend went to the barn for their horses. The others conferred a moment with the two slaves and Mrs. Brimstead. Then the latter went out into the garden lot to a woman in a sunbonnet who was working with a hoe some fifteen rods from the house. Mrs. Brimstead seemed to be conveying a message to the woman by signs. Evidently the latter was deaf and dumb.

"That is the third slave," Brimstead whispered. "I don't believe they'll discover her."

Soon Peasley and Samson got into the wagon with the negroes and drove away, followed by the two horsemen.

In a little village on the river they stopped at a low frame house.   A woman came to the door.

"Is Freeman Collar here?" Peasley demanded.

"He is back in the garden," the woman answered.

"Please ask him to come here."

In a moment Collar came around the house with a hoe on his shoulder.   He was a slim, sandy bearded, long-haired man of medium height, with keen gray eyes.

"Good morning, Mr. Constable," said Peasley. "This is Eliphalet Biggs of St. Louis, and here is a warrant for his arrest."

He passed a paper to the officer.

"For my arrest!" Biggs exclaimed.   "What is the charge?"

"That you hired a number of men to burn the house of Samson Henry Traylor, near the village of New Salem, in Sangamon County, and, by violence, to compel him to leave said county; that, on the 29th of 'August, said men—the same being eight in number —attempted to carry out your design and, being captured and overpowered, all confessed their guilt and your connection with it, their sworn confessions being now in the possession of one Stephen Nuckles, a minister of this county.   I do not need to remind you that it is a grave offense and likely to lead to your confinement for a term of years."

"Well, by G—," Biggs shouted, in anger.   "You

suckers will have some traveling to do before you arrest me."

He struck the spurs in his horse and galloped away, followed by his servant. Samson roared with laughter.

"Now, Collar, get on your horse and hurry 'em along, but don't ketch up with 'em if you can help it," said Peasley. "We've got them on the run now. They'll take to the woods an' be darn careful to keep out of sight."

When the Constable had gone, Peasley said to Samson: "We'll drop these slaves at Nate Haskell's door. He'll take care of 'em until dark and start 'em on the north road. Late in the evening I'll pick 'em up an' get 'em out o' this part o' the country."

Meanwhile Brimstead and Harry had stood for a moment in the dooryard of the former, watching the party on its way up the road. Brimstead blew out his breath and said in a low tone:

"Say, I'll tell ye, I ain't had so much excitement since Samson Traylor rode into Flea Valley. The women need a chance to wash their faces and slick up a little. Le's you and me go back to the creek and go in swimmin' an' look the farm over."

"What become of the third nigger?" Harry asked.

"She went out in the field in a sunbonnet an' went to work with a hoe and they didn't discover her," said Brimstead.

"It must have been a nigger that didn't belong to him," Harry declared.

"I guess it was one that the others picked up on the road."

They set out across the sown fields, while Brimstead, in his most divulging mood, confided many secrets to the young man. Suddenly he asked:

"Say, did you take partic'lar notice o' that yaller nigger?"

"I didn't see much of him."

"Well, I'll tell ye, he was about as handsome a feller as you'd see in a day's travel—straight as an arrow and about six feet tall and well spoken and clean faced. He told me that another master had taught him to read and write and cipher. He's read the Bible through, and many of the poems of Scott and Byron and Burns. Don't it rile ye up to think of a man like that bein' bought and sold and pounded around like a steer? It ain't decent."

"It's king work; it isn't democracy," Harry answered. "We've got to put an end to it."

"Say, who's that?" Brimstead asked, as he pointed to a pair of horsemen hurrying down the distant road.

"It's Biggs and his servant," Harry answered.

"Whew! They ain't lettin' the grass grow under their feet. They'll kill them horses."

"Biggs is a born killer. I'd like to give him one more licking."

In a moment they saw another horseman a quarter of a mile behind the others and riding fast.

"Ha, ha! That explains their haste," said Brimstead. "It's ol' Free Collar on his sorrel mare. Say, I'll tell ye," Brimstead came close to Harry and added in a low tone: "If Biggs tries any fightin' business with Collar he'll git killed sure. That man loves excitement. He don't take no nonsense at all, and he can put a bullet into a gimlet hole at ten rods."

They had their swim in the creek and got back to the house at dinner time. Samson had returned and, as they sat down at the table, he told what had happened at the Constable's house and learned of the passing of Biggs and his friend in the road, followed by Collar on his sorrel mare.

"We must hurry back, but we will have to give the horses a rest," said Samson.

"And the young people a chance to play checkers?" said Mrs. Brimstead.

"I have no heart for play," said Annabel, with a sigh.

"The excitement and the sight o' those poor slaves have taken all the fun out of her," the woman remarked.

Then Harry asked: "What have you done with the third slave?"

"She's been up-stairs, getting washed and dressed," said Mrs. Brimstead.

As she spoke, the stairway door opened and Bim entered the room—in a silk gown and slippers. Sorrow had put its mark upon her face, but had not extinguished her beauty. All rose from the table. Harry walked toward her. She advanced to meet him. Face to face, they stopped and looked into each other's eyes. The moment long desired, the moment endeared and sublimated by the dreams of both, the moment toward which their thoughts had been wont to hasten, after the cares of the day, like brooks coming down from the mountains, had arrived suddenly. She was in a way prepared for it. She had taken thought of what she would do and say. He had not. Still it made no difference. This little point of time had been so filled with the power which had flowed into it out of their souls there was no foretelling what they would do when it touched them. Scarcely a second of that moment was wasted in hesitation, as a matter of fact. Quickly they fell into each other's embrace, and the depth of their feeling we may guess when we read in the diary of the rugged and rather stoical Samson that no witness of the scene spoke or moved "until I turned my back upon it for shame of my tears."

Soon Bim came and kissed Samson's cheek and said:

"I am not going to make trouble. I couldn't help this. I heard what he said to you last night. It made me happy in spite of all my troubles. I love him but

above all I shall try to keep his heart as clean and noble
as it has always been.   I really meant to be very strong
and upright.   It is all over now.   Forgive us.   We
are going to be as respectable as—as we can."

Samson pressed her hand and said:

"You came with the slaves and I guess you heard
our talk in the wagon."

"Yes, I came with the slaves, and was as black as
either of them.   We had all suffered.   I should have
come alone, but they had been good and faithful to
me.   I could not bear to leave them to endure the
violence of that man.   We left together one night
when he was in a drunken stupor.   We took a boat
to Alton and caught *The Star of the North* to Beardstown—they traveling as my servants.   There I hired
a team and wagon.   It brought us to the grove near
your house."

"Why did you disguise yourself before you came
in?"

"I longed to see Harry, but I did not want him to
see me.   I did not know that he would care to see
me," she answered.   "I longed to see all of you."

"Isn't that like Bim?" Samson asked.

"I am no longer the fool I was," she answered.   "It
was not just a romantic notion.   I wanted to share the
lot of a runaway slave for a few days and know what
it means.   That mulatto—Roger Wentworth—and his
wife are as good as I am, but I have seen them kicked

and beaten like dogs. I know slavery now and all the days of my life I am going to fight against it. Now I am ready to go to my father's house—like the Prodigal Son coming back after his folly."

"But you will have some dinner first," said Mrs. Brimstead.

"No, I can not wait—I will walk. It is not far to Hopedale."

"Percy is at the door now with his buggy," said Brimstead.

Bim kissed Samson's cheek and embraced Annabel and her mother and hurried out of the house. Harry carried her bag to the buggy and helped her in.

"Harry, I want you to fall in love with this pretty girl," she said. "Don't you dare think of me any more or come near me. If you do, I'll shoo you away. Go on, Percy."

She waved her hand as the buggy went up the road.

"It's the same old Bim," Harry said to himself, as he stood watching her. "But I think she's lovelier than she ever was."

The next day Samson wrote in his diary:

"Bim was handsomer, but different. She had a woman's beauty. I noticed her loose clothes and that gentle look in her face that used to come to Sarah's when her time was about half over. I am glad she got away before she was further along."

CHAPTER XV

ILLINOIS was growing. In June scores of prairie schooners, loaded with old and young, rattled over the plains from the East. There were many Yankees from Ohio, New York and New England in this long caravan. There were almost as many Irish, who had set out for this land of golden promise as soon as they had been able to save money for a team and wagon, after reaching the new world. There were some Germans and Scandinavians in the dust clouds of the National Road. Steamers on the Illinois River scattered their living freight along its shores. These were largely from Kentucky, southern Ohio, Pennsylvania, Maryland and Virginia. The call of the rich and kindly lands had traveled far and streams of life were making toward them, to flow with increasing speed and volume for many years.

People in Sangamon County had begun to learn of the thriving village of Chicago in the North. Abe said that Illinois would be the Empire State of the West;

that a new era of rapid development and great prosperity was near. Rumors of railroad and canal
projects and river improvements were on every tongue.
Samson and Sarah took new heart of the prospect and
decided to try another year in New Salem, although an
Irishman had made a good offer for their farm. Land
was in great request and there were many transfers
of title. Abe had more surveying to do than he was
able to accomplish that summer. Harry was with him
for some weeks. He could earn two dollars a day
with Abe, whereas Samson was able to hire a helper
for half that sum. Harry made a confident of his
friend, and when they were working at the northern
end of the county they borrowed a pair of horses and
rode up to Kelso's house and spent a Sunday there.

Bim met them down the road a mile or so from
Hopedale. She, too, was on the back of a horse.
She recognized them before they were in hailing distance and waved her hand and hurried toward them
with a happy face.

"Where are you going?" she asked.

"To see you and your father and mother," said
Harry.

A sad look came into her eyes.

"If I had a stone I would throw it at you," she
said.

"Why?" Harry asked.

"Because I have to get used to being miserable, and
just as I begin to be resigned to it, you come along

and make me happy, and I have it all to do over again."

The young man stopped his horse.

"I hadn't thought of that," he said, with a sad face. "It isn't fair to you, is it? It's rather—selfish."

"Why don't you go to Brimstead's," Bim suggested. "A beautiful girl over there is in love with you. Honestly, Harry, there isn't a sweeter girl in all the world."

"I ought not to go there, either," said the young man.

"Why?"

"Because I mustn't let her think that I care for her. I'll go over to Peasley's and wait for Abe there."

"Look here," said the latter. "You both remind me of a man in a Kentucky village who couldn't bear to hear a rooster crow. It kept him awake nights, for the roosters did a lot o' crowing down there. He moved from one place to another, trying to find a cockless town. He couldn't. There was no such place in Kentucky. He thought of taking to the woods, but he hated loneliness more than he hated roosters. So he did a sensible thing. He started a chicken farm and got used to it. He found that a little crowing was too much, and that a lot of it was just what he needed. You two have got to get used to each other. What you need is more crowing. If you saw each other every day you wouldn't look so wonderful as when you don't."

"I reckon that's a good idea," said Bim. "Come on,

Harry, let's get used to crowing. We'll start in to-day to fall out of love with each other. We must be very cold and distant and haughty and say every mean thing we can think of."

So it happened that Harry went on with Bim and Abe to the little house in Hopedale. Jack Kelso sat reading in the shade of a tree by his door-step.

"I hope you feel as good as you look," Abe called, as they rode up.

"I've been feeling like a fly in a drum," Jack answered. "I've just heard a sermon by Peter Cartwright."

"What do you think of him?"

"He is saturated in the statistics of vice. His Satan is too busy; his hell is too big, too hot and too durable. He is a kind of human onion designed to make women weep."

Abe answered with a laugh:

"It is said that General Jackson went into his church one Sunday and that a deacon notified Mr. Cartwright of the presence of the great man. They say that the stern preacher exclaimed in a clearly audible tone: 'General Jackson! What does God care for General Jackson? If he don't repent, God will damn him as quick as he would damn a Guinea nigger.'"

"He's just that thumping, downright kind of a man," Kelso remarked. "How are you getting on with the books?"

"I have *Parsons on Contracts* strapped to the pommel," said Abe. "I did my stint coming over, but I had to walk and lead the pony."

"Every book you read gets a baptism of Democracy," said Kelso. "An idle aristocracy of the shelves loafing in fine coats and immaculate linen is not for the wise man. Your book has to roll up its sleeves and go to work and know the touch of the sweaty hand. Swift used to say that some men treat books as they do Lords—learn their titles and then brag of having been in their company. There are no Lords and Ladies among your books. They are just men and women made for human service."

"I don't read long at once," Abe remarked. "I scratch into a book, like a hen on a barn floor, until my crop is full, and then I digest what I have taken."

Harry and Bim had put out the horses. Now the girl came and sat on her father's knee. Harry sat down by the side of Abe on the grass in the oak's shadow.

"It is a joy to have the little girl back again," said Kelso, as he touched her hair with his hand. "It is still as yellow as a corn tassel. I wonder it isn't gray."

"Her eyes look as bright as ever to-day," said Harry.

"No compliments, please. I want you to be downright mean," Bim protested.

Kelso looked up with a smile: "My boy, it was Leonardo da Vinci who said that a man could have neither a greater nor a less dominion than that over himself."

"What a cruel-looking villain he is!" Bim exclaimed, with a smile. "I wouldn't dare say what I think of him."

"If you keep picking on me I'll cut loose and express my opinion of you," he retorted.

"Your opinions have ceased to be important," she answered, with a look of indifference.

"I think this is a clear case of assault and flattery," said Kelso.

"It pains me to look at you," Bim went on.

"Wait until I learn to play the flute and the snare drum," Harry threatened.

"I'm glad that New Salem is so far away," she sighed.

"I'll go and look at the new moon through a knot hole," he laughed.

"My dears, no more of this piping," said Kelso. "Bim must tell us what she has learned of the great evil of slavery. It is most important that Abe should hear it."

Bim told of revolting scenes she had witnessed in St. Louis and New Orleans—of flogging and buying and selling and herding. It was a painful story, the like of which had been traveling over the prairies of Illinois for years. Some had accepted these reports; many, among whom were the most judicious men, had thought they detected in them the note of gross exaggeration. Here, at last, was a witness whose word it was impossible for those who knew her to doubt. Abe put many questions and looked very grave when the testimony was all in.

"If you have any doubt," said Bim, "I ask you to look at that mark on my arm. It was made by the whip of Mr. Eliphalet Biggs."

The young men looked with amazement at a scar some three or four inches long on her forearm.

"If he would do that to his wife, what treatment could you expect for his niggers?" Bim asked. "There are many Biggses in the South."

"What so vile as a cheap, rococo aristocracy—growing up in idleness, too noble to be restrained, with every brutal passion broad blown as flush as May?" Kelso growled.

"Nothing is long sacred in the view of any aristocracy—not even God," Abe answered. "They make a child's plaything of Him and soon cast Him aside."

"But I hold that if our young men are to be trained to tyranny in a lot of little nigger kingdoms, our Democracy will die."

Abe made no answer. He was always slow to commit himself.

"The North is partly to blame for what has come," said Samson. "I guess our Yankee captains brought over most of the niggers and sold them to the planters of the South."

"There was a demand for them, or those Yankee

pirates wouldn't have brought the niggers," Harry answered. "Both seller and buyer were committing a crime."

"They established a great wrong and now the South is pushing to extend and give it the sanction of law," said Abe. "There is the point of irritation and danger."

"I hear that in the next Legislature an effort will be made to endorse slavery," said Kelso. "It would be like endorsing Nero and Caligula."

"It is a dangerous subject," Abe answered. "Whatever happens, I shall not fail to express my opinion of slavery if I go back."

"The time is coming when you will take the bull by the horns," said Kelso. "There's no fence that will keep him at home."

"I hope that isn't true," Abe answered.

Soon Mrs. Kelso called Bim to set the table. She and Harry brought it out under the tree, where, in the cool shade, they had a merry dinner.

When the dishes were put away Percy Brimstead arrived with his sister Annabel in their buggy. Bim went out to meet them and came into the dooryard with her arm around Annabel's waist.

"Did any one ever see a lovelier girl than this?" Bim asked, as they stood up before the dinner party.

"Her cheeks are like wild roses, her eyes like the dew on them when the sun is rising," said Kelso.

"But look at her mouth and the teeth in it the next time she smiles," Bim went on.

"Aye, they are well wrought," her father answered.

"If you don't stop, I shall run," Annabel protested.

"I haven't said a word, but I want you to know that I am deeply impressed," said Harry. "No girl has a right to be as handsome as you are and come and look into the face of a young man who has resolved to look at the new moon through a knot hole."

"Well, who would have thought it!" Bim exclaimed. "Such a wonderful compliment, and from Harry Needles!"

"Of course he didn't mean it," said Annabel, whose cheeks were now very red.

"Of course I mean it," Harry declared. "That's why I keep away from your house. I am bound to stay single."

"Did you ever see a fairy going to mill on a butterfly's back?" Bim asked, looking at Harry.

"Not as I remember," he answered.

"If you had, you wouldn't expect us to believe it," Bim asserted.

"There was a soldier in Colonel Taylor's regiment who always ran when the enemy was in sight," Abe began. "When he was brought up for discipline, he said 'My heart is as brave as Julius Cæsar's, but my legs can't be trusted.' I know Harry's legs are all right, but I don't believe his heart can be trusted in a battle of this kind."

"I've heard all about his brave adventures in the war," said Bim. "He'll find that girls are worse than Indians."

"If they're as well armed as you two, I guess you're right," said Samson.

Abe rose and said: "The day is passing. I'll start on with Parsons and the pony and read my stint afoot. You come along in a few minutes. By the time you overtake me I'll be ready to get into the saddle."

Half an hour or so after Abe had gone, Harry's horse, which had been whinnying for his mate, bounded out of the stable and went galloping down the road, having slipped his halter.

"He will not stop until he overtakes the other horse," said Harry.

"You can ride with us," Annabel suggested.

So the young man brought his saddle and bridle and put it under the seat of the buggy and got in with Annabel and her small brother.

"Don't let us go too far," said Bim, as she stood by the side of the buggy. "You haven't offered to shake hands."

"It was a deliberate slight—just to please you," Harry answered, as they shook hands.

"You are behaving terribly well," Bim exclaimed,

merrily. "Now, Annabel, here is your chance to convert him."

She laughed and shook her hand, as they rode away, and went into the house and sat down and for a time was like one whose heart is broken.

"Oh, the troubles of the young!" her mother exclaimed, as she kissed her.

"They are ever the wonder of the old!" said Kelso, who stood near.

"I love him! I love him!" the girl moaned.

"I don't wonder," her father answered. "He is a big, brave, clean lad, and handsome as a Greek god. He will love you all the better for your self-restraint. It makes me proud of you, my daughter—proud of you! Be of good cheer. The day of your emancipation may not be long delayed."

Some two miles down the road Harry found Abe standing between the horses, holding the runaway by his forelock. The latter was saddled and bridled, while the buggy went on ahead.

"That is a wonderful girl," said Harry, as he and Abe were riding along together. "She is very modest and gentle hearted."

"And as pleasant to look at as the flowery meadows," Abe answered.

"I have promised to stop there a few minutes on our way back."

"It is possible Bim could get a divorce," said Abe,

looking down thoughtfully at the mane of his horse. "I'll ask Stuart what he thinks about it when I see him again."

"I hope you'll see him soon."

"As soon as I can get to Springfield."

Brimstead and Abe had a talk together, while Harry went into the house.

"Say, there's a good many kinds o' trouble," said the former, in a low tone, "but one o' the worst is skunks. Say, I'll tell ye, there's a feller lives over in the woods a few miles from here that had a skunk in a pen. His name is Hinge. Somebody had been stealin' his grain, so the other night he hitched that skunk right under the barn door. The thief came and the skunk punished him tolerable severe. The next day Free Collar, the famous Constable, was comin' up the road from Sangamon County and met that man Biggs on a horse. Say—"

Brimstead looked about him and stepped close to Abe and added in a tone of extreme confidence: "Biggs had left a streak behind him a mile long. Its home was Biggs. It had settled down and gone into business on him and was doin' well and gettin' a reputation. Collar coughed and backed away. For four days he had been chasin' that man to arrest him. Biggs had been hid in the woods near Hinge's cabin an' had stole grain for his horses.

" 'Here I am,' said Biggs. 'You can have me. I'm lonesome.'

" 'You'll be lonesomer 'fore I go near ye,' says Collar.

" 'I thought you wanted to arrest me,' says Biggs.

" 'Say, man, I'd 'a' been glad to see you go to prison for a year or two, but now I'm plum sorry for ye,' says Collar. 'A constable who wouldn't run if he smelt you comin' would be a durn fool.'

"They started in opposite directions. In half a minute the Constable hollered to Biggs:

" 'Say, they've got a railroad train on a track over in Ohio, but they can't make it run. I wouldn't wonder if you could help 'em.' "

Brimstead added in a half whisper:

"Biggs went on, but the poor devil is livin' a God lonesome life. He can't sleep in a buildin' an' his food'll have to be throwed to him. It's a new way to defeat justice."

Abe's laughter was like the neigh of a horse. It brought Harry out of the house. He mounted his pony and, as they rode away, Abe told him of the fate of Biggs.

"I don't believe he'll take another Illinois girl away with him," Abe laughed.

"Talk about the chains of bondage! He's buried in 'em," Harry exclaimed.

In a moment he said: "That lovely girl gave me a necktie and a pair of gloves that she has knit with her own hands. I'll never forget the way she did it and the look of her. It rather touched my heart."

"She's as innocent as a child," said Abe. "It's hard on a girl like that to have to live in this new country. Her father and mother have promised to let her come for a visit with Ann. I'll go up next Saturday and take her down to New Salem with me."

This kindly plan of Abe's—so full of pleasant possibilities—fell into hopeless ruin next day, when a letter came from Dr. Allen, telling him that Ann was far gone with a dangerous fever. Both Abe and Harry dropped their work and went home. Ann was too sick to see her lover.

The little village was very quiet those hot summer days. The sorrow of the pretty maiden had touched the hearts of the simple kindly folk who lived there. They would have helped her bear it—if that had been possible—as readily as they would have helped at a raising. For a year or more there had been a tender note in their voices when they spoke of Ann. They had learned with great gladness of her engagement to marry Abe. The whole community were as one family with its favorite daughter about to be crowned with good fortune greater than she knew. Now that she was stricken down, their feeling was more than sympathy. The love of justice, the desire to see a great wrong righted, in a measure, was in their hearts when they sought news of the little sufferer at the tavern.

There was no shouting in the street, no story-telling in the dooryards, no jesting in the stores and houses, no merry parties, gladdened by the notes of the violin, in the days and nights of Ann's long illness.

Samson writes in his diary that Abe went about like a man in a dream, with no heart for work or study. He spent much time at the Doctor's office, feeling for some straw of hope.

One day late in August, as he stood talking with Samson Traylor in the street, Dr. Allen called him from his door-step. Abe turned very pale as he obeyed the summons.

"I've just come from her bedside," said Dr. Allen. "She wants to see you. I've talked it over with her parents, and we've decided to let you and her have a little visit together. You must be prepared for a great change in Ann. There's not much left of the poor girl. A breath would blow her away. But she wants to see you. It may be better than medicine. Who knows?"

The two men went across to the tavern. Mrs. Rutledge and Abe tiptoed up the stairway. The latter entered the room of the sick girl. The woman closed the door. Ann Rutledge was alone with her lover. There were none who knew what happened in that solemn hour save the two—one of whom was on the edge of eternity, and the other was never to speak of it.

The only record of that hour is to be found in the face and spirit of a great man.

Years later Samson wrote in a letter.

"I saw Abe when he came out of the tavern that day. He was not the Abe we had all known. He was different. There were new lines in his face. It was sorrowful. His steps were slow. He had passed out of his young manhood. When I spoke to him, he answered with that gentle dignity now so familiar to all who know him. From that hour he was Abraham Lincoln."

Ann passed away before the month ended and became, like many of her kind, an imperishable memory. In her presence the spirit of the young man had received such a baptism that henceforward, taking thought of her, he was to love purity and all cleanness, and no Mary who came to his feet with tears and ointment was ever to be turned away.

CHAPTER XVI

WHEREIN YOUNG MR. LINCOLN SAFELY PASSES TWO
GREAT DANGER POINTS AND TURNS INTO THE HIGH-
WAY OF HIS MANHOOD.

FOR days thereafter the people of New Salem were
sorely troubled. Abe Lincoln, the ready helper in
time of need, the wise counselor, the friend of all—
"old and young, dogs and horses," as Samson was
wont to say—the pride and hope of the little cabin
village, was breaking down under his grief. He
seemed to care no more for work or study or friendship. He wandered out in the woods and upon the
prairies alone. Many feared that he would lose his
reason.

There was a wise and merry-hearted man who lived
a mile or so from the village. His name was Bowlin
Green. Every one on Salem Hill and in the country
round about it laid claim to the friendship of this remarkable man. Those days when one of middle age
had established himself in the affections of a community, its members had a way of adopting him. So
Mr. Green had been adopted into many families from

Beardstown to Springfield. He was everybody's
"Uncle Bowlin." He had a most unusual circumference and the strength to carry it. He was indeed a
man of extended boundaries, embracing noble gifts,
the best of which was good nature. His jests, his loud
laughter and his quaking circumference were the three
outstanding factors in his popularity. The loss of
either would have been a misfortune to himself and
neighbors. His ruddy cheeks and curling locks and
kindly dark eyes and large head were details of importance. Under all were a heart with the love of
men, a mind of unusual understanding and a hand
skilled in all the arts of the Kentucky pioneer. He
could grill a venison steak and roast a grouse and broil
a chicken in a way which had filled the countryside
with fond recollections of his hospitality; he could
kindle a fire with a bow and string, a pine stick and
some shavings; he could make anything from a splint
broom to a rocking horse with his jack-knife. Abe
Lincoln was one of the many men who knew and loved
him.

On a warm, bright afternoon early in September,
Bowlin Green was going around the pasture to put
his fence in repair, when he came upon young Mr.
Lincoln. The latter sat in the shade of a tree on the
hillside. He looked "terribly peaked," as Uncle Bowlin
has said in a letter.

"Why, Abe, where have you been?" he asked. "The

whole village is scared. Samson Traylor was here last night lookin' for ye."

"I'm like a deer that's been hurt," said the young man. "I took to the woods. Wanted to be alone. You see, I had a lot of thinking to do—the kind of thinking that every man must do for himself. I've got the brush cleared away, at last, so I can see through. I had made up my mind to go down to your house for the night and was trying to decide whether I have energy enough to do it."

"Come on; it's only a short step," urged the big-hearted Bowlin. "The wife and babies are over to Beardstown. We'll have the whole place to ourselves. The feather beds are ladder high. I've got a haunch of venison buried in the hide and some prairie chickens that I killed yesterday, and, besides, I'm lonesome."

"What I feel the need of, just now, is a week or two of sleep," said Mr. Lincoln, as he rose and started down the long hill with his friend.

Some time later Bowlin Green gave Samson this brief account of what happened in and about the cabin:

"He wouldn't eat anything. He wanted to go down to the river for a dip, and I went with him. When we got back, I induced him to take off his clothes and get into bed. He was fast asleep in ten minutes. When night came I went up the ladder to bed. He was still asleep when I came down in the morning. I went out and did my chores. Then I cut two venison steaks, each about the size o' my hand, and a half moon of bacon. I pounded the venison to pulp with a little salt and bacon mixed in. I put it on the broiler and over a bed o' hickory coals. I got the coffee into the pot and up next to the fire and some potatoes in the ashes. I basted a bird with bacon strips and put it into the roaster and set it back o' the broiling bed. Then I made some biscuits and put 'em into the oven. I tell you, in a little while the smell o' that fireplace would have 'woke the dead—honest! Abe began to stir. In a minute I heard him call:

" 'Say, Uncle Bowlin, I'm goin' to get up an' eat you out o' house and home. I'm hungry and I feel like a new man. What time is it?'

" 'It'll be nine o'clock by the time you're washed and dressed,' I says.

" 'Well, I declare,' says he, 'I've had about sixteen hours o' solid sleep. The world looks better to me this morning.'

"He hurried into his clothes and we sat down at the table with the steak and the chicken and some wild grape jelly and baked potatoes, with new butter and coffee and cream and hot biscuit and clover honey, and say, we both et till we was ashamed of it.

"At the table I told him a story and got a little laugh out of him. He stayed with me three weeks, choring around the place and taking it easy. He read all the books I had, until you and Doc Allen came with the law books. Then he pitched into them. I think he has changed a good deal since Ann died. He talks a lot about God and the hereafter."

In October young Mr. Lincoln returned to his surveying, and in the last month of the year to Vandalia for an extra session of the Legislature, where he took a stand against the convention system of nominating candidates for public office. Samson went to Vandalia for a visit with him and to see the place before the session ended. The next year, in a letter to his brother, he says:

"Vandalia is a small, crude village. It has a strong flavor of whisky, profanity and tobacco. The night after I got there I went to a banquet with Abe Lincoln. Heard a lot about the dam nigger-loving Yankees who were trying to ruin the state and country with abolition. There were some stories like those we used to hear in the lumber camp, and no end of powerful talk, in which the names of God and the Savior were roughly handled. A few of the statesmen got drunk, and after the dinner was over two of them jumped on the table and danced down the whole length of it, shattering plates and cups and saucers and glasses. Nobody seemed to be able to stop them. I hear that they had to pay several hundred dollars for the damage done. You will be apt to think that there is too much liberty here in the West, and perhaps that is so, but the fact is these men are not half so bad as they seem to be. Lincoln tells me that they are honest almost to a man and sincerely devoted to the public good as they see it. I asked Abe Lincoln, who all his life has associated with rough tongued, drinking men, how he had managed to hold his own course and keep his talk and habits so clean.

" 'Why, the fact is,' said he, 'I have associated with the people who lived around me only part of the time, but I have never stopped associating with myself and with Washington and Clay and Webster and Shakespeare and Burns and DeFoe and Scott and Blackstone and Parsons. On the whole, I've been in pretty good company.'

"He has not yet accomplished much in the Legislature. I don't think that he will until some big issue comes along. 'I'm not much of a hand at hunting squirrels,' he said to me the other day. 'Wait till I see a bear.' The people of Vandalia and Springfield have never seen him yet. They don't know him as I do. But they all respect him—just for his good fellowship, honesty and decency. I guess that every fellow with a foul mouth hates himself for it and envies the man who isn't like him. They begin to see his skill as a politician, which has shown itself in the passage of a bill removing the capitol to Springfield. Abe Lincoln was the man who put it through. But he has not yet uncovered his best talents. Mark my word, some day Lincoln will be a big man.

"The death of his sweetheart has aged and sobered him. When we are together he often sits looking down with a sad face. For a while not a word out of him. Suddenly he will begin saying things, the effect of which will go with me to my grave, although I can not

call back the words and place them as he did.   He is
what I would call a great Captain of words.   Seems
as if I heard the band playing while they march by
me as well dressed and stepping as proud and regular
as The Boston Guards.   In some great battle between
Right and Wrong you will hear from him.   I hope
it may be the battle between Slavery and Freedom,
although at present he thinks they must avoid coming
to a clinch.   In my opinion, it can not be done.   I expect to live to see the fight and to take part in it."

Late in the session of 1836-1837 the prophetic truth
of these words began to reveal itself.   A bill was being put through the Legislature denouncing the growth
of abolition sentiment and its activity in organized so-
cieties and upholding the right of property in slaves.

Suddenly Lincoln had come to a fork in the road.
Popularity, the urge of many friends, the counsel of
Wealth and Power, and Public Opinion, the call of
good politics pointed in one direction and the crowd
went that way.   It was a stampede.   Lincoln stood
alone at the corner.   The crowd beckoned, but in
vain.   One man came back and joined him.   It was
Dan Stone, who was not a candidate for re-election.
His political career was ended.   There were three
words on the sign-board pointing toward the perilous
and lonely road that Lincoln proposed to follow. They
were the words Justice and Human Rights.   Lincoln
and Dan Stone took that road in a protest, declaring

that they "believed the institution of slavery was founded upon injustice and bad policy." Lincoln had followed his conscience, instead of the crowd.

At twenty-eight years of age he had safely passed the great danger point in his career. The declaration at Decatur, the speeches against Douglas, the miracle of turning 4,000,000 beasts into 4,000,000 men, the sublime utterance at Gettysburg, the wise parables, the second inaugural, the innumerable acts of mercy, all of which lifted him into undying fame, were now possible. Henceforth he was to go forward with the growing approval of his own spirit and the favor of God.

BOOK THREE

CHAPTER XVII

WHEREIN YOUNG MR. LINCOLN BETRAYS IGNORANCE OF TWO HIGHLY IMPORTANT SUBJECTS, IN CONSEQUENCE OF WHICH HE BEGINS TO SUFFER SERIOUS EMBARRASSMENT.

THERE were two subjects of which Mr. Lincoln had little understanding. They were women and finance. Up to this time his tall, awkward, ill clad figure had been a source of amusement to those unacquainted with his admirable spirit. Until they had rightly appraised the value of his friendship, women had been wont to regard him with a riant curiosity. He had been aware of this, and for years had avoided women, save those of old acquaintance. When he lived at the tavern in the village often he had gone without a meal rather than expose himself to the eyes of strange women. The reason for this was well understood by those who knew him. The young man was an exceedingly sensitive human being. No doubt he had suffered more than any one knew from ill concealed ridicule, but he had been able to bear it with composure in his callow youth. Later nothing roused his anger like an attempt to ridicule him. No man who came in his way in after life was so quickly and completely floored as one George Forquer, who, in a moment of folly, had attempted to make light of him.

Two women he had regarded with great tenderness —his foster mother, the second wife of Thomas Lincoln, and Ann Rutledge. Others had been to him, mostly, delightful but inscrutable beings. The company of women and of dollars had been equally unfamiliar to him. He had said more than once in his young manhood that he felt embarrassed in the presence of either, and knew not quite how to behave himself—an exaggeration in which there was no small amount of truth.

In 1836 the middle frontier had entered upon a singular phase of its development. Emigrants from the East and South and from overseas had been pouring into it. The summer before the lake and river steamers had been crowded with them, and their wagons had come in long processions out of the East. Chicago had begun its phenomenal growth. A frenzied speculation in town lots had been under way in that community since the autumn of '35. It was spreading through the state. Imaginary cities were laid out on the lonely prairies and all the corner lots sold to eager buyers and paid for with promises. Fortunes of imaginary wealth were created by sales of future greatness. Millions of conversational, promissory dollars, based upon the gold at the foot of the rainbow, were changing hands day by day. The Legislature, with an empty treasury behind it, voted twelve millions for river improvements and imaginary railroads and canals, for which neither surveys nor estimates had been made, to serve the dream-built cities of the speculator. If Mr. Lincoln had had more experience in the getting and use of dollars and more acquaintance with the shrinking timidity of large sums, he would have tried to dissipate these illusions of grandeur. But he went with the crowd, every member of which had a like inexperience.

In the midst of the session Samson Traylor arrived in Vandalia on his visit to Mr. Lincoln.

"I have sold my farm," said Samson to his old friend the evening of his arrival.

"Did you get a good price?" Mr. Lincoln asked.

"All that my conscience would allow me to take," said Samson. "The man offered me three dollars an acre in cash and ten dollars in notes. We compromised on seven dollars, all cash."

"It's a mistake to sell now. The river is going to be deepened and improved for navigation."

"I've made up my mind that it can't be done, unless you can invent a way to run a steamboat on moist ground," said Samson. "You might as well try to make a great man out of 'Colonel Lukins.' It hasn't the water-shed. To dig a deep channel for the Sanga-mon would be like sending 'Colonel Lukins' to Harvard. We're going too fast. We have little to sell yet but land. The people are coming to us in great numbers, but most of them are poor. We must give them time to settle down and create something and increase the wealth of the state. Then we shall have a solid base to build upon; then we shall have the confidence of the capital we require for improvements. Now I fear that we are building on the sands."

"Don't you think that our bonds would sell in the East?"

"No; because we have only used our lungs in all these plans of ours. No one has carefully considered the cost. For all we know, it may cost more than the entire wealth of the state to put through the improvements already planned. The eastern capitalists will want to know about costs and security. Undoubtedly Illinois is sure to be a great state. But we're all looking at the day of greatness through a telescope. It seems to be very near. It isn't. It's at least ten years in the future."

Young Mr. Lincoln looked very grave for a moment. Then he laughed and said: "I don't know but we're all a lot of fools. I begin to suspect myself. The subject of finance is new to me. I don't know much about it, but I'm sure if I were to say what you have said, in the House of Representatives, they would throw me out-of-doors."

"Just at present the House is a kind of insane asylum," said Samson. "You'll have to stick to the procession now. The road is so crowded that nobody can turn around. The folly of the state is so unanimous no one will be more to blame than another when the crash comes. You have meant well, anyhow."

"You make me feel young and inexperienced."

"You are generally wise, Abe, but there's one thing you don't know—that's the use of capital. For two years Sarah and I have been studying the subject of finance."

"I've seen too little of you in the last year or so," said the young statesman. "What are you going to do now that you have sold out?"

"I was thinking of going up to Tazewell County."

"Why don't you go to the growing and prosperous town of Springfield," Mr. Lincoln asked. "The capitol will be there, and so will I. It is going to be a big city. Men who are to make history will live in Springfield. You must come and help. The state will need a man of your good sense. It would be a great comfort to me to have you and Sarah and Harry and the children near me. I shall need your friendship, your wisdom and your sympathy. I shall want to sit often by your fireside. You'll find a good school there for the children. If you'll think of it seriously, I'll try to get you into the public service."

"We need you plenty," Samson answered. "We kind o' think o' you as one o' the family. I'll talk it over with Sarah and see. Never mind the job. If I keep you behavin' yourself, it'll be job enough. Anyway, I guess we can manage to get along. Sarah's uncle in Boston died last month and left her a little money. If we can get what we have well invested, all I shall need will be a few acres and a few tools and some friends to swap stories with."

"I've had a talk with Stuart and have some good news for Harry and Bim," said young Mr. Lincoln. "Stuart thinks she can get a divorce under the law of 1827. I suppose they are still interested in each other."

"He's like most of the Yankees. Once he gets set, it's hard to change him. The Kelsos have moved to Chicago, and I don't know how Bim stands. If Harry knows, he hasn't said a word to us about it."

"I'm interested in that little romance," said the legislator. "It's our duty to do what we can to secure the happiness of these young lovers. We mustn't neglect that in the pressure of other things. They and their friends are dear to me. Tell Harry to come over here. I want to talk with him."

This dialogue was about the last incident in the visit of Samson Traylor.

Late in the historic session of that spring, wherein

the Whigs adopted the convention system of nominations and many plans were made for the expenditure of visionary millions, young Mr. Lincoln received a letter from his friend, Mrs. Bennet Able of New Salem, which conveyed a shock to his nerves. Before he had gone to the session, Mrs. Able had said to him lightly:

"Abe, I'll ask my sister Mary to come up here for a visit if you'll agree to marry her."

"All right," the young man had answered playfully.

He remembered Mary. When he had left Kentucky, years before, Mary—a slender, sweet-faced girl—had been one of those who bade him good-by.

The letter had said among other things: "Mary has come, and now we expect you to keep your word."

No knight of old had a keener sense of chivalry than the young statesman of Salem Hill. It was almost as Quixotic as the excesses at which Cervantes aimed his ridicule. An appalling fear took possession of him—a fear that Mrs. Able and the girl had taken him seriously. It worried him.

About this time Harry Needles arrived in Vandalia. The Legislature had adjourned for a week-end. It was a warm, bright Saturday, early in March. The two friends went out for a stroll in the woods.

"Have you seen Mrs. Able's sister, Mary Owens?" Abe Lincoln asked.

"I've seen her often."

"What kind of a girl is she?"

"A good kind, but—heavy."

"Fat?"

"Massive and most of her front teeth gone."

Lincoln looked thoughtful.

"You look as if she had stepped on your foot," Harry remarked.

"The fact is I'm engaged to her in a kind of a way."

"Of course that's a joke."

"You're right; it's a joke, but I'm afraid she and her sister have taken it seriously. A man must be careful of the heart of a young woman. After all, it isn't a thing to play with. As usual, when I try to talk with women, I make a fool of myself."

"It would be easier to make a whistle out of a pig's tail than a fool out of you," said Harry. "I have joked like that with Annabel and other girls, but they knew that it was only fun."

"Still true to your old love?"

"As firm as a nail driven in oak," said Harry. "I seem to be built that way. I shall never care much for any other girl."

"Do you hear from Bim?"

"Once in a while I get a long, playful letter from her, full of things that only Bim could write."

"Stuart says she can get a divorce. We know the facts pretty well. If you say so, we'll prepare the papers and you can take them up to Chicago and get them signed and attested. Stuart tells me that we can serve them by advertising."

"Good!" Harry exclaimed. "Get the papers ready as soon as you can and send them up to me. When they come I'll mount that new pony of mine and start for Chicago. If she won't have me, let her take a better man."

"In my opinion Bim will want you," said the legislator. "I'll be coming home in a few days and will bring the papers with me. The session is about over. If the rich men refuse to back our plans, there's going to be a crowd of busted statesmen in Illinois, and I'll be one of 'em."

"Shall you spend the summer in New Salem?"

"I don't know yet what I shall do. First I must tackle the delicate task of getting disengaged from Mary."

"I shouldn't think it would take long," said Harry, with a smile.

"I can tell better after a preliminary survey."

"No doubt Mrs. Able would like to have you marry her sister. She knows that you have a promising future ahead of you. But don't allow her to look serious over that little joke."

Abe Lincoln laughed and said: "Mary would be like the man who traded horses unsight and unseen and drew a saw horse."

Harry returned to New Salem. After the session, young Mr. Lincoln went to Springfield and did not reach New Salem until the first week of May. When he arrived there, Mrs. Able met the stage from which he alighted and asked him to come to supper at her house that evening. Not a word was said of Mary in the excitement, about all the folk of the village having assembled to meet and cheer the triumphant Captain of Internal Improvements. Abe Lincoln went to supper and met Mary, who had a cheerful heart and good manners, and a schooled and active intellect, as well as the defects which Harry had mentioned. She and the young statesman had a pleasant visit together, recalling scenes and events which both remembered from beyond the barrier of a dozen years. On the whole, he was agreeably impressed. The neighbors came in after supper. Mrs. Able kept the comedy moving along by a playful reference to the pseudo engagement of the young people. Mr. Lincoln laughed with the others and said that it reminded him a little of the boy who decided to be president and only needed the consent of the United States.

CHAPTER XVIII

MR. LINCOLN had brought the papers which Harry was to take to Bim, and made haste to deliver them. The boy was eager to be off on his mission. The fields were sown. The new buyer was coming to take possession in two weeks. Samson and Harry had finished their work in New Salem.

"Wait till to-morrow and maybe I'll go with ye," said Samson. "I'm anxious to see the country clear up to the lake and take a look at that little mushroom city of Chicago."

"And buy a few corner lots?" Abe Lincoln asked, with a smile.

"No; I'll wait till next year. They'll be cheaper then. I believe in Chicago. It's placed right—on the waterway to the north and east, with good country on three sides and transportation on the other. It can go into partnership with Steam Power right away and begin to do business. Your grain and pork can go straight from there to Albany and New York and Boston and Baltimore without being rehandled. When

283

railroads come—if they ever do—Steam Power will be shoving grain and meat and passengers into Chicago from every point of the compass."

Abe Lincoln turned to Sarah and said: "This is a growing country. You ought to see the cities springing up there in the Legislature. I was looking with great satisfaction at the crop when Samson came along one day and fell on it. He was like a frost in midsummer."

"The seed was sown too early," Samson rejoined. "You and I may live to see all the dreams of Vandalia come true."

"And all the nightmares, too," said the young statesman.

"Yes, we're going to wake up and find a cold morning and not much to eat in the house and the wolf at the door, but we'll live through it."

Then the young statesman proposed: "If you are going with Harry, I'll go along and see what they've done on the Illinois and Michigan Canal. Some contractors who worked on the Erie Canal will start from Chicago Monday to look the ground over and bid on the construction of the southern end of it. I want to talk with them when they come along down the line."

"I guess a few days in the saddle would do you good," said Samson.

"I reckon it would. I've been rloyed on house air

and oratory and future greatness. The prairie wind
and your pessimism will straighten me up."

Harry rode to the village that afternoon to get
"Colonel" and Mrs. Lukins to come out to the farm
and stay with Sarah while he and Samson were away.
Harry found the "Colonel" sitting comfortably in a
chair by the door of his cabin, roaring with laughter.
He had not lived up to his title and was still generally
known as "Bony" Lukins.

"What are you roaring at?" Harry demanded.

The "Colonel" was dumb with joy for a moment.
Then, with an effort, he straightened his face and
managed to say: "Laughin' just 'cause I'm alive."
The words were followed by a kind of spiritual ex-
plosion followed by a silent ague of merriment. It
would seem that his brain had discovered in the human
comedy some subtle and persuasive jest which had
gone over the heads of the crowd. Yet Harry seemed
to catch it, for he, too, began to laugh with the fortunate "Colonel."

"You see," said the latter, as, with great difficulty,
he restrained himself for half a moment, "this is my
busy day."

Again he roared and shook in a fit of ungovernable
mirth. In the midst of it Mrs. Lukins arrived.

"Don't pay no 'tention to him," she said. "The
'Colonel' is wearin' himself out restin'. He's kep' his

head bobbin' all day like a woodpecker's. Jest laughs till he's sick every time he an' ol' John gits together. It's plum ridic'lous."

The "Colonel" turned serious long enough to give him time to explain in a quivering, joyous tone: "Ol' John, he just sets beside me and says the gol' darndest funniest things!"

He could get no further. His last words were blown out in a gale of laughter. Mrs. Lukins had sat down with her knitting.

"Ol' John Barleycorn will leave to-night, an' to-morrow the 'Colonel' will be the soberest critter in Illinois—kind o' lonesome like an' blubberin' to himself," she explained. The faithful soul added in a whisper of confidence: "He's a good man. There don't nobody know how deep an' kind o' coralapus like he is."

She now paused as if to count stitches. For a long time the word "coralapus" had been a prized possession of Mrs. Lukins. Like her feathered bonnet, it was used only on special occasions by way of putting her best foot forward. It was indeed a family ornament of the same general character as her husband's title. Just how she came by it nobody could tell, but of its general significance, as it fell from her lips, there could be no doubt whatever in any but the most obtuse intellect. For her it had a large and noble, although a rather indefinite meaning, entirely favorable to the person or the object to which it was applied.

There was one other word in her lexicon which was in the nature of a jewel to be used only on special occasions. It was the word "copasetic." The best society of Salem Hill understood perfectly that it signalized an unusual depth of meaning.

In half a moment she added: "He's got some grand idees. If they was ever drawed out an' spread on the ground so that folks could see them, I reckon they'd be surprised."

"I'm sorry to find him in this condition," said Harry. "We wanted you and him to come out and help Mrs. Traylor to look after the place while we are gone to Chicago."

"You needn't worry about Ol' John," said she. "He'll git lonesome an' toddle off when the 'Colonel' goes to bed an' won't come 'round ag'in till snow flies. That man will be just as steady as an ox all the summer an' fall—not a laugh out o' him—you see."

"Can you be there at six in the morning?"

"We'll be there—sure as sunrise—an' ready to go to work."

They were on hand at the hour appointed, the "Colonel" having acquired, meanwhile, his wonted look of solemnity.

Josiah, now a sturdy boy of thirteen, stood in the dooryard, holding the two saddle ponies from Nebraska which Samson had bought of a drover. Betsey, a handsome young miss almost fifteen years old, stood beside him. Sambo, a sober old dog with gray hairs in his head, sat near, looking at the horses. Sarah, whose face had begun to show the wear of years full of loneliness and hard work, was packing the saddle-bags, now nearly filled, with extra socks and shirts and doughnuts and bread and butter. As the travelers were saying good-by, Mrs. Lukins handed a package to Samson.

"I heard Philemon Morris readin' 'bout Chicago in the paper," said she. "I want you to take that money an' buy me some land thar—jest as much as ye kin. There's two hundred an' fifty dollars in the foot o' that ol' sock, and most of it shiny gold."

"I wouldn't risk my savings that way," Samson advised. "It's too much like gambling. You couldn't afford to lose your money."

"You do as I tell ye," the "Colonel's" wife insisted. "I alwus obey your orders. Now I want you to take one from me."

"All right," the man answered. "If I see anything that looks good to me, I'll buy it if I can."

As the two men were riding toward the village, Samson said: "Kind o' makes my heart ache to leave home even for a little while these days. We've had six long, lonesome years on that farm. Not one of our friends have been out to see us. Sarah was right. Movin' west is a good deal like dyin' and goin' to an-'other world. It's a pity we didn't settle further north, but we were tired of travel when we got here. We didn't know which way to turn and felt as if we'd gone far enough. When we settle down again, it'll be where we can take some comfort and see lots o' folks every day."

"Have you decided where to go?" Harry asked.

"I think we shall go with Abe to Springfield."

"That's good. Next year I hope to be admitted to the bar, and I'd like to settle in Springfield."

For nearly two years Abe Lincoln had been passing the law books that he had read to Harry before they went back to John T. Stuart.

The gray horses, Colonel and Pete, stood by the fence in the pasture lot and whinnied as the men passed.

"They know us all right," said Samson. "I guess they feel slighted, but they've had their last journey. They're about worn out. We'll give 'em a vacation this summer. I wouldn't sell 'em. They're a part o' the family. You can lay yer hand on either one and say that no better hoss was ever wrapped in a surcingle."

They met Abe Lincoln at the tavern, where he was waiting on a big horse which he had borrowed for the trip from James Rutledge. Without delay, the three men set out on the north road in perfect weather. From the hill's edge they could look over a wooded plain running far to the east.

"It's a beautiful place to live up here, but on this side you need a ladder to get to it. The little village

is going to die—too much altitude. It's a horse killer.
No team can draw anything but its breath going up
that hill. It's all right for a generation of walkers,
but the time has come when we must go faster than
a walk and carry bigger burdens than a basket or a
bundle. Every one will be moving—mostly to Peters-
burg."

As they rode on, the young statesman repeated a
long passage from one of the sermons of Dr. William
Ellery Channing on the Instability of Human Affairs.

"I wish that I had your memory," Samson remarked.

"My memory is like a piece of metal," said the
young legislator. "Learning is not easy for me. It's
rather slow work—like engraving with a tool. But
when a thing is once printed on my memory it seems
to stay there. It doesn't rub out. When I run across
a great idea, well expressed, I like to put it on the
wall of my mind where I can live with it. In this way
every man can have his own little art gallery and be in
the company of great men."

They forded a creek in deep water, where a bridge
had been washed away.

As they came out dripping on the farther shore,
Lincoln remarked: "The thing to do in fording a
deep stream is to keep watch o' your horse's ears. As
long as you can see 'em you're all right."

"Mr. Lincoln, I'm sorry—you got into a hole," said
Samson.

"I don't mind that, but while we're traveling together, please don't call me 'Mr. Lincoln.' I don't think
I've done anything to deserve such lack of respect."

Samson answered: "If you're nice to us, I don't
know but we'll call ye 'Abe' again, just for a few
days. You can't expect us to go too far with a man
who associates with Judges and Generals and Gov-
ernors and such trash. If you keep it up, you're bound
to lose standing in our community."

"I know I've changed," said Abe. "I've grown older
since Ann died—years older—but I don't want you
fellows to throw me over. I'm on the same level that
you are and I intend to stay there. It's a fool notion
that men go up some heavenly stairway to another
plane when they begin to do things worth while. That's
a kind of feudalistic twaddle. The wise man keeps
his feet on the ground and lifts his mind as high as
possible. The higher he lifts it, the more respect he
will have for the common folk. Have either of you
seen McNamar since he got back?"

"I saw him the day he drove into the village,"
Harry answered. "He was expecting to find Ann and
make good his promise to marry her."

"Poor fool! It's a sad story all around," said Abe
Lincoln. "He's not a bad fellow, I reckon, but he
broke Ann's heart. Didn't realize what a tender thing
it was. I can't forgive him."

In the middle of the afternoon they came in sight
of the home of Henry Brimstead.

"Here's where we stop and feed, and listen to Henry's secrets," said Samson.

The level fields were cut into squares outlined by wooden stakes.

Brimstead was mowing the grass in his dooryard. He dropped his scythe and came to welcome the travelers.

"Say, don't you know that you are standing in the center of a large and promising city?" he said to Samson. "You fellers ought to dress up a little when ye come to town."

"Boys, we've stumbled on to a dream city, paved with gold and arched with rainbows," said Samson.

"You are standing at the corner of Grand Avenue and Empire Street, in the growing city of El Dorado, near the great water highway of Illinois," Brimstead declaimed.

"Where's the growin'?" Samson demanded.

Brimstead came closer and said in a confidential tone: "If you stand right where you are an' listen, you'll hear it growin'."

"It sounds a good deal like a turnip growin' in a garden," Samson remarked, thoughtfully.

"Give it a fair chance," Brimstead went on. "Two cellars have been dug over there in the pasture. One is for the Town Hall and the other for the University which the Methodists are going to build. A railroad has been surveyed and is expected this summer."

"That same railroad has been expected in a thousand places since '32," said Samson.

"I know, it's the most expected thing in the United States but that won't scare it away," Brimstead went on. "Everybody is yellin' for it."

"You can't call a railroad as you would a dog by whistling," Abe warned him.

"But it's got beyond Buffalo on its way," said Brimstead.

"A team of healthy snails would get here sooner," Samson insisted.

"El Dorado can make out with a canal to Lake Michigan, carrying its manufactures and the product of the surrounding country straight to the big cities of the East," said Brimstead. "Every corner lot in my city has been sold and paid for, half cash and half notes."

"The brokers in Chicago got the cash and you got the notes?"

"You've said it. I've got a drawer full of notes."

"And you've quit farmin'?"

"Say, I'll tell ye the land has gone up so it wouldn't pay. Peasley an' I cal'ate that we're goin' to git rich this summer sellin' lots."

"Wake up, man. You're dreamin'," said Samson.

Henry came close to Samson and said in a confidential tone: "Say, mebbe the whole state is dreamin' an' yellin' in its sleep 'bout canals an' schools an' factories an' mills an' railroads. We're havin' a good time anyway."

This reminded Abe Lincoln of the story:

"There was a man in Pope County who came home one evening and sat down in the middle of the barn floor and began to sing. His wife asked him:

" 'Are you drunk or crazy or a fool?'

" 'I don't know what you'd call it, but I know I ain't got a darn bit to spare,' he answered, with a whoop of joy."

"You're all goin' to roll out o' bed and hit the floor with a bump," said Samson.

Brimstead declared in his usual tone of confidence:

"The worst part o' bein' a fool is lonesomeness. I was the only one in Flea Valley. Now I shall be in the company of a Governor an' dozens o' well known statesmen. You'll be the only lonesome man in Illinois."

"I sometimes fear that he will enjoy the loneliness of wisdom," said Honest Abe.

"In some parts of the state every farmer owns his own private city," Samson declared. "I hope Henry Brimstead does as well raising cities as he did raising grain. He was a very successful farmer."

"I knew you'd make fun o' me but when you come again you'll see the towers an' steeples," said Brimstead. "Put up your horses and come into the house and see the first lady of El Dorado."

Mrs. Brimstead had their dinner cooking before the horses were cared for. Samson went into the house while Henry was showing his El Dorado map to the others.

"Well, what do you think of Henry's plans?" she asked.

"I like the farm better."

"So do I," the woman declared. "But the men around here have gone crazy with dreams of sudden wealth. I kept Henry busy on the farm as long as I could."

"I've only a word of advice about it. If those Chicago men sell any more of your land make them take the notes and you take the money. Where is Annabel?"

"Teaching the school at Hopedale."

"We're going up to Chicago to see the Kelsos," said Samson.

"Glad you are. Some rich feller up there by the name of Davis has fallen in love with Bim an' he don't give her any peace. He left here last night goin' north. Owns a lot o' land in Tazewell County an' wears a diamond in his shirt as big as your thumb nail. Bim has been teaching school in Chicago this winter. It must be a wonderful place. Every one has loads of money. The stores an' houses are as thick as the hair on a dog's back—some of 'em as big as all outdoors."

She added in a moment as she stirred her pudding: "Something ought to be done for Bim to get her free."

"We're going to see about that," Samson assured her.

"Harry had better look out," said Mrs. Brimstead.

"Abe is going to get a divorce for her an' I guess from now on the grass won't have a chance to grow under Harry's feet. The boy has worried a good deal lately. Wouldn't wonder if he'd heard o' those rich fellers but he hasn't let on about it."

Abe Lincoln and Harry entered with their host and the travelers sat down to a luncheon of pudding and milk and doughnuts and pie.

"There's no El Dorado about this," said Samson. "Women have to have something more than hopes to work with."

"The women in this country have to do all their dreaming at night," said Mrs. Brimstead.

"El Dorado will not stay long," Samson averred.

"It wouldn't cost much to shoo it off your land," Abe laughed.

"You can't either shoo or shoot it," said Brimstead.

"I look for it just to take the rickets an' die," was the comment of his wife.

"How far do you call it to the sycamore woods?" Lincoln asked as they rose from the table.

"About thirty mile," said Brimstead.

"We must be off if we are to get there before dark," the young statesman declared.

They saddled their horses and mounted and rode up to the door. After their acknowledgments and farewells Brimstead came close to Samson and said in confidence: "I enjoy bein' a millionaire for a few minutes now an' then. It's as good as goin' to a circus an' cheaper."

"The feelings of a millionaire are almost as good as the money while they last," said Abe Lincoln with a laugh.

Brimstead came up to him and whispered: "They're better 'cause if you can keep away from Samson Traylor you don't have any fear o' bein' robbed."

"It reminds me o' the time I used to play I was a horse," said Samson as they rode away. In a moment he added: "Abe, the state is getting in a bad way."

"It looks as if you were right," said the member from Sangamon County. "It's a bad sign to find men like Peasley and Brimstead going crazy."

Up the road they passed many farms unsown and staked into streets and avenues. The hand of industry had been checked by dreams of wealth.

"The land that once laughed with fatness now has a lean and solemn look," Abe admitted. "But I reckon you'll find that kind of thing going on all over the country—east and west."

"It reminds me of those fellers that danced on the table an' smashed the dishes at the banquet," said Samson.

"They had the same kind o' feelin's that Brimstead has," said the legislator. "I wish we had had you in the House."

"They would have thrown me out of a window."

"I wouldn't wonder but I reckon the time is near when they would urge you to come in at the door. You've got more good sense than all of us put together. I've heard you accuse me of growing but your own growth has astonished me."

"No one can stand still in this country especially if he's got a wife like mine," Samson answered. "Even Mr. and Mrs. Peter Lukins want to be movin' on, an' a city is likely to come an' sit down beside ye when ye ain't lookin'."

"Your wife is a wonderful woman," said Abe.

"She's been a great help to me," Samson declared. "We read together and talk the matter over. She's got better sense than I have."

"And yet they say women ought not to vote," said Lincoln. "That's another relic of feudalism. I think that the women you and I know are as well qualified to vote as the men."

"On the whole better. They are more industrious, thrifty and dependable. Have you ever seen a 'Colonel' Lukins or a Bap McNoll in woman's dress?"

"Never. Democracy has much ground to win. For my part I believe that the Declaration of Independence is a practical document. My ambition is to see its truth accepted everywhere. As a contribution to human welfare its principles are second only to the law of Moses. It should be our work to keep the structure of America true to the plan of its architects."

After a moment of silence Lincoln added: "What is your ambition?"

"It is very modest," said Samson. "I've been thinking that I'd like to go into some kind of business and help develop the West."

"Well some one has got to provide our growing population with food and clothing and tools and transportation."

"And see that they don't get El Doradoed," said Harry.

At early candlelight they reached the sycamore woods very hungry. It was a beautiful grove-like forest on the shore of a stream. The crossing was a rough bridge of corduroy. A crude log tavern and a cruder store stood on the farther shore of the creek. The tavern was a dirty place with a drunken proprietor. Three ragged, shiftless farmers and a half-breed Indian sat in its main room in varying stages of inebriacy. A well dressed, handsome, young man with a diamond in his shirt-front was leading a horse back and forth in the stable yard. The diamond led Samson to suspect that he was the man Davis of whom Mrs. Brimstead had spoken. Our travelers, not liking the look of the place, got some oats and rode on, camping near the farther edge of the woods, where they built a fire, fed and tethered their horses and sat down and ate from the store in their saddle-bags.

"I was hankering for a hot supper," said Abe as they began eating. "Washington Irving wrote in his journal that if he couldn't get a dinner to suit his taste he endeavored to get a taste to suit his dinner. That is what we must do."

They made out very well in the undertaking and then with their knives Abe and Samson cut big armfuls of grass from the near prairie for the horses and a bed upon which the three men lay down for the night. Harry had dried out their saddle-blankets by the fire and these were their bed clothing.

"This hay may have some bugs in it but they won't tickle so bad as those in the tavern," Abe laughed.

Then Harry remarked: "There was lots of bad company in that tavern. The towel that hung over the washstand was as black as the ground."

"It reminded me of the tavern down in Pope County," Abe yawned. "A traveler found fault with the condition of its one towel and the landlord said: 'Go to h—l, stranger. More than fifty men have used that towl to-day an' you're the first one that's complained of it.'"

Samson had that gift of "sleeping with one eye open" which the perils of the wilderness had conferred upon the pioneer. He had lain down on the side of their bed near the horses, which were tethered to trees only a few feet away. He had gone to sleep with his pistol under his right hand. Since the beginning of that long journey overland from Vermont Samson had been wont to say that his right hand never slept. Late in the night he was awakened by an unusual movement among the horses. In the dim light of the fire he could see a man in the act of bridling Abe's horse.

"Hold up your hands," Samson shouted as he covered the man with his pistol. "If ye stir a foot I'll bore a hole in ye."

The man threw up his hands and stood still.

In half a moment Abe Lincoln and Harry had got up and captured the man and the loosed horse.

This is part of the entry which Samson made in his diary a week or so later:

"Harry put some wood on the fire while Abe and I led him up into the light. He was one of the dirty white men we had seen at the tavern.

"'I'll give ye four hundred dollars for a hoss in good Michigan money,' he said.

"'If ye can't steal a horse you're willin' to buy one,' I says.

"'No, sir. I only come to buy,' says he.

"I flopped him sudden and asked him why he was putting on the bridle.

"He owned up then.   Said a man had hired him to steal the horse.

" 'That man has got to have a hoss,' he said.   'He'll give ye any price ye want to ask.   If you'll give me a few dollars I'll take ye to him.'

" 'You go and bring him here and I'll talk to him,' I said.

"I let the feller go.   I didn't suppose he'd come back but he did.   Came a little before sunrise with that well dressed feller we saw at the tavern.

" 'Do you want to buy a horse?' I says.

" 'Yes, sir, I've got to get to Chicago to-day if possible.'

" 'What's your hurry?'

" 'I have engagements to-morrow and land to sell.'

" 'How did ye get here?'

" 'Came up from Tazewell County to-day on a horse.   It died last evening.'

" 'What's your name?' I says.

"He handed me a card on which I read the words 'Lionel Davis, Real Estate, Loans and Insurance, 14 South Water Street, Chicago, Ill.'

" 'There's one branch o' your business that isn't mentioned on the card,' I says.

" 'What's that?' says he.

" 'Horse-thief,' says I.   'You sent that feller here to steal a horse and he got caught.'

" 'Well I told him if he'd get me a good horse I'd give him five hundred dollars and that I didn't care how he got him.   The fact is I'm desperate.   I'll give you a thousand dollars for one of your horses.'

" 'You couldn't buy one of 'em at any price,' I said. 'There's two reasons. I wouldn't do business with a horse-thief and no money would tempt me to sell an animal to be ridden to death.'

"The two thieves had had enough of us and they got out."

That night our party camped on the shore of the Kankakee and next day they met the contractors. Lincoln joined the latter party and Harry and Samson went on alone. Late that afternoon they crossed the nine mile prairie, beyond which they could see the shimmer of the lake and the sunlit structures of the new city. Pink and white moccasin flowers and primroses were thick in the grass. On the lower ground the hoofs of their horses plashed in wide stretches of shallow water.

Chicago looked very bare on the high prairie above the lake. It was Mr. William Cullen Bryant who said that it had the look of a huckster in his shirt-sleeves.

"There it is," said Samson. "Four thousand, one hundred and eighty people live there. It looks like a sturdy two-year-old."

The houses were small and cheaply built and of many colors. Some were unpainted. Near the prairie they stood like people on the outer edge of a crowd, looking over one another's shoulders and pushing in a disordered mass toward the center of interest. Some seemed to have straggled away as if they had given up trying to see or hear. So to one nearing it the town had a helter-skelter look.

Our travelers passed rough boarded houses with grand-looking people in their dooryards and on their small porches—men in broadcloth and tall hats and ladies in silk dresses. It was six o'clock and the men had come home to supper. As the horsemen proceeded larger buildings surrounded them, mostly two stories high. There were some stores and houses built of red brick. Beyond the scatter of cheap, wooden structures they came to streets well laid out and crowded and busy and "very soft" to quote a phrase from the diary. Teams were struggling in the mud, drivers shouting and lashing. Agents for hotels and boarding-houses began to solicit the two horsemen from the plank sidewalks. The latter were deeply impressed by a negro in scarlet clothes, riding a horse in scarlet housings. He carried a scarlet banner and was advertising in a loud voice the hour and place of a great land sale that evening.

A sound of many hammers beating upon boards could be heard above the noises of the street and behind all was the constant droning of a big steam saw and the whir of the heavy stones in the new grist mill. It was the beginning of that amazing diapason of industry which accompanied the building of the cities of the West.

They put out in the livery stable of the City Hotel and at the desk of the latter asked about the price of board. It was three dollars a day and no politeness in the offer.

"It's purty steep," said Samson. "But I'm too hungry for argument or delay and I guess we can stand it to be nabobs for a day or so."

"I shall have to ask you to pay in advance," the clerk demanded.

Samson drew out the pig's bladder in which he carried his money and paid for a day's board.

Samson writes that Harry spent half an hour washing and dressing himself in the clean clothes and fine shoes which he had brought in his saddle-bags and adds:

"He was a broad-shouldered, handsome chap those days, six feet and an inch high and straight as an arrow with a small blond mustache. His clothes were rumpled up some and he wore a gray felt hat instead of a tall one but there was no likelier looking lad in the new city."

After supper the office of the hotel was crowded with men in tall hats and tail coats smoking "seegars" and gathered in groups. The earnestness of their talk was signalized by little outbursts of profanity coupled with the name of Jackson. Some denounced the President as a traitor. One man stood in the midst of a dozen others delivering a sort of oration, embellished with noble gestures, on the future of Illinois. His teeth were clenched on his "seegar" that tilted out of the corner of his mouth as he spoke. Now and then he would pause and by a deft movement of his lips roll the "seegar" to the other corner of his mouth, take a fresh grip on it and resume his oration.

Samson wrote in his diary:

"He said a lot of foolish things that made us laugh."

Twenty years later he put this note under that entry:

"The funny thing about it was really this; they all came true."

The hotel clerk had a *Register of the Residents of the City of Chicago* wherein they found the name and address of John Kelso. They went out to find the house. Storekeepers tried to stop them as they passed along the street with offers of land at bargains which would make them millionaires in a week. In proceeding along the plank sidewalks they were often ascending or descending steps to another level.

They went to a barber shop and got "trimmed and shaved." For change the barber gave them a sort of shinplaster money, each piece of which bore the legend: "Good for one shave or ten cents at the Palace Shaving Parlors, 16 Dearborn Street, Chicago, Ill."

The barber assured them it was as good as coin anywhere in the city which they found to be true. The town was flooded with this "red dog money" issued by stores or work-shops and finding general acceptance among its visitors and inhabitants. On the sidewalks were emigrant families the older members of which carried heavy bags and bundles. They were followed by troops of weary, dirty children.

On La Salle Street they found the home of Jack Kelso. It was a rough boarded small house a story and a half high. It had a little porch and dooryard enclosed by an unpainted picket fence. Bim in a handsome, blue silk gown came running out to meet them.

"If you don't mind I'm going to kiss you," she said to Harry.

"I'd mind if you didn't," said the young man as he embraced her.

"We must be careful not to get the habit," she laughed.

"It grows on one."

"It also grows on two," she answered.

"I'd enjoy being careless for once," said Harry.

"Women can be extravagant with everything but carelessness," she insisted. "Do you like this gown?"

"It is lovely—like yourself."

"Then perhaps you will be willing to take me to the party to-night. My mother will chaperon us."

"With these clothes that have just been hauled out of a saddle-bag?" said Harry with a look of alarm.

"Even rags could not hide the beauty of him," said Kelso as he came down from the porch to greet them. "And look at her," he went on. "Was there ever a fairer maid in spite of all her troubles? See the red in her cheeks and the diamond glow of youth and health in her eyes. You should see the young men sighing and guitaring around her."

"You'll hear me tuning up," Harry declared.

"That is father's way of comforting my widowhood," said Bim. "He has made a wonderful beauty mask and often he claps it on me and whistles up a band of sighing lovers. As a work of the imagination I am a great success."

"The look of you sets my heart afire again," the boy exclaimed.

"Come—put up your guitar and take mother and me to the party at Mrs. Kinzie's," said Bim. "A very grand young man was coming to take us in a wonderful carriage but he's half an hour late now. We won't wait for him."

So the three set out together afoot for Mrs. Kinzie's, while Samson sat down for a visit with Jack Kelso.

"Mrs. Kinzie enjoys the distinction of owning a piano," said Bim as they went on. "There are only three pianos in the city and so far we have discovered only two people who can play on them—the music teacher and a young gentleman from Baltimore. When they are being played on people gather around the houses where they are."

The Kinzies' house was of brick and larger and more pretentious than any in Chicago. Its lawn, veranda and parlor were crowded with people in a curious variety of costumes.

Nearly all the festive company wore diamonds. They scintillated on fingers, some of which were knotted with toil; they glowed on shirt bosoms and morning as well as evening gowns; on necks and ears which should have been spared the emphasis of jewels. They were the accepted badge and token of success. People who wore them not were either new arrivals or those of questionable wealth and taste. So far had this singular vanity progressed that a certain rich man, who had lost a finger in a saw mill, wore an immense solitaire next to the stub, it may be presumed, as a memorial to the departed.

Colonel Zachary Taylor, who had lately arrived from Florida and was presently returning with a regiment of recruits for the Seminole War, was at Mrs. Kinzie's party. He was then a man of middle age with iron gray hair and close cropped side whiskers. A splendid figure he was in his uniform. He remembered Harry and took him in hand and introduced him to many of his friends as the best scout in the Black Hawk War, and, in spite of his dress, the young man became one of the lions of the evening.

"I reckon I could tell you some things about this boy," the Colonel said to Bim.

"He may not be afraid of guns or Indians but he has always been scared of women," said she.

"Which shows that he has a just sense of the relative importance of perils," the Colonel answered. "A man of the highest chivalry is ever afraid in the presence of a lovely woman and chiefly for her sake. I once held a beautiful vase in my hands. They said it was worth ten thousand dollars. I was afraid until I had put it down."

"A great piano player from New York" was introduced. She played on Mrs. Kinzie's instrument, after which Bim sang a number of Scottish ballads and "delightfully" if one may believe a chronicler so partial as Harry Needles, the value of whose judgment is somewhat affected by the statement in his diary that as she stood by the piano her voice and beauty set his heart thumping in his breast. However of the charm and popularity of this young lady there is ample evidence in copies of *The Democrat* which are still preserved and in sundry letters and journals of that time.

The refreshment table was decorated with pyramids of quartered oranges in nets of spun sugar and large frosted cakes. There were roasted pigeons and turkeys and chickens and a big ham, served with jelly, and platters of doughnuts and bread and butter and cabbage salad. Every one ate heartily and was served often, for the supper was thought to be the most important feature of a party those days.

After refreshments the men went outside to smoke and talk—some with pipes—of canals, railroads and corner lots while the younger people were dancing and being proudly surveyed by their mothers.

As Harry and the ladies were leaving Colonel Taylor came to them and said:

"Young man, I am the voice of your country. I call you to Florida. Will you go with us next week?"

Harry looked into Bim's eyes.

"The campaign will be over in a year and I need you badly," the Colonel urged.

"I can not say no to the call of my country," Harry answered. "I will join your regiment at Beardstown on its way down the river."

That night Harry and Bim stood by the gate talking after Mrs. Kelso had gone into the house.

"Bim, I love you more than ever," said the boy. "Abe says you can get a divorce. I have brought the papers for you to sign. They will make you free. I have done it for your sake. You will be under no obligation. I want you to be free to marry whom you will. I would be the happiest man in the world if you were to choose me. I haven't the wealth of some of these city men. I can only offer you my love."

"Be careful and please let go of my hand," she

said. "The time has come when it would be possible to spoil our story. I'm not going to say a word of love to you. I am not free yet. We couldn't marry if we wanted to. I wish you to be under no sense of obligation to me. Many things may happen in a year. I am glad you are going to see more of the world before you settle down, Harry. You will stop in New Orleans and see some of its beautiful women. It will help you to be sure to know yourself a little better and to be sure of what you want to do."

There was a note of sadness in her voice as she spoke these words which he recalled with a sense of comfort on many a lonely day.

"I think that I know myself fairly well," he answered. "There are so many better men who want to marry you! I shall go away with a great fear in me."

"There are no better men," she answered. "When you get back we shall see what comes of our little romance. Meanwhile I'm going to pray for you."

"And I for you," he said as he followed her into the house where the older people sat waiting for them. Harry gave the papers to Bim to be signed and attested and forwarded to Mr. Stuart in Springfield.

On their way to the hotel Samson said to Harry:

"I don't believe Bim is going to be carried away by any of these high-flyers. She's getting to be a very sensible person. Jack is disgusted by what he calls 'the rank commercialism of the place.' I told him about that horse-thief Davis. He was the man who was going to the party to-night with the ladies. He's in love with Bim. Jack says that the men here are mostly of that type. They seem to have gone crazy in the scramble for riches. Their motto is: 'Get it; do it honestly if you can, but get'it.' I guess that was exactly the plan of Davis in trying to get a horse.

"Poor Jack has caught the plague. He has invested in land. Thinks it will make him rich. He's in poor health too—kidney trouble—and Bim has a baby with all the rest—a beautiful boy. I went up-stairs and saw him asleep in his cradle. Looks like her. Hair as yellow as gold, light complexion, blue eyes, handsome as a picture."

That night in the office of the City Hotel they found Mr. Lionel Davis in the midst of a group of excited speculators. In some way he had got across the prairies and was selling his land and accepting every offer on the plea that he was going into the grain business in St. Louis and had to leave Chicago next day. Samson and Harry watched him while he exercised the arts of the auctioneer in cleaning his slate. Diamonds and gold watches were taken and many thousands of dollars in bank bills and coin came into his hands. He choked the market with bargains. The buyers began to back off. They were like hungry dogs laboring with a difficult problem of mastication. Mr. Davis closed his carpet bag and left.

"It was a kind of horse stealin'," said Samson as they were going to bed. "He got news down there on the main road by pony express on its way to St. Louis. I'll bet there's been a panic in the East. He's awake and the others are still dreamin'."

CHAPTER XIX

SAMSON and Harry saw the bursting of the great bubble of '37. Late that night Disaster, loathsome and thousand legged, crept into the little city. It came on a steamer from the East and hastened from home to home, from tavern to tavern. It bit as it traveled. Great banks had suspended payment; New York had suffered a panic; many large business enterprises in the East had failed; certain agents for the bonds of Illinois had absconded with the state's money; in the big cities there had been an ominous closing of doors and turning of locks; a great army of men were out of employment. Those of sound judgment in Chicago knew that all the grand schemes of the statesmen and speculators of Illinois were as the visions of an ended dream. The local banks did not open their doors next day. The little city was in a frenzy of excitement. The streets were filled with a shouting, half crazed throng. New fortunes had shrunk to nothing and less than nothing in a night. Lots in the city were

offered for a tithe of what their market value had
been. Davis had known that the storm would arrive
with the first steamer and in the slang of business
had put on a life-preserver. Samson knew that the
time to buy was when every one wanted to sell. He
wore a belt with some two thousand dollars of gold
coin tucked away in its pockets. He bought two corner lots for himself in the city and two acres for Mrs.
Lukins on the prairie half a mile from town. They
got their deeds and went to the Kelsos to bid them
good-by.

"Is there anything I can do for you?" Samson asked.

"Just give us a friendly thought now and then,"
said Kelso.

"You can have my horse or my wallet or the
strength of my two hands."

"I have heard you called a damned Yankee but I
can think of no greater blessing than to be damned
in a like manner," Kelso answered. "Keep your
largess for those who need it more, good friend."

After these hearty farewells Samson and Harry
set out for their home. They were not again to see
the gentle face and hear the pleasant talk of Jack Kelso.
He had once said, in the presence of the writer, that
it is well to remember, always, that things can not go
on with us as they are. Changes come—slowly and
quite according to our calculations or so swiftly and
unexpectedly that they fill us with confusion. Learned

and wise in the weighty problems of humanity he had little prudence in regulating the affairs of his own family.

Kelso had put every dollar he had and some that he hoped to have into land. Bim, who had been teaching in one of the schools, had invested all her savings in a dream city on the shore of an unconstructed canal.

Like many who had had no experience with such phenomena they underestimated the seriousness of the panic. They thought that, in a week or so, its effect would pass and that Illinois would then resume its triumphal march toward its high destiny. Not even Samson Traylor had a correct notion of the slowness of Time.

The effect of the panic paralyzed the city. Men whose "red dog money" was in every one's pocket closed their shops and ran away. The wild adventurers cleared out. Their character may be judged by the words of one of them reported by the editor of *The Democrat*.

"I failed for a hundred thousand dollars and could have failed for a million if Jackson had kept his hands off."

Hard times hung like a cloud over the city. Its population suffered some diminishment in the next two years in spite of its position on the main highway of trade. Dream cities, canals and railroads built without hands became a part of the poetry of American commerce. Indeed they had come of the prophetic vision and were therefore entitled to respect in spite of the fact that they had been smirched and polluted by speculators.

That autumn men and women who had come to Mrs. Kinzie's party in jewels and in purple and fine linen had left or turned their hands to hard labor. The Kelsos suffered real distress, the schools being closed and the head of the house having taken to his bed with illness. Bim went to work as a seamstress and with the help of Mrs. Kinzie and Mrs. Hubbard was able to keep the family from want. The nursing and the care of the baby soon broke the health of Mrs. Kelso, never a strong woman. Bim came home from her work one evening and found her mother ill.

"Cheer up, my daughter," said Jack. "An old friend of ours has returned to the city. He is a rich man—an oasis in the desert of poverty. He has loaned me a hundred dollars in good coin."

"Who has done this?" Bim asked.

"Mr. Lionel Davis. He has just come from New Orleans. He is a successful speculator in grain."

"We must not take his money," said Bim.

"I had a long talk with him," Kelso went on. "He has explained that unfortunate incident of the horse. It was a bit of offhand folly born of an anxious moment."

"But the man wants to marry me."

"He said nothing of such a purpose."

"He will be in no hurry about that," said Bim. "He is a shrewd operator. Every one hates him. They say that he knew what was coming when he sold out."

That evening Bim wrote a long letter to Samson Traylor telling of the evil days which had come to them. This letter, now in the possession of a great grandson of Samson and Sarah Traylor, had a singular history. It reached the man to whom it was addressed in the summer of 1844. It was found with many others that summer in Tazewell County under a barn which its owner was removing. It brought to mind the robbery of the stage from Chicago, south of the sycamore woods, in the autumn of '37, by a man who had ridden with the driver from Chicago and who, it was thought, had been in collusion with him. A curious feature of the robbery had been revealed by the discovery of the mail sack. It was unopened, its contents undisturbed, its rusty padlock still in place. The perpetrator of the crime had not soiled his person with any visible evidence of guilt and so was never apprehended.

Then for a time Bim entered upon great trials. Jack Kelso weakened. Burning with fever, his mind wandered in the pleasant paths he loved and saw in its fancy the deeds of Ajax and Achilles and the topless towers of Illium and came not back again to the vul-

gar and prosaic details of life. The girl knew not
what to do. A funeral was a costly thing. She had
no money. The Kinzies had gone on a hunting trip
in Wisconsin. Mrs. Hubbard was ill and the Kelsos
already much in her debt. Mr. Lionel Davis came.

He was a good-looking young man of twenty-nine,
those days, rather stout and of middle stature with
dark hair and eyes. He was dressed in the height of
fashion. He used to boast that he had only one vice—
diamonds. But he had ceased to display them on his
shirt-front or his fingers. He carried them in his
pockets and showed them by the glittering handful
to his friends. They had come to him through trad-
ing in land where they were the accepted symbol of
success and money was none too plentiful. He had
melted their settings and turned them into coin. The
stones he kept as a kind of surplus—a half hidden evidence of wealth and of superiority to the temptation
to vulgar display. Mr. Davis was a calculating, masterful, keen-minded man, with a rather heavy jaw.
In his presence Bim was afraid for her soul that night.
He was gentle and sympathetic. He offered to lend
her any amount she needed. She made no answer but
sat trying to think what she would best do. The Traylors had paid no attention to her letter although a
month had passed since it was written.

In a moment she rose and gave him her hand.

"It is very kind of you," said she. "If you can

spare me five hundred dollars for an indefinite time I will take it."

"Let me lend you a thousand," he urged. "I can do it without a bit of inconvenience."

"I think that five hundred will be enough," she said.

It carried her through that trouble and into others of which her woman's heart had found abundant signs in the attitude of Mr. Davis. He gave the most assiduous attention to the comfort of Bim and her mother. He had had a celebrated physician come down from Milwaukee to see Mrs. Kelso and had paid the bill in advance. He bought a new and wonderful swinging crib of burnished steel for the baby.

"I can not let you be doing these things for us," Bim said one evening when he had called to see them.

"And I can not help loving you and doing the little I can to express it," he answered. "There is no use in my trying to keep it from you when I find myself lying awake nights planning for your comfort. I would like to make every dollar I have tell you in some way that I love you. That's how I feel and you might as well know it."

"You have been kind to us," Bim answered. "We feel it very deeply but I can not let you talk to me like that. I am a married woman."

"We can fix that all right. It will be easy for you to get a divorce."

"But I do not love you, Mr. Davis."

"Let me try to make you love me," he pleaded. "Is there any reason why I shouldn't?"

"Yes. If there were no other reason, I love a young soldier who is fighting in the Seminole War in Florida under Colonel Taylor."

"Well, at least, you can let me take the place of your father and shield you from trouble when I can."

"You are a most generous and kindly man!" Bim exclaimed with tears in her eyes.

So he seemed to be, but he was one of those men who weave a spell like that of an able actor. He excited temporary convictions that began to change as soon as the curtain fell. He was in fact a performer. That little midnight scene at the City Hotel had sounded the key-note of his character. He was no reckless villain of romance. If he instigated the robbery of the south-bound mail wagon, of which the writer of this little history has no shadow of doubt, he was so careful about it that no evidence which would satisfy a jury has been discovered to this day.

On account of the continued illness of her mother Bim was unable to resume her work in the academy. She took what sewing she could do at home and earned enough to solve the problems of each day. But the payment coming due on the house in December loomed ahead of them. It was natural, in the circumstances, that Mrs. Kelso should like Mr. Davis and favor his aims. Now and then he came and sat with her of an evening while Bim went out to the shops—an act of accommodation which various neighbor women were ever ready to perform.

Mrs. Kelso's health had improved slowly so that she was able then to spend most of each day in her chair.

One evening when Davis sat alone with her, she told him the story of Bim and Harry Needles—a bit of knowledge he was glad to have. Their talk was interrupted by the return of Bim. She was in a cheerful mood. When Mr. Davis had gone she said to her mother:

"I think our luck has turned. Here's a letter from John T. Stuart. The divorce has been granted."

"Thank the Lord," Mrs. Kelso exclaimed. "Long ago I knew bad luck was coming; since the day your father carried an axe through the house."

"Pshaw! I don't believe in that kind of nonsense."

"My father would sooner break his leg than carry an edged tool through the house," Mrs. Kelso affirmed. "Three times I have known it to bring sickness. I hope a change has come."

"No. Bad luck comes when you carry all your money through the house and spend it for land. I am going to write to Harry and tell him to hurry home and marry me if he wants to. Don't say a word about the divorce to our friend Davis. I want to make him keep his distance. It is hard enough now."

Before she went to bed that night she wrote a long

letter to Harry and one to Abe Lincoln thanking him for his part in the matter and telling him of her father's death, of the payment coming due and of the hard times they were suffering. Two weeks passed and brought no answer from Mr. Lincoln.

The day before the payment came due in December, a historic letter from Tampa, Fla., was published in *The Democrat*. It was signed "Robert Deming, private, Tenth Cavalry." It gave many details of the campaign in the Everglades in which the famous scout Harry Needles and seven of his comrades had been surrounded and slain. When Mr. Davis called at the little home in La Salle Street that evening he found Bim in great distress.

"I throw up my hands," she said. "I can not stand any more. We shall be homeless to-morrow."

"No, not that—so long as I live," he answered. "I have bought the claim. You can pay me when you get ready."

He was very tender and sympathetic.

When he had left them Bim said to her mother: "Our old friends do not seem to care what becomes of us. I have no thought now save for you and the baby. I'll do whatever you think best for you two. I don't care for myself. My heart is as dead as Harry's."

CHAPTER XX

WHICH TELLS OF THE SETTLING OF ABE LINCOLN AND
THE TRAYLORS IN THE VILLAGE OF SPRINGFIELD
AND OF SAMSON'S SECOND VISIT TO CHICAGO.

BIM's judgment of her old friends was ill founded. It was a slow time in which she lived. The foot
of the horse, traveling and often mired in a rough
muddy highway, was its swiftest courier. Letters carried by horses or slow steamboats were the only media
of communication between people separated by wide
distances. The learned wrote letters of astonishing
length and literary finish—letters which were passed
from hand to hand and read aloud in large and small
assemblies. They presented the news and the comment it inspired. In these old and generous letters,
which antedate the railroad and the telegraph, critics
have discovered one of the most delicate and inform-
ing of the lost arts—the epistolary. But to the av-
erage hand, wearied by heavy tools, the lightsome
goose quill, committing its owner to dubious spelling
and clumsy penmanship, and exposing the interior of
his intellect, was a dreaded thing. When old Black
Hawk signed a treaty he was wont to say that he had
"touched it with the goose quill." He made only a
little mark whereupon a kind of sanctity was imparted

to the document. Every man unaccustomed to its use stood in like awe of this implement. When he "took his pen in hand" he had entered upon an adventure so unusual that his letter always mentioned it as if, indeed, it were an item of news not to be overlooked. So it is easy to understand that many who had traveled far were as the dead, in a measure, to the friends they had left behind them and that those separated by only half a hundred miles had to be very enterprising to keep acquainted.

In March Abe Lincoln had got his license to practise law. On his return from the North he had ridden to Springfield to begin his work as a lawyer in the office of John T. Stuart. His plan was to hire and furnish a room and get his meals at the home of his friend, Mr. William Butler. He went to the store of Joshua Speed to buy a bed and some bedding. He found that they would cost seventeen dollars.

"The question is whether you would trust a man owing a national debt and without an asset but good intentions and a license to practise law for so much money," said Honest Abe. "I don't know when I could pay you."

Speed was also a young man of good intentions and a ready sympathy for those who had little else. He had heard of the tall representative from Sangamon County.

"I have a plan which will give you a bed for nothing if you would care to share my room above the store and sleep with me," he answered.

"I'm much obliged but for you it's quite a contract."

"You're rather long," Speed laughed.

"Yes, I could lick salt off the top of your hat. I'm about a man and a half but by long practice I've learned how to keep the half out of the way of other people. They say that when Long John Wentworth got to Chicago he slept with his ·feet sticking out of a window and that they had to take down a partition because he couldn't stand the familiarity of the woodpeckers, but he is eight inches taller than I am."

"I'm sure we shall get along well enough together," said Speed.

They went up to the room. In a moment Mr. Lincoln hurried away for his saddle-bags and returned shortly.

"There are all my earthly possessions," he said as he threw the bags on the floor.

So his new life began in the village of Springfield. Early in the autumn Samson arrived and bought a small house and two acres of land on the edge of the village and returned to New Salem to move his family and furniture. When they drove along the top of Salem Hill a number of the houses were empty and deserted, their owners having moved away. Two of the stores were closed. Only ten families remained. They stopped at Rutledge's tavern whose entertainment was little sought those days. People from the near houses came to bid them good-by. Dr. John Allen was among them.

"Sorry to see you going," he said. "With you and Abe and Jack Kelso gone it has become a lonely place. There's not much left for me but the long view from the end of the hill and the singing in the prairie grass."

Pete and Colonel, invigorated by their long rest, but whitened by age and with drooping heads, drew the wagon. Sambo and the small boy rode between Sarah and Samson. Betsey and Josiah walked ahead of the wagon, the latter leading a cow. That evening they were comfortably settled in their new home. Moving was not such a complicated matter those days. Abe Lincoln was on hand to bid them welcome and help get their goods in place. He had borrowed fire and cut some wood and there was a cheering blaze in the fireplace on the arrival of the newcomers. When the beds were set up and ready for the night Sarah made some tea to go with the cold victuals she had brought. Mr. Lincoln ate with them and told of his new work.

"So far I've had nothing more important to do than proving damage in cases of assault and battery," he said. "There is many a man who, when he thinks he has been wronged, proceeds to take it out of the hide of the other feller. The hides of Illinois have suffered a good deal in that way. It is very annoying.

Generally I stand for the hides. They need a friend and protector. When people take the law in their hands it gets badly worn and mussed up. In a little while there isn't any law. Next week I begin my first turn on the circuit."

"It seems good to see folks around us," said Sarah. "I believe we shall enjoy ourselves here."

"It's a wonderful place," Lincoln declared with enthusiasm. "There are fine stores and churches and sociables and speeches and theater shows."

"Yes. It's bigger than Vergennes," said Sarah.

"And you're goin' to have time to enjoy it," Samson broke in. "There'll be no farm work and Betsey and Josiah are old enough to be quite a help."

"How the girl is developing!" Abe exclaimed. "I believe she will look like Bim in a year or two."

Betsey was growing tall and slim. She had the blonde hair and fair skin of Samson and the dark eyes of her mother. Josiah had grown to be a bronzed, sturdy, good-looking lad, very shy and sensitive.

"There's a likely boy!" said Samson as he clapped the shoulder of his eldest son. "He's got a good heart in him."

"You'll spoil him with praise," Sarah protested and then asked as she turned to the young statesman. "Have you heard from Bim or any of the Kelsos?"

"Not a word. I often think of them."

"There's been a letter in the candle every night for

a week or so, but we haven't heard a word from Harry or from them," said Sarah. "I wonder how they're getting along in these hard times."

"I told Jack to let me know if I could do anything to help," Samson assured them.

Sarah turned to Abe Lincoln with a smile and said: "As we were coming through the village Mary Owens asked me to tell you that on account of the hard times she was not going to have a public wedding."

The chairman of the finance committee laughed and answered: "That old joke is still alive. She writes me now and then and tells me what she is doing in the way of preparation. It's really a foolish little farce we have been playing in—a kind of courtship to avoid marriage. We have gone too far with it."

A bit later he wrote a playful letter to Mary and told her that there was so much flourishing about in carriages and the like in Springfield he could not recommend it to a lady of good sense as a place of residence. He said that owing to certain faults in his disposition he could not recommend himself as a husband; that he felt sure she could never be happy with him. But he manfully offered to marry her as soon as his circumstances would allow if, after serious consideration, she decided that she cared to accept him. It was, on the whole, one of the most generous acts in the history of human affairs.

There is some evidence that Mary was displeased

with these and other lines in the little drama and presently rang down the curtain. Some of the spectators were informed by her that Abe Lincoln was crude and awkward and without a word to please a lady of her breeding. But she had achieved the credit, with certain people, of having rejected a young man for whom great honors were thought to be in store.

Late in November Mr. Lincoln went out on the circuit with the distinguished John T. Stuart who had taken him into partnership. Bim's letter to him bears an endorsement on its envelope as follows:

"This letter was forwarded from Vandalia the week I went out on the circuit and remained unopened in our office until my return six weeks later.—A. Lincoln."

The day of his return he went to Sarah and Samson with the letter.

"I'll get a good horse and start for Chicago tomorrow morning," said Samson. "They have had a double blow. Did you read that Harry had been killed?"

"Harry killed!" Mr. Lincoln exclaimed. "You don't mean to tell me that Harry has been killed?"

"*The Chicago Democrat* says so but we don't believe it," said Samson. "Here's the article copied into *The Sangamon Journal*. Read it and then I'll tell you why I don't think it's so."

Abe Lincoln read the article.

"You see it was dated in Tampa, November the fifth," said Samson. "Before we had read that article we had received a letter from Harry dated November the seventh. In the letter he says he is all right and I calculate that he ought to know as much about it as any one."

"Thank God! Then it's a mistake," said Lincoln. "We can't afford to lose Harry. I feel rather poor with Jack Kelso gone. It will comfort me to do what I can for his wife and daughter. I'll give you every dollar I can spare to take to them."

A moment of sorrowful silence followed.

"I'll never forget the kindly soul of Jack or his wit or his sayings, many of which are in my notebook," said Lincoln as he sat looking sadly into the fire.

They talked much of the great but humble man who had so loved honor and beauty and whose life had ended in the unholy turmoil of the new city.

"The country is in great trouble," was a remark of Abe Lincoln inspired by the reflections of the hour. "We tried to allay it in the special session of July. Our efforts have done no good. The ail is too deep seated. We must first minister to a mind diseased and pluck from the heart a rooted sorrow. You were right about it, Samson. We have been dreaming. Some one must invent a new system. Wildcat money will do no good.

These big financial problems are beyond my knowledge.
I don't know how to think in those terms.   Next session I propose to make a clean breast of it.   We're
all wrong but I fear that not all of us will be brave
enough to say so."

Samson hired horses for the journey and set out
early next morning with his son, Josiah, bound for
the new city.   The boy had begged to go and both
Samson and Sarah thought it would be good for him
to take a better look at Illinois than his geography
afforded.

"Joe is a good boy," his mother said as she embraced him.   He was, indeed, a gentle-hearted, will-
ing-handed, brown-eyed youth who had been a great
help to his father.   Every winter morning he and
Betsey had done the chores and ridden on the back
of Colonel to Mentor Graham's school where they
had made excellent progress.

Joe and his father set out on a cold clear morning in
February.   They got to Brimstead's in time for dinner.

"How d'y do?" Samson shouted as Henry came to
the door.

"Better!" the latter answered.   He put his hand on
Samson's pommel and said in a confidential tone:
"El Dorado was one of the wickedest cities in his-
tory.   It was like Tyre and Babylon.   It robbed me.
Look at that pile of stakes."

Samson saw a long cord of stakes along the road in the edge of the meadow.

"They are the teeth of my city," said Brimstead in a low voice. "I've drawed 'em out. They ain't goin' to bite me no more."

"They are the towers and steeples of El Dorado," Samson laughed. "Have any of the notes been paid?"

"Not one and I can't get a word from my broker about the men who drew the notes—who they are or where they are."

"I'm going to Chicago and if you wish I'll try to find him and see what he says."

"That's just what I wish," said Brimstead. "His name is Lionel Davis. His address is 14 South Water Street. He put the opium in our pipes here in Tazewell County. It was his favorite county. He spent two days with us here. I sold him all the land I had on the river shore and he gave me his note for it."

"If you'll let me take the note I'll see what can be done to get the money," Samson answered.

"Say, I'll tell ye," Brimstead went on. "It's for five thousand dollars and I don't suppose it's worth the paper it was wrote on. You take it and if you find it's no good you lose it just as careful as you can. I don't want to see it again. Come into the house. The woman is making a johnny-cake and fryin' some sausage."

They had a happy half-hour at the table, Mrs. Brimstead being in better spirits since her husband had got back to his farming. Annabel, her form filling with the grace and charm of womanhood, was there and more comely than ever.

They had been speaking of Jack Kelso's death.

"I heard him say once that when he saw a beautiful young face it reminded him of noble singing and the odor of growing corn," said Samson.

"I'd rather see the face," Joe remarked, whereupon they all laughed and the boy blushed to the roots of his blond hair.

"He's become a man of good judgment," said Brimstead.

Annabel's sister Jane who had clung to the wagon in No Santa Claus Land was a bright-eyed, merry-hearted girl of twelve. The boy Robert was a shy, good-looking lad a little older than Josiah.

"Well, what's the news?" Samson asked.

"Nothin' has happened since we saw you but the fall of El Dorado," Brimstead answered.

"There was the robbery of the mail stage last summer a few miles north of here," said Mrs. Brimstead. "Every smitch of the mail was stolen. I guess that's the reason we haven't had no letter from Vermont in a year."

"Maybe that's why we haven't heard from home," Samson echoed.

"Why don't you leave Joe here while you're gone to Chicago?" Annabel asked.

"It would help his education to rassle around with Robert an' the girls," said Brimstead.

"Would you like to stay?" Samson asked.

"I wouldn't mind," said Josiah who, on the lonely prairie, had had few companions of his own age.

So it happened that Samson went on alone. As he was leaving, Brimstead came close to his side and whispered:

"Don't you ever let a city move into you and settle down an' make itself to home. If you do you want to keep your eye on its leading citizens."

"Nobody can tell what'll happen when he's dreamin'," Samson remarked with a laugh as he rode away, waving his hand to the boy Josiah who stood looking up the road with a growing sense of loneliness.

Near the sycamore woods Samson came upon a gray-haired man lying by the roadside with a horse tethered near him. The stranger was sick with a fever. Samson got down from his horse.

"What can I do for you?" he asked.

"The will of God," the stranger feebly answered. "I prayed for help and you have come. I am Peter Cartwright, the preacher. I was so sick and weak I had to get off my horse and lie down. If you had not come I think that I should have died here."

Samson gave him some of the medicine for chills and fever which he always carried in his pocket, and water from his canteen. The sun shone warm but the ground was damp and cold and there was a chilly breeze. He wrapped the stricken man in his coat and sat down beside him and rubbed his aching head.

"Is there any house where I could find help and shelter for you?" he asked presently.

"No, but I feel better—glory to God!" said the preacher. "If you can help me to the back of my horse I will try to ride on with you. There is to be a quarterly meeting ten miles up the road to-night. With the help of God I must get there and tell the people of His goodness and mercy to the children of men. Nothing shall keep me from my duty. I may save a dozen souls from hell—who knows?"

Samson was astonished at the iron will and holy zeal of this lion-hearted, strong-armed, fighting preacher of the prairies of whom he had heard much. He looked at the rugged head covered with thick, bushy, gray hair, at the deep-lined face, smooth-shaven, save for a lock in front of each ear, with its keen, dark eyes and large, firm mouth and jaw. Samson lifted the preacher and set him on the back of his horse.

"God blessed you with great strength," said the latter. "Are you a Christian?"

"I am."

They rode on in silence. Presently Samson observed that the preacher was actually asleep and snoring in the saddle. They proceeded for an hour or more in this manner. When the horses were wallowing through a swale the preacher awoke.

"Glory be to God!" he shouted. "I am better. I shall be able to preach to-night. A little farther on is the cabin of Brother Cawkins. He has been terribly pecked up by a stiff-necked, rebellious wife. We'll stop there for a cup of tea and if she raises a rumpus you'll see me take her by the horns."

Mrs. Cawkins was a lean, sallow, stern-eyed woman of some forty years with a face like bitter herbs; her husband a mild mannered, shiftless man who, encouraged by Mr. Cartwright, had taken to riding through the upper counties as a preacher—a course of conduct of which his wife heartily disapproved. Solicited by her husband she sullenly made tea for the travelers. When it had been drunk the two preachers knelt in a corner of the room and Mr. Cartwright began to pray in a loud voice. Mrs. Cawkins shoved the table about and tipped over the chairs and dropped the rolling-pin as a counter demonstration. The famous circuit rider, being in no way put out by this, she dashed a dipper of cold water on the head of her husband. The praying stopped. Mr. Cartwright rose from his knees and commanded her to desist. On her declaration that she would not he laid hold of the

woman and forced her out of the door and closed and
bolted it and resumed his praying.

Having recorded this remarkable incident in his
diary Samson writes:

"Many of these ignorant people in the lonely, prairie
cabins are like children. Cartwright leads them on
like a father and sometimes with the strong hand. If
any of them deserve a spanking they get it. He and
others like him have helped to keep the cabin people
clean and going up hill instead of down. They have
established schools and missions and scattered good
books and comforted sorrows and kindled good desire
in the hearts of the humble."

As they were leaving Mr. Cawkins told them that
the plague had broken out in the settlement on Honey
Creek, where the quarterly meeting was to be held,
and that the people had been rapidly "dyin' off." Samson knew from this that the smallpox—a dreaded and
terrible scourge of pioneer days—had come again.

"It's dangerous to go there," said Cawkins.

"Where is sorrow there is my proper place," Cartwright answered. "Those people need comfort and the
help of God."

"But are you not afraid of the plague?" Samson
asked.

"I fear only the wrath of my Master."

"I got a letter from a lady there," Cawkins went
on. "As nigh as I can make out they need a minister.

I can read print handy but writin' bothers me. You read it, brother."

Mr. Cartwright took the letter and read as follows:

"Dear Sir: Mr. Barman gave me your name. We need a minister to comfort the sick and help bury the dead. It is a good deal to ask of you but if you feel like taking the chance of coming here I am sure you could do a lot of good. We have doctors enough and it seems a pity that the church should fail these people when they need it most. The ministers in Chicago seem to be too busy to come. One of them came out for a funeral and unfortunately took the disease. If you have the courage to come you would win the gratitude of many people. For a month I have been taking care of the sick and up to now no harm has come to me.   Yours respectfully,
                                        "Bim Kelso."

" 'A man's heart deviseth his way but the Lord directeth his steps,' " said Cartwright. "For three days I have felt that He was leading me."

"I begin to think that He has been leading me," Samson declared. "Bim Kelso is the person I seek."

"I would have gone but my wife took on so I couldn't get away," said Cawkins.

"I'll come back some day soon and you and I will pry the Devil out of her with the crowbar of God's truth and mercy," Cartwright assured him as he and Samson took the road to the north.

On their way to the Honey Creek settlement the

lion-hearted minister told of swimming through flooded rivers, getting lost on the plains and suffering for food and water, of lying down to rest at night in wet clothes with no shelter but the woods, of hand to hand fights with rowdies who endeavored to sell drink or create a disturbance at his meetings. Such was the zeal for righteousness woven by many hands into the fabric of the West. A little before sundown they reached the settlement.

Samson asked a man in the road if he knew where they could find the nurse Bim Kelso.

"Do ye mean that angel o' God in a white dress that takes keer o' the sick?" the man asked.

"I guess that would be Bim," said Samson.

"She's over in yon' house," the other answered, pointing with his pipe to a cabin some twenty rods beyond them. "Thar's two children sick thar an' the mammy dead an' buried in the ground."

"Is the plague getting worse?" Cartwright asked.

"No, I reckon it's better. Nobody has come down since the day before yestiddy. Thar's the doctor comin'. He kin tell ye."

A bearded man of middle age was approaching them in the saddle.

"Gentlemen, you must not stop in this neighborhood," he warned them. "There's an epidemic of smallpox here. We are trying to control it and every one must help."

"I am Peter Cartwright—the preacher sent of God to comfort the sick and bury the dead," said Samson's companion.

"We welcome you, but if you stop here you will have to stay until the epidemic is over."

"That I am prepared to do."

"Then I shall take you where you can find entertainment, such as it is."

"First, this man wishes to speak to Miss Kelso, the nurse," said Cartwright. "He is a friend of hers."

"You can see her but only at a distance," the Doctor answered. "I must keep you at least twenty feet away from her. Come with me."

They proceeded to the stricken house. The Doctor entered and presently Bim came out. Her eyes filled with tears and for a moment she could not speak. She wore a white dress and cap and was pale and weary. "But still as I looked at her I thought of the saying of her father that her form and face reminded him of the singing of birds in the springtime, she looked so sweet and graceful," Samson writes in his diary.

"Why didn't you let me know of your troubles?" he asked.

"Early last summer I wrote a long letter to you," she answered.

"It didn't reach me. One day in June the stage

was robbed of its mail down in Tazewell County. Your letter was probably on that stage."

"Harry's death was the last blow. I came out here to get away from my troubles—perhaps to die. I didn't care."

"Harry is not dead," said Samson.

Her right hand touched her forehead; her lips fell apart; her eyes took on a look of tragic earnestness.

"Not dead!" she whispered.

"He is alive and well."

Bim staggered toward him and fell to her knees and lay crouched upon the ground, in the dusky twilight, shaking and choked with sobs, and with tears streaming from her eyes but she was almost as silent as the shadow of the coming night. She looked like one searching in the dust for something very precious. The strong heart of Samson was touched by the sorrowful look of her so that he could not speak.

Soon he was able to say in a low, trembling voice:

"In every letter he tells of his love for you. That article in the paper was a cruel mistake."

After a little silence Bim rose from the ground. She stood, for a moment, wiping her eyes. Her form straightened and was presently erect. Her soul resented the injustice she had suffered. There was a wonderful and touching dignity in her voice and manner when she asked: "Why didn't he write to me?"

"He must have written to you."

Sadly, calmly, thoughtfully, she spoke as she stood looking off at the fading glow in the west:

"It is terrible how things can work together to break the heart and will of a woman. Write to Harry and tell him that he must not come to see me again. I have promised to marry another man."

"I hope it isn't Davis," said Samson.

"It is Davis."

"I don't like him. I don't think he's honest."

"But he has been wonderfully kind to us. Without his help we couldn't have lived. We couldn't even have given my father a decent burial. I suppose he has his faults. I no longer look for perfection in human beings."

"Has he been out here to see you?"

"No."

"And he won't come. That man knows how to keep out of danger. I don't believe you'll marry him."

"Why?"

"Because I intend to be a father to you and pay all your debts," said Samson.

The Doctor called from the door of the cabin.

Bim said: "God bless you and Harry!" as she turned away to take up her task again.

That night both of them began, as they say, to put two and two together. While he rode on in the growing dusk the keen intellect of Samson saw a convincing sequence of circumstances—the theft of the mail sack, the false account of Harry's death, the failure of his letters to reach their destination, and the fact that Bim had accepted money from Davis in time of need. A strong suspicion of foul play grew upon him and he began to consider what he could do in the matter.

Having forded a creek he caught the glow of a light in the darkness a little way up the road. It was the lighted window of a cabin, before whose door he stopped his horse and hallooed.

"I am a belated and hungry traveler on my way to Chicago," he said to the man who presently greeted him from the open doorway.

"Have you come through Honey Creek settlement?" the latter asked.

"Left there about an hour ago."

"Sorry, mister, but I can't let you come into the house. If you'll move off a few feet I'll lay some grub on the choppin' block an' up the road about a half-mile you'll find a barn with some hay in it where you and your horse can spend the night under cover."

Samson moved away and soon the man brought a package of food and laid it on the block and ran back to the door.

"I'll lay a piece of silver on the block," Samson called.

"Not a darned cent," the man answered. "I hate

like p'ison to turn a feller away in the night, but we're awful skeered here with children in the house. Goodby. You can't miss the barn. It's close ag'in' the road."

Samson ate his luncheon in the darkness, as he rode, and presently came upon the barn and unsaddled and hitched and fed his horse in one end of it— the beast having drunk his fill at the creek they had lately forded—and lay down to rest, for the night, with the saddle blanket beneath him and his coat for a cover. A wind from the north began to wail and whistle through the cracks in the barn and over its roof bringing cold weather. Samson's feet and legs had been wet in the crossing so that he found it difficult to keep warm. He crept to the side of his horse, which had lain down, and found a degree of comfort in the heat of the animal. But it was a bad night, at best, with only a moment, now and then, of a sort of one-eyed sleep in it.

"I've had many a long, hard night but this is the worst of them," Samson thought.

There's many a bad night in the history of the pioneers, its shadows falling on lonely, ill-marked roads cut by rivers, creeks and marshes and strung through unnumbered miles of wild country. Samson was up and off at daylight in a bitter wind and six inches of snow. It was a kind of work he would not have undertaken upon any call less commanding than that of friendship. He reached Chicago at noon having had nothing to eat that day. There was no such eager, noisy crowd in the streets as he had seen before. The fever of speculation had passed. Some of the stores were closed; he counted a score of half-built structures getting weather-stained inside and out. But there were many people on the main thoroughfares, among whom were Europeans who had arrived the autumn before. They were changing but the marks of the yoke were still upon them. In Chicago were the vitals of the West and they were very much alive in spite of the panic.

Samson bought some new clothes and had a bath and a good dinner at the City Hotel. Then he went to the office of Mr. Lionel Davis. There to his surprise he met his old acquaintance, Eli Fredenberg, who greeted him with great warmth and told of having settled in Chicago.

A well-dressed young man came out of an inner office and informed the Jew that Mr. Davis could not see him that day.

"I'd like to see Mr. Davis," said Samson as Eli went away.

"I'm Mr. Davis's secretary," the young man politely informed him.

"What's a secretary?" Samson asked.

"It's a man who helps another with his work."

"I don't need any help myself—thank you," said

Samson. "You tell him that I've got some money that belongs to him and that I'm ready to deliver it."

The young man disappeared through the door of the private office and soon returned and conducted Samson into the presence of Mr. Davis who sat at a handsome desk, smoking, in a room with fine old mahogany furnishings brought up from New Orleans. The two men recognized each other.

"Well, sir, what is it about?" the young speculator demanded.

"The daughter of my old friend, Jack Kelso, owes you some money and I want to pay it," said Samson.

"Oh, that is a matter between Miss Kelso and me." Mr. Davis spoke politely and with a smile.

"Not exactly—since I knew about it," Samson answered.

"I refuse to discuss her affairs with you," Davis declared.

"I suppose you mistrust me," said Samson. "Well, I've offered to pay you and I'm going to make it plain to them that they don't have to worry any more about the money you loaned them."

"Very well, I bid you good morning."

"Don't be in a hurry," Samson answered. "I have a note of five thousand dollars against you. It is endorsed to me by Henry Brimstead and I want to collect it."

"I refuse to pay it," Davis promptly answered.

"Then I shall have to put it in the hands of a lawyer," said Samson.

"Put it where you like but don't consume any more of my time."

"But you'll have to hear me say that I don't think you're honest."

"I have heard you," Davis answered calmly.

Samson withdrew and went to the home of Mrs. Kelso. He found her with Bim's boy in her lap—a handsome little lad, then a bit over two years old,—at the house on La Salle Street. The good woman gave Samson an account of the year filled with tearful praise of the part Mr. Davis had played in it. Samson told of the failure of Bim's letter to reach him and of his offer to return the money which Davis had paid for their relief.

"I don't like the man and I don't want you to be under obligation to him," said Samson. "The story of Harry's death was false and I think that he is responsible for it. He wanted her to marry him right away after that—of course. And she went to the plague settlement to avoid marriage. I know her better than you do. She has read him right. Her soul has looked into his soul and it keeps her away from him."

But Mrs. Kelso could believe no evil of her benefactor, nor would she promise to cease depending on his bounty.

Samson was a little disheartened by the visit. He went to see John Wentworth, the editor of *The Democrat,* of whose extreme length Mr. Lincoln had humorously spoken in his presence. The young New Englander was seven feet tall. He welcomed the broad-shouldered man from Sangamon County and began at once to question him about Honest Abe and "Steve" Douglas and O. H. Browning and E. D. Baker and all the able men of the middle counties. Then he wanted to know of the condition of the people since the collapse of the land boom. The farmer's humorous comment and sane views delighted the young editor. At the first opportunity Samson came to the business of his call—the mischievous lie regarding Harry's death which had appeared in *The Democrat.* Mr. Wentworth went to the proof room and found the manuscript of the article.

"We kept it because we didn't know and do not now know the writer," said Wentworth.

Samson told of the evil it had wrought and conveyed his suspicions to the editor.

"Davis is rather unscrupulous," said Wentworth. "We know a lot about him in this office."

Samson looked at the article and presently said: "Here is a note that he gave to a friend of mine. It looks to me as if the note and the article were written by the same hand."

Mr. Wentworth compared the two and said: "You

are right. The same person wrote them. But it was not Davis."

When Samson left the office of *The Democrat* he had accomplished little save the confirmation of his suspicions. There was nothing he could do about it.

He went to Eli Fredenberg. Eli, having sold out at the height of the boom in Springfield, had been back to Germany to visit his friends.

"I haf money—plendy money," said Eli. "In de ol' country I vas rich. I thought maybe I stay dere an' make myself happy. It vas one big job. Mein frients dey hate me becos I haf succeed so much. De odders hate me becos de butcher haf mein fadder been. Dey laugh at my good close. Nobody likes me not. I come avay. Dey don't blame you here becos you vos born."

"What has Davis done to you?" Samson asked, recalling where he had met Eli that morning.

Eli explained that he had borrowed money from Davis to tide him over the hard times and was paying twelve per cent. for it.

"Dis morning I get dot letter from his secretary," he said as he passed a letter to Samson.

It was a demand for payment in the handwriting of the Brimstead note and had some effect on this little history. It conveyed definite knowledge of the authorship of a malicious falsehood. It aroused the anger and sympathy of Samson Traylor. In the con-

ditions then prevailing Eli was unable to get the money.
He was in danger of losing his business. Samson
spent a day investigating the affairs of the merchant.
His banker and others spoke well of him. He was
said to be a man of character and credit embarrassed
by the unexpected scarcity of good money. So it
came about that, before he left the new city, Samson
bought a fourth interest in the business of Eli Fredenberg. The lots he owned were then worth less than
when he had bought them, but his faith in the future
of Chicago had not abated.

He wrote a long letter to Bim recounting the history of his visit and frankly stating the suspicions to
which he had been led. He set out on the west road
at daylight toward the Riviere des Plaines, having
wisely decided to avoid passing the plague settlement.
Better weather had come. In the sunlight of a clear
sky he fared away over the vast prairies, feeling that
it was a long road ahead and a most unpromising visit
behind him.

CHAPTER XXI

THE boy Joe had had a golden week at the home of the Brimsteads. The fair Annabel knowing not the power that lay in her beauty had captured his young heart scarcely fifteen years of age. He had no interest in her younger sister, Mary. But Annabel with her long skirts and full form and glowing eyes and gentle dignity had stirred him to the depths. When he left he carried a soul heavy with regret and great resolutions. Not that he had mentioned the matter to her or to any one. It was a thing too sacred for speech. To God in his prayers he spoke of it but to no other.

He asked to be made and to be thought worthy. He would have had the whole world stopped and put to sleep for a term until he was delivered from the bondage of his tender youth. That being impossible it

353

was for him a sad but not a hopeless world. Indeed he rejoiced in his sadness. Annabel was four years older than he. If he could make her to know the depth of his passion perhaps she would wait for him. He sought for self-expression in *The Household Book of Poetry*—a sorrowful and pious volume. He could find no ladder of rhyme with an adequate reach. He endeavored to build one. He wrote melancholy verses and letters, confessing his passion, to Annabel, which she did not encourage but which she always kept and valued for their ingenuous and noble ardor. Some of these Anacreontics are among the treasures inherited by her descendants. They were a matter of slight importance, one would say, but they mark the beginning of a great career. Immediately after his return to the new home in Springfield the boy Josiah set out to make himself honored of his ideal. In the effort he made himself honored of many. His eager brain had soon taken the footing of manhood.

A remarkable school of political science had begun its sessions in that little western village. The world had never seen the like of it. Abraham Lincoln, Stephen A. Douglas, E. D. Baker, O. H. Browning, Jesse B. Thomas, and Josiah Lamborn—a most unusual array of talent as subsequent history has proved —were wont to gather around the fireplace in the rear of Joshua Speed's store, evenings, to discuss the issues of the time. Samson and his son Joe came often to hear the talk. Douglas looked like a dwarf among those long geared men. He was slight and short, being only about five feet tall, but he had a big, round head covered with thick, straight, dark hair, a bull-dog look and a voice like thunder. The first steamboat had crossed the Atlantic the year before and The Future of Transportation was one of the first themes discussed by this remarkable group of men. Douglas and Lincoln were in a heated argument over the admission of slavery to the territories the first night 'that Samson and Joe sat down with them.

"We didn't like that little rooster of a man, he had such a high and mighty way with him and so frankly opposed the principles we believe in. He was an out and out pro-slavery man. He would have every state free to regulate its domestic institutions, in its own way, subject only to the Constitution of the United States. Lincoln held that it amounted to saying 'that if one man chose to enslave another no third party shall be allowed to object.' "

In the course of the argument Douglas alleged that the Whigs were the aristocrats of the country.

"That reminds me of a night when I was speaking at Havana," said Honest Abe. "A man with a ruffled shirt and a massive gold watch chain got up and charged that the Whigs were aristocrats. Douglas in his broadcloth and fine linen reminds me of that man. I'm going to answer Douglas as I an-

swered him. Most of the Whigs I know are my kind
of folks. I was a poor boy working on a flat boat
at eight dollars a month and had only one pair of
breeches and they were buckskin. If you know the
nature of buckskin, you know that when it is wet
and dried by the sun it will shrink and my breeches
kept shrinking and deserting the sock area of my legs
until several inches of them were bare above my
shoes. Whilst I was growing longer they were growing shorter and so much tighter that they left a blue
streak around my legs which can be seen to this day.
If you call that aristocracy I know of one Whig that
is an aristocrat."

"But look at the New England type of Whig ex-
emplified by the imperious and majestic Webster,"
said Douglas.

"Webster was another poor lad," Lincoln answered.
"His father's home was a log cabin in a lonely land
until about the time Daniel was born when the family
moved to a small frame house. His is the majesty of
a great intellect."

There was much talk of this sort until Mr. Lincoln
excused himself to walk home with his two friends
who had just returned from the North, being eager to
learn of Samson's visit. The latter gave him a full
account of it and asked him to undertake the collec-
tion of Brimstead's note.

"I'll get after that fellow right away," said Lincoln.

"I'm glad to get a chance at one of those men who have been skinning the farmers. I suppose he has other creditors in Tazewell County?"

"I presume there are many of them."

"I'll find out about that," said Lincoln.

They sat down by the fireside in Samson's house.

"Joe has decided that he wants to be a lawyer," said Samson.

"Well, Joe, we'll all do what we can to keep you from being a shot-gun lawyer," Abe Lincoln began. "I've got a good first lesson for you. I found it in a letter which Rufus Choate had written to Judge Davis. In it he says that we rightly have great respect for the decisions of the majority, but that the law is something vastly greater and more sacred than the verdict of any majority. 'It is a thing,' says he, 'which has stood the test of long experience—a body of digested rules and processes bequeathed to us by all the ages of the past. The inspired wisdom of the primeval east, the robust genius of Athens and Rome, the keener modern sense of righteousness are in it. The law comes down to us one mighty and continuous stream of wisdom and experience accumulated, ancestral, widening and deepening and washing itself clearer as it runs on, the agent of civilization, the builder of a thousand cities. To have lived through ages of unceasing trial with the passions, interests, and affairs of men, to have lived through the drums and tramplings of conquest,

through revolution and reform and all the changing
cycles of opinion, to have attended the progress of the
race and gathered unto itself the approbation of civilized humanity is to have proved that it carries in it
some spark of immortal life.' "

The face of Lincoln changed as he recited the
lines of the learned and distinguished lawyer of Massachusetts.

"His face glowed like a lighted lantern when he
began to say those eloquent words," Samson writes in
his diary.   "He wrote them down so that Josiah could
commit them to memory."

"That is a wonderful statement," Samson remarked.
Abe answered: "It suggests to me that the voice of
the people in any one generation may or may not be inspired, but that the voice of the best men of all ages,
expressing their sense of justice and of right, in the
law, is and must be the voice of God.   The spirit and
body of its decrees are as indestructible as the throne
of Heaven.   You can overthrow them but until their
power is reestablished as surely it will be, you will live
in savagery."

"You do not deny the right of revolution."

"No, but I can see no excuse for it in America.   It
has remained for us to add to the body of the law the
idea that men are created free and equal.   The lack
of that saving principle in the codes of the world has
been the great cause of injustice and oppression.   The

voice of revolution here would be like that of Iago in the play and worse. It would be like the unscrupulous lawyer, anxious for a fee, who says to a client, living happily with his wife: 'I know she is handsome and virtuous and intelligent and loving but she has her faults. There are lovelier women. I could easily get a divorce for you.' We would quickly throw such a man out of the door. A man's country is like his wife. If she is virtuous and well-disposed he should permit no meddling, odious person to come between them, or to suggest to him that he put poison into her tea. Least of all should he look for perfection in her, knowing that it is not to be found in this world of ours."

Honest Abe rose and walked up and down the room in silence for a moment. Then he added:

"Choate phrased it well when he said · 'We should beware of awaking the tremendous divinities of change from their long sleep. Let us think of that when we consider what we shall do with the evils that afflict us.' "

The boy Joe has been deeply interested in this talk.

"If you'll lend me a book I'd like to begin studying," he said.

"There's time enough for that," said Lincoln. "First I want you to understand what the law is and what the lawyer should be. You wouldn't want to be a pettifogger. Choate is the right model. He has a dignity suited to the greatness of his chosen master. They say that before a Justice of the Peace in a room no bigger than a shoemaker's shop his work is done with the same dignity and care that he would show in the supreme court of Massachusetts. A newspaper says that in a dog case at Beverly he treated the dog as if he were a lion and the crabbed old squire with the consideration due a chief justice."

"He knows how to handle the English language," Samson observed.

"He got that by reading. He is the best read man at the American bar and the best Bible student. There's a lot of work ahead of you, Joe, before you are a lawyer and when you're admitted success comes only of the capacity for work. Brougham wrote the peroration of his speech in defense of Queen Caroline nineteen times."

"I want to be a great orator," the boy exclaimed with engaging frankness.

"Then you must remember that character is the biggest part of it," Honest Abe declared. "Great thoughts come out of a great character and only out of that. They will come even if you have little learning and none of the graces which attract the eye. But you must have a character that is ever speaking even when your lips are silent. It must show in your life and fill the spaces between your words. It will help you to choose and charge them with the love of great things that carry conviction.

"I remember when I was a boy over in Gentryville a shaggy, plain-dressed man rode up to the door one day. He had a cheerful, kindly face. His character began to speak to us before he opened his mouth to ask for a drink of water.

" 'I don't know who you are,' my father said. 'But I'd like it awful well if you'd light an' talk to us.' He did and we didn't know till he had gone that he was the Governor of the state. A good character shines like a candle on a dark night. You can't mistake it. A firefly can't hold his light long enough to compete with it.

"Webster said in the Knapp trial: 'There is no evil that we can not either face or fly from but the consciousness of duty disregarded.'

"A great truth like that makes wonderful music on the lips of a sincere man. An orator must be a lover and discoverer of such unwritten laws."

It was nearing midnight when they heard footsteps on the board walk in front of the house. In a moment Harry Needles entered in cavalry uniform with fine top boots and silver spurs, erect as a young Indian brave and bronzed by tropic suns.

"Hello!" he said as he took off his belt and clanking saber. "I hang up my sword. I have had enough of war."

He had ridden across country from the boat landing and arriving so late had left his horse at a livery stable.

"I'm lucky to find you and Abe and Joe all up and

waiting for me," he said as he shook their hands.
"How is mother?"

"I'm well," Sarah called from the top of the stairway. "I'll be down in a minute."

For an hour or more they sat by the fireside while
Harry told of his adventures in the great swamps of
Southern Florida.

"I've done my share of the fighting," he said at
length. "I'm going north to-morrow to find Bim and
her mother."

"I shall want you to serve a complaint on one Lionel
Davis," said Mr. Lincoln.

"I have one of my own to serve on him," Harry
answered. "But I hope that our case can be settled
out of court."

"I think that I'll go with you as far as Tazewell
County and draw the papers there," said Lincoln.

When the latter had left for his lodgings and Joe
and his mother had gone to bed, Samson told Harry
the details of his visit to Chicago.

"She may have taken the disease and died with it
before now," said the young man. "I'll be on my way
to Honey Creek in the morning. If she's sick I'll
take care of her. I'm not going to worry about Davis.
But when I get there I wouldn't wonder if he'd have
to worry a little about me."

CHAPTER XXII

WHEREIN ABE LINCOLN REVEALS HIS METHOD OF CON-
DUCTING A LAWSUIT IN THE CASE OF HENRY BRIM-
STEAD ET AL., VS. LIONEL DAVIS.

THEY found many of Davis's notes in Tazewell
County. Abe Lincoln's complaint represented seven
clients and a sum exceeding twenty thousand dollars.

"Now, Harry, you don't like Davis and I can't blame
you for it," said Honest Abe before they parted.
"Don't spoil our case by trying to take it out of his
hide. First we've got to take it out of his pocket.
When I get through there may not be any hide on him
worth speaking of, but if there is you can have it
and welcome."

With the papers in his pocket Harry went on to
the Honey Creek settlement. There he found that the
plague had spent itself and that Bim had gone to a
detention camp outside the city of Chicago. He rode
on to the camp but was not permitted to see her, the
regulations having become very strict. In the city
he went to the store of Eli Fredenberg. The merchant received him with enthusiasm. Chicago had
begun to recover from the panic. Trade was lively.

Eli wanted Harry to go to work in the store until he was prepared for the law.

"You must stay here until you haf got a wife already," said the thoughtful Eli. "It is bat for you and Bim to be not marrit so much."

The young man favored both the commercial and the sentimental suggestions of Eli. He had long felt the lure of that promising little city on the lake shore.

"I wish you'd take this complaint and serve it on Davis," he said. "I don't want to see him if I can help it. If you don't mind, you can tell him that I've come to life and am here in the city and that if he kills me again he'd better do it while I'm looking. It would be more decent."

Eli was delighted with a task which promised a degree of discomfort to the man who had endeavored to ruin him. Harry spent the afternoon with Mrs. Kelso and Bim's baby boy. The good woman was much excited by the arrival of the young soldier.

"We have had a terrible year," she said. "We couldn't have lived through it without the help of a friend. Bim went away to take care of the sick in the smallpox neighborhood. She was rather discouraged. Our friend, Mr. Davis, is in love with her. She promised to marry him. It seemed to be the only way out of our troubles. But she will not even write to him now. I think that she is very unhappy."

"I shall not try to increase her troubles, but I shall

prevent her from marrying Davis if I can," said Harry.

"Why?"

"Because I think he is dishonest."

"He has convinced me that all the reports are wrong," Mrs. Kelso declared. "I think that he is one of the kindest and best of men."

"I shall not argue with you as to the character of my rival," Harry answered. "The facts will be on record one of these days and then you can form your own judgment. I hope you won't mind my coming here to see you and the baby now and then."

"You are always welcome. But Mr. Davis comes often and feeling as you do it might be unpleasant for you to meet him."

"It would. I'll keep away until the air clears," said Harry.

He wrote a very tender letter to Bim that day. He told her that he had come to Chicago to live so that he might be near her and ready to help her if she needed help. "The same old love is in my heart that made me want you for my wife long ago, that has filled my letters and sustained me in many an hour of peril," he wrote. "If you really think that you must marry Davis, I ask you at least to wait for the developments of a suit which Abe Lincoln is bringing in behalf of many citizens of Tazewell County. It is likely that we shall know more than we do now be-

fore that case ends. I saw your beautiful little boy.
He looks so much like you that I long to steal him and
keep him with me."

In a few days he received this brief reply:

"Dear Harry: Your letter pleased and pained me.
I have been so tossed about that I don't know quite
where I stand. My brain is like a bridge that has
been washed out by floods. I am picking up the frag-
ments and trying to rebuild it. For a long time my
life has been nothing but a series of emotions. What
Honest Abe may be able to prove I know not, but I
am sure that he can not disprove the fact that Mr.
Davis has been kind and generous to me. For that I
can not ever cease to be grateful. I should have married him before now but for one singular circumstance.
My little boy can not be made to like him. He will
have nothing to do with Mr. Davis. He will not be
bribed or coerced. Time and kindness do not seem
to diminish his dislike. My soul has been drugged
with argument and—I can not help saying it—bribed
with favors. But the boy has been steadfast. He has
kept his frankness and honesty. I saw in this a
prophecy of trouble. I left home and went down into
the very shadow of death. It may be that we have
been saved for each other by the wisdom of childhood.
I must not see you now. Nor shall I see him until
I have found my way. Even your call can not make
me forget that I am under a solemn promise. I must
keep it without much more delay unless something
happens to release me.

"I'm glad you like the boy. He is a wonderful

child. I named him Nehemiah for his grandfather.
We call him Nim and sometimes 'Mr. Nimble' because
he is so lively. I'm homesick to see him and you. I
am going to Dixon to teach and earn money for mother and the baby. Don't tell any one where I am and
above all don't come to see me until in good heart I
can ask you to come.

"God bless you!

"Bim."

In a few weeks the suit came on. It was tried in the
new brick Court-House in Chicago. Davis's defense,
as given in the answer, alleged that the notes were to
be paid out of the proceeds of the sale of lots and
that in consequence of the collapse of the boom there
had been no such proceeds. His claim was supported
by the testimony of his secretary and another and by
certain letters of his, promising payment as soon as
the land was sold, and by letters from the plaintiffs
allowing that grace. As to the understanding upon
which the notes were drawn, there was a direct issue
of veracity for which Abe Lincoln was exceedingly
well prepared. He had gained possession of many
facts in the history of the young speculator, including
the important one that he had been convicted of fraud
in New Orleans. Mr. Lincoln's cross-examination
was as merciless as sunlight "falling round a helpless
thing." It was kindly and polite in tone but relent-
less in its searching. When it ended, the weight of

Davis's character had been accurately established. In his masterly summing up Mr. Lincoln presented every circumstance in favor of the defendant's position. With remarkable insight he anticipated the arguments of his attorney. He presented them fairly and generously to the court and jury. According to Samson the opposing lawyers admitted in a private talk that Lincoln had thought of presumptions in favor of Davis which had not occurred to them. Therein lay the characteristic of Mr. Lincoln's method in a lawsuit.

"It was a safe thing for him to do for he never took a case in which justice was not clearly on his side," Samson writes. "If he had been deceived as to the merits of a case he would drop it. With the sword of justice in his hand he was invincible."

First he put the thing to be weighed on the scale fully and fairly. Then, one by one, he put the units of gravity on the other side so that the court and jury saw the turning of the balance.

He covered the point at issue with a few words "every one of which drew blood," to quote a phrase from the diary. He showed that the validity of such claims rested wholly on the character of the man who made them, especially when they were opposed to the testimony of people whose honesty had been questioned only by that man.

"Now as to the secretary," said Mr. Lincoln, "I

honestly regret that he has disagreed with himself.
A young man ought not to disagree with himself as to
the truth and especially when he contradicts the oath
of witnesses whom we have no reason to discredit. I
want to be kind to him on account of his youth. He
reminds me of the young man who hired out to a
Captain in Gloucester and shipped for the China coast
and learned presently that he was on a pirate vessel.
He had been a young man of good intentions but he
had to turn to and help the business along. When
the ship was captured he said:

" 'I didn't want to be a pirate, but there was only
one kind o' politics on that ship and the majority was
so large I thought that the vote might as well be
unanimous. At first I was in favor of reform but
the walkin' was that bad I had to decide between a
harp and a cutlass.'

"This parable serves to illustrate the history of most
young men who fall into bad company. The walking
becomes more or less bad for them. They get into
the bondage of Fear. We know not how it may have
influenced the action of Cap'n Davis's First Mate.
Probably since the hard times began, the walking has
looked bad to him but still there was walking. I am
sorry it must be said that there was walking and I
hope that he will now make some use of it."

He did and in time confessed to Samson Traylor
that Mr. Lincoln's reproach had been the saving of

him. A judgment was rendered in favor of the plaintiffs for the full amount of their claim with costs. The character of Lionel Davis had been sufficiently revealed. Even the credulous Mrs. Kelso turned against him. Mr. Lincoln's skill as a lawyer was recognized in the north as well as in the middle counties. From that day forth no man enjoyed a like popularity in Tazewell County.

When Samson and Harry Needles left the Court-House, there seemed to be no obstacle between the young man and the consummation of his wishes. Unfortunately, as they were going down the steps Davis, who blamed Samson for his troubles, flung an insult at the sturdy Vermonter. Samson, who had then arrived at years of firm discretion, was little disturbed by the anger of a man so discredited. But Harry, on the sound of the hateful words, had leaped forward and dealt the speculator a savage blow in the face which for a few seconds had deprived him of the power of speech. That evening a friend of Davis called at the City Hall with a challenge. The hot-blooded young soldier accepted it against the urgent counsel of Samson Traylor, Mr. Lincoln having left the city. It was a fashion of the time for gentlemen to stand up and shoot at each other after such a quarrel. But Davis, since the trial, had no character to defend and therefore no right to enter the field of honor with a man

of Harry's standing. But the young officer had promised to fight and was not to be dissuaded.

As to the details of the tragic scene that followed
next day, the writer has little knowledge. Samson
was not the type of man for such a chronicle. The
diary speaks of his part in it with shame and sorrow
and remorse. His mind seems to have been too much
engaged with its own fears and thoughts to take note
of the color. We may infer from one remark in it
that the sky was clear. We know, too, that it was
at day-break when he and Harry rode to a point on
the prairie "something more than a mile from the
city limits." There he tells us they met Davis and
one friend of the latter and two surgeons who had
driven to the scene in a box wagon. It is evident, too,
that great secrecy had been observed in the plan and
its execution and that, until sometime after the last
act, Lincoln knew nothing of the later developments
in the drama of Davis's downfall. For the rest of the
deplorable scene the historian must content himself
with the naked details in the diary of a puritan pioneer. They are, at least, direct and derive a certain
vividness from their haste to be done with it as a proceeding of which the less said the better.

"I went because there was no escape from it and
with the shadow of God's wrath in my soul," Samson writes. "The sun rose as we halted our horses.

We paced the field. The two men took their places twenty yards apart. Harry was a little pale but he stood up as straight and steady as a hitching post. The pistols rang out at the command to fire and both men fell. Davis had been hit in the left shoulder. My handsome boy lay on his face. The bullet had bored through his right lung. Before I could reach him he had risen to his feet ready to go on with the battle. Davis lay like one paralyzed by the shock of the bullet. His seconds declared they were satisfied. The surgeons began their work. I saw them take the bullet out of Harry's back where it had lodged under his skin. I helped them put the wounded men into the wagon and rode to the house of one of the doctors near the city wherein were rooms for the accommodation of critical cases, leading Harry's horse and praying for God's help and forgiveness. I took care of the boy until Steve Nuckles came to help me. Bim arrived when Harry was out of his head and didn't know her. She was determined to stay and do the nursing but I wouldn't let her. She did not look strong. I loaned her the money to pay the debt to Davis and persuaded her to go back to her work in Dixon. She went and was rather heart-broken about it.

"As she was leaving she looked into my face and said: 'Don't tell him or any one what has happened to me. I want to tell him.'

"I promised to keep her secret and did it. Soon I learned that she was down sick of her worries. I sent her mother to her and kept the small boy with me.

"The surgeon said that Harry would live if lung fever didn't set in. It set in but he pulled through.

He mended slowly. I had some fear of arrest but the conspiracy of silence kept the facts under cover. It was partly due, I guess, to the friendship of John Wentworth for me and Honest Abe. He kept it out of the papers. There were no complaints and the rumors soon fell into silence. I spent about six weeks at Harry's bedside and in the store which has begun to prosper.

"The boy, 'Mr. Nimble,' is a cunning little man. When he began to get better, Harry loved to play with him and listen to his talk about fairies. The young man was able to leave his bed, by and by, but he didn't get over his weakness and pallor. He had no appetite. I sent him with Nuckles into the Wisconsin woods to live in the open. Then I took the small boy to Dixon with me in the saddle. Bim had just got back to her work. She was distressed by the news of Harry's condition.

" 'I fear he has got his death-blow,' she said with a sad look in her face. 'I had hoped that we could be married this autumn. But something comes between us always. First it was my folly and now it is his folly. It seems as if we hadn't sense enough to get married when there's nothing in the way of it.'

"She told me that Eliphalet Biggs had been there. He had heard of the boy and wished to see him and demanded to know where he was. For fear that Biggs would try to get possession of 'Mr. Nimble' I took him with me to Springfield in the saddle.

"I learn that Davis has recovered his health and left the city. A man can not do business without friends and after the trial Chicago was no place for him."

CHAPTER XXIII

WHICH PRESENTS THE PLEASANT COMEDY OF INDI-
VIDUALISM IN THE NEW CAPITAL, AND THE COURT-
SHIP OF LINCOLN AND MARY TODD.

SAMSON, with "Mr. Nimble" on a pad stuffed with
straw in front of him, jogged across the prairies and
waded the creeks and sloughs on his way to Springfield. The little lad was in his fourth year that summer. He slept and talked much on the way and kept
Samson busy with queries about the sky and the creeks
and the great flowery meadows. They camped the
first night in a belt of timber and Samson writes that
the boy "slept snug against me with his head on my
arm. He went to sleep crying for his mother." He
adds:

"It reminded me of the old days of my young
fatherhood. 'Mr. Nimble' wanted to pick all the
the flowers and splash his bare feet in every stream.
In the evening he would talk to the stars as if he
were playing with them. To him the whole world is
a plaything. He is like some of the grown folks in
Chicago. He would sit hanging on to the reins and
talk to the horse and to God by the hour. He used
to tell me that God was a friend of his and I think he

374

was right.   It was good luck to get back to Sarah and
the children.   They took the little stranger into
their hearts.   'Heart room, house room' is the motto
of this part of the country."

It was a new town to which Samson returned. The
Governor and the state officers had moved to Springfield. The new Capitol was nearing completion. The
hard times which had followed the downfall of '37
had unjustly diminished Mr. Lincoln's confidence in
his ability as a legislator. He enjoyed the practice
of the law which had begun to turn his interest from
the affairs of state. But the pot of political science
boiled before the fireplace in the rear of Joshua
Speed's store every evening that Lincoln and his associates were in Springfield. The wit and wisdom
which bubbled into its vapors and the heat that surrounded it were the talk of the town. Many came
to witness the process and presently it was moved, for
a time, to more accommodating quarters. Before a
crowd of people in the Presbyterian Church, Lincoln,
Logan, Baker and Browning for the Whigs, and
Douglas, Calhoun, Lamborn and Thomas for the
Democrats, having assiduously prepared for the trial,
debated the burning issues of the time. The effort of
each filled an evening and Lincoln's speech gave him
new hope of himself. Wise men began to have great
confidence in his future. He had taken the style of
Webster for his model. He no longer used the broad

humor which had characterized his efforts on the stump. A study of the best speeches of the great New Englander had made him question its value in a public address. Dignity, clear reasoning and impressiveness were the chief aims of his new method, the latter of which is aptly illustrated by this passage from his speech in reply to Douglas in the debate mentioned:

"If I ever feel the soul within me elevate and expand to those dimensions not wholly unworthy of its Almighty Architect it is when I contemplate the cause of my country deserted by all the world besides, and I standing up boldly and alone and hurling defiance at her victorious oppressors. Here without contemplating consequences before high heaven and in the face of the world I swear eternal fidelity to the just cause, as I deem it, of the land of my life, my liberty and my love."

In these perfervid utterances one may find little to admire save a great spirit seeking to express itself and lacking as yet the refinement of taste equal to his undertaking. He was no heaven-born genius "sprung in full panoply from the head of Jove." He was just one of the slow, common folk, with a passion for justice and human rights, slowly feeling his way upward. His spirit was growing. Strong in its love and knowledge of common men and of the things necessary to their welfare, it was beginning to seek and know "the divine power of words." Every moment of leisure he

gave to the study of Webster and Burke and Byron
and Shakespeare and Burns. He had begun to study
the art of Irving and Walter Scott and of a new writer of the name of Dickens. There were four men
who slept with him, in the room above Speed's store,
and one of them has told how he used to lie sprawled
on the floor, with his pillow and candle, reading long
after the others had gone to sleep. Samson writes that
he never knew a man who understood the art of using
minutes as he did. A detached minute was to him a
thing to be filled with value. Yet there were few
men so deeply in love with fun. He loved to laugh
at a story-telling and to match his humor with Thomp-
son Campbell—a famous raconteur—and to play with
children. Fun was as necessary to him as sleep. He
searched for it in people and in books.

He came often to Samson's house to play with "Mr.
Nimble" and to talk with Joe. Some of his best
thoughts came when he was talking with Joe and some
of his merriest moments when he was playing with
"Mr. Nimble." He confessed that it was the latter that
reminded him that he had better be looking for a wife.

But Lincoln was only one of many remarkable per-
sonalities in Springfield who had discovered themselves
and were seeking to be discovered. Sundry individuals
were lifting their heads above the crowd but not with
the modesty and self-distrust of Honest Abe. "Steve"
Douglas, whom Samson had referred to as "that little

rooster of a man," put on the stilts of a brave and pon-
derous vigor. His five-foot stature and his hundred
pounds of weight did not fit the part of Achilles. But
he would have no other. He blustered much with a
spear too heavy for his hands. Lincoln used to call
him a kind of popgun.

This free-for-all joust of individualism—one of the
first fruits of Freedom in the West—gave to the life
of the little village a rich flavor of comedy. The great
talents of Douglas had not been developed. His character was as yet shifty and shapeless. Some of the
leading citizens openly distrusted him. He sought to
command respect by assaulting men of full size and
was repeatedly and soundly thumped for his presump-
tion. He had endeavored publicly to chastise the
sturdy Simeon Francis and had been bent over a market cart and severely wigged by the editor. Lincoln
used to call these affairs "the mistakes of Douglas due
wholly to the difference between the size of his body
and the size of his feelin's." He never liked this little
man, in opposing whom he was to come to the fulness
of his power on the platform. It is evident that Lincoln regarded him as an able advocate of small sin-
cerity looking chiefly for personal advancement.

There is a passage in the diary which illustrates the
character of Douglas and Lincoln's knowledge of it.
The passage relates to a day in the famous debates of
1858. Lincoln had not reached Havana in time to

hear the speech of his opponent. A great crowd had come by train and in wagons. Taking advantage of his absence Douglas had called Lincoln "a liar, a coward and a sneak" and declared that he was going to fight him.

Lincoln heard of this and said in his speech:

"I shall not fight with Judge Douglas. A fight could prove nothing at issue in this campaign. It might prove that he is a more muscular man than I or that I am a more muscular man than he, but this subject is not mentioned in either platform. Again he and I are really very good friends and when we are together he would no more think of fighting me than of fighting his wife. Therefore when the Judge talked about fighting he was not giving vent to any ill feeling but was trying to excite—well, let us say enthusiasm against me on the part of his audience."

Justice accomplished her ends now and then with comic displays of violence in the prairie capital. One night Abe Lincoln and certain of his friends captured a shoe-maker who had beaten his wife and held him at the village pump while the aggrieved woman gave him a sound thrashing. So this phase of imperialism was cured in Springfield by "hair off the same dog" as Lincoln put it.

One evening while E. D. Baker was speaking in the crowded village court room above Lincoln's office and was rudely interrupted and in danger of assault, the

long legs of Honest 'Abe suddenly appeared through
a scuttle hole in the ceiling above the platform. He
leaped upon it and seizing a stone water pitcher defied any one to interfere with the right of free speech
in a worthy cause.

So it will be seen that there were zestful moments
in these sundry vindications of the principles of Democracy in the prairie capital.

About this time Miss Mary Todd, the daughter of a
Kentucky banker, arrived in Springfield to visit her
sister, Mrs. Ninian W. Edwards. She was a fashionably dressed, good-looking girl of blue-gray eyes and
dark hair. She had been well educated in the schools
of Lexington and could speak French as well as English.

"Well, Mary, haven't you found the fortunate young
man yet?" Mr. Edwards playfully asked the day of
her coming.

"You know my husband is going to be President
of the United States and I hoped that I would find him
in Springfield," Mary answered in a like vein.

"There's great fishing here," said Mr. Edwards.
"I know the very man you are looking for. He has
come up from the ranks and is now the most popular
member of the Legislature. He can make a stirring
speech and they say he is going to be the President
of the United States. He's wise and witty and
straight as a string but a rough diamond—big, awk-

ward and homely. You're just the girl to take him in
hand and give him a little polish and push him along.
His name is Abraham Lincoln."

Speed knew the Todds—a distinguished Kentucky
family with a Governor of Virginia and other historic
figures in its record. When he called upon Mary she
asked about Mr. Lincoln and said she would like to
meet him.

"She's just the girl for you, 'Abe," Speed said to
him that evening. "She is bright and well educated
and her family has influence. She could be a great
help to you."

This interested the member from Sangamon County who was indeed eager to get along. The companion-
ship of a refined young lady was the very thing he
needed.

"Let's go over and pay our respects to her," Speed
suggested. They went, Lincoln being carefully dressed
in his first suit of black clothes. Miss Todd was a
bright, vivacious girl of middle stature, twenty-two
years old. She was fashionably dressed and carried
her head proudly—a smart-looking, witty, well spoken
girl but not especially handsome. She was most agreeable to the young men. Honest Abe was deeply impressed by her talk and fine manners and general come-
liness. He felt her grace and charm and spoke of it
with enthusiasm. But to him and to her there seemed
to be an impassable gulf between them. She changed

her mind about that, however, when she heard him speak and felt the power of his personality and saw his face lighted by the candle of his spirit. It was a handsome face in those moments of high elation. Hardship and malarial poison had lined and sallowed his skin. He used to say that every time the fever and ague walked over him, they left a track on his face. The shadows of loneliness and sorrow were in its sculpturing. But when his eyes glowed with passion one saw not the rough mask which the life of the pioneer had given him. His form lost its awkwardness; his face took on a noble and impressive beauty. Those times every eye looked longingly upon him because of the great and wonderful things with which he was interfused. To quote his own words to the boy, Josiah Traylor, his character was speaking as well as his lips. Mary had the insight to recognize his power. She felt the strength of his spirit. She agreed with her friends that here was a man of great promise. She felt the need of him.

To one who loved beauty and respected women as he did the grace and refinement of this young lady had a singular appeal coupled as it was with the urge of his strong, masculine nature. It was a revelation. He was like a young poet going out into the open and seeing for the first time the mysterious beauty of the mountains or "the exquisite, delicate, thin curve of the new moon in spring." He began to seek and study refinement of thought, of manner, of dress, of expression. He knew that he needed Mary but had the feeling that she was not for him.

A woman who lived near the Edwards's house had a small, hairy, poodle dog. One day as Abe and Mary were walking along the street, they met this woman who asked if they had seen her dog.

"I wouldn't wonder if some one down the street had got him tied to the end of a pole and is using him to swab off his windows," said Abe Lincoln with a good-natured laugh. "I'll try to find him for you."

Mary enjoyed fun and this and like sallies of the young legislator added a certain zest to their friendship. Women are like children in their love of humor.

The diminutive Douglas saw in Miss Todd an asset of much value and his attentions began to be assiduous. Mary was indifferent to his lofty manner and sonorous vocalism. Abe Lincoln liked her better for that.

She encouraged the visits of the latter and invited his confidence. The fact filled him with a great joy. They went about together. In the Edwards parlor he modestly told her of his work and his life plan. She differed with him on certain subjects which were unfortunately fundamental. He did not love her as he had loved Ann. But her personality pleased and fascinated the young legislator. One evening under the spell of it he asked her to be his wife. She consented. Then he began to think it over.

It was like Lincoln in his relations with women to get the cart before the horse so to speak. The points upon which they disagreed came up for consideration. She could not think as he did on the subject of slavery and the kindred one of State Rights. His manners were not like hers. He was thirty-one years old that summer. It was rather late in life to undertake any great change in his manners. They grew naturally out of one's history and character. He could be kind and gentle in his way. But, mainly, his manners would have to be like the rugged limbs of the oak. The grace and elegance of the water-willow and the white birch were not for him. It saddened him to conclude that he would have to be for a long time just what he was—crude, awkward, unlearned in the graces and amenities of cultivated people. He rightly judged that his crudeness would be a constant source of irritation to the proud Mary. As their acquaintance progressed the truth of his conviction grew more apparent. This, however, did not so much concern him as her lack of sympathy with some of his deepest motives. He decided that, after all, he did not love her and that to marry her would be committing a great wrong.

Some of the unhappiest days of his life followed.

His conscience gave him no rest. He knew not what to do. He told a friend that if his misery were equally distributed to the whole human race each would have a troublesome burden. He was wont to take long walks into the country with "Mr. Nimble" those days, often carrying the boy on his shoulders. It is likely that the little lad was a great comfort to him. He wrote a letter to Miss Todd in which he reviewed the history of his thinking on the subject of their marriage and frankly but tenderly stated his conviction that it would imperil her happiness to marry him. Before sending it he submitted the letter to his friend Speed.

The latter read it over and looked very grave.

"What do you think of it?" Lincoln asked.

"I would never send a letter like that to a lady," Speed answered. "If you feel as you say go and tell her so, but don't put it in a letter."

Lincoln went to see her that evening and returned to his friend in a more cheerful mood.

"Did you tell her?" Speed asked.

"Yes, I told her."

"What happened?"

"She burst out crying and I threw my arms around her and kissed her and that settled it. We are going to be married."

What an illustration of the humanity and chivalry of Honest Abe was in the proceeding!

"I'm sure you'll get along all right together," said

Speed. "Your spirit is jealous of any one likely to get in its way. But she won't. She'll fall in line and do what she can to help you."

Now a little before this time Henry Brimstead and other creditors of Davis had gone to Chicago in the matter of the satisfaction of their judgment against him. Henry had driven a wagon across the prairies and, returning, had brought Bim and her mother to his home and then to Springfield. It was while they were there that Harry had come down to Chicago out of the woods in a condition of health which had alarmed his physician. The latter had put him on a steamboat and sent him east. He was bound for the mountain country in northern New York.

Bim and her mother returned to Chicago on the stage, the former to take a place in the store as the representative of Samson's interest.

Harry was three years in the wilderness trying to regain his health. Success came to him in the last year of his banishment.

Toward the end of it he received a letter from Mr. Lincoln. It was written soon after that curious climax in the courting of Mary Todd. In this letter he said:

"I am serving my last term in the Legislature. I learn that you are in better health and I hope that you will have the strength and inclination to return soon and be a candidate for my seat in the house. Samson

will not do it, being so busy with large affairs. You
are young. You have won distinction in the service
of your country. You have studied the problems of
the county and the state. Samson and Baker and
Logan and Browning agree with me that you are the
man for the place.

"As for myself I am going to be married in a year
or so. I shall have to give all my time to the practice
of the law. I am now in partnership with Stephen T.
Logan and am slowly clearing my conscience of debt.
I have done what I could for the state and for Sangamon County. It hasn't been much. I want you to
take up the burden, if you can, until I get free of my
debts at least. By and by I may jump into the ring
again."

Harry was glad to obey the summons. Soon after
the arrival of Mr. Lincoln's letter his doctor gave the
young man what he called "an honorable discharge."
The magic of youth and its courage and of good air
had wrought a change of which the able doctor had had
little hope in the beginning.

In his travels through the great forest Harry had
met David Parish and Stephen Van Renssalaer at
whose homes on the shore of the St. Lawrence he had
spent many a happy, summer day. Three years had
passed since that fateful morning on the prairie.
Through the winters he had lived in a comfortable
hunter's camp on the shore of Lake Placid. Summers
he had wandered with a guide and canoe through the
lakes and rivers of the wilderness hunting and fishing

and reading the law books which he had borrowed from Judge Fine of Ogdensburg. Each summer he worked down the Oswegatchie to that point for a visit with his new friends. The history of every week had been written to Bim and her letters had reached him at the points where he was wont to rest in his travels. The lovers had not lost their ardor. Theirs was the love "that hopes and endures and is patient."

On a day in June, 1841, he boarded a steamboat at Ogdensburg on his way to Chicago. He arrived in the evening and found Samson at the home of Bim and her mother—a capacious and well-furnished house on Dearborn Street. Bim was then a little over twenty-five years old. A letter from John Wentworth says that she was "an exquisite bit of womanhood learned in the fine arts of speech and dress and manner." He spoke also of her humor and originality and of her gift for business "which amounted to absolute genius."

The store had doubled in size under her management and with the help of the capital of Samson and Sarah Traylor. Its wholesale and retail business was larger than any north of St. Louis. The epidemic had seized her toward the last of her nursing and left the marks of its scourge upon her. It had marred her beauty but Samson writes, "the girl was still very handsome. She was well filled out and stood as straight as an arrow and was always dressed as neat as a pin. I fear she was a little extravagant about that. She

carried her head like a sleek, well-fed Morgan colt.
She was kind of scared to meet Harry for fear of
what he'd think of those little marks on her face but
I told her not to worry."

"You are the smartest and loveliest looking creature
that I ever saw in my life," said Harry after he had
held her in his arms a moment.

"But see what has happened to me—look at my
face," she answered.

"It is more beautiful than ever," he said. "Those
marks have doubled my love for you. They are medals
of honor better than this one that I wear."

"Then I think that I'll take you off and marry you
before you have a chance to fight another duel or find
another war to go to," said Bim. "There is the
mustache that I used to long for and which wouldn't
come," she added with a smile.

"Is there anything else that I seem to need?" Harry
asked. "I could grow whiskers now."

"Don't," she answered. "The great need of the
West is shears and razors and a law to compel their
use. There can be little romance in the midst of so
much hair."

"I shall be careful not to offend you," Harry
laughed. "I want to marry you as soon as possible.
I've been looking forward to that since I was sixteen."

"I don't hear of anything but love and marriage,"
said Samson. "We've been rassling down at our

house to keep Josiah from running off and getting married. He's engaged already."

"Engaged! To whom?" Harry asked.

"To Annabel Brimstead. She's a little older than he is. She laughed at him and promised to marry him as soon as he was nominated for President by all his friends. She would now vote for him herself. He has become a good athlete and the best scholar in school. He has every boy and girl in the village working for him evenings and Saturdays."

"What are they doing?" Harry asked.

"Making those newfangled things they call lucifers. You can build a fire in a second with 'em. They cut splinters out of soft wood, dip their ends in brimstone —which Joe learned how to make—and put them in a hot oven until the brimstone is baked. Then a scratch will bring a flame. Joe puts them up in bundles and sells them to the merchants and calls them lucifer matches. He has invented a machine that will cut and dip a thousand splinters an hour. I tell you Annabel is in danger."

He took a lucifer out of his pocket and scratched it on the bottom of his boot. The party looked with wonder at its flame which quickly consumed the slender thread of pine in his fingers.

"I have always thought that Joe would make a whale of a man," said Harry.

"We all seem to be threatened with immediate and overwhelming happiness," Bim exclaimed.

"The only thing in the way of mine is the national debt that I have accumulated," Harry remarked.

"I knew he'd think of something," said Bim ruefully. "If I wanted to abolish the noble institution of marriage I'd make him chairman of the ways and means committee."

"Harry, your credit is still good with me, and I'm prosperous," Samson began. "I want you to know that 'Bim's energy and skill are mostly responsible for my success. I guess we owe more to your sickness than you're aware of. If it hadn't been for that we would be plodding along at the same old pace. We would not have felt the need of speeding up. It was your misfortune that brought Bim into the store. If she wants to retire and marry you I rather think she is entitled to do it. I don't want any more fooling around about this matter. Sarah and I couldn't stand it. She's kept me awake nights talking about it. The thing has worried us plenty. We rebel and demand action before anything else happens. We feel as if we had some rights in this case."

"I concede them and second your demand," Harry answered. "Bim must name a near day. I only need a week to get some clothes made and to go up to Milwaukee on a little matter of business."

"I don't know whether we'll give him a week or not," said Bim playfully. "A great many things may happen to him in a week."

CHAPTER XXIV

Two days later Bim suggested that they should take
a day's ride in the open and spend the night at the home
of a friend of hers in a settlement known as Plain's
End, Harry having expressed a wish to get out on the
prairies in the saddle after his long term of travel on
a steamboat.

"Are you sure that you can stand an all day's journey?" Bim asked.

"I! I could kill a bear with my hands and carry him
home on my back and eat him for dinner," the young
man boasted.

"I've got enough of the wild West in me to like
a man who can eat bears if there's nothing better,"
said Bim. "I didn't know but you'd been spoiled in
the homes of those eastern millionaires. If you're
willing to take what comes and make the best of it,
I'll give you a day that you will remember. You will
have to put up with a very simple hospitality but I
wouldn't wonder if you'd enjoy it."

"I can put up with anything so long as I have your help," the young man answered.

"Then I shall send word that we are coming. We will leave here day after to-morrow. Our horses will be at the door at eight o'clock in the morning. We shall take some luncheon and reach our destination late in the afternoon and return next day. It will give us a good long visit with each other and you'll know me better before we get back."

"I want to know you as well as I love you," he said. "I suppose it will be like studying law—one never gets through with it."

"I've found myself a rather abstruse subject—as bad as Coke, of which Abe used to talk so much with my father," she declared. "I shall be glad if it doesn't discourage you."

"The mystery of woman can not be solved by intellectual processes," the young man remarked. "Observation is the only help and mine has been mostly telescopic. We have managed to keep ourselves separated by a great distance even when we were near each other. It has been like looking at a star with a very limited parallax. It's a joy to be able to see you with the naked eye."

"You will have little to look at on this holiday but me and the prairies," said Bim.

"I think the prairies will be neglected. I shall wear

my cavalry uniform and try to get a pair of the best horses in Chicago for the trip."

"Then you would have to get mine. I have a handsome pair of black young horses from Ohio—real high steppers. It is to be my party. You will have to take what comes and make the best of it."

The day of their journey arrived—a warm, bright, cloudless day in September 1841. The long story of those years of separation was told as they rode along. Biggs had been killed in a drunken brawl at Alton. Davis had gone to the far West—a thoroughly discredited man. Henry Brimstead had got his new plow on the market and was prospering beyond all his hopes. Eli had become a merchant of unusual ability and vision. His square dealing and good sense had done much to break down prejudice against the Jews in the democracy of the West. Agents of the store were traveling in Wisconsin, Illinois and Indiana selling its goods to country dealers. They carried with them the progressive and enlightened spirit of the city and the news. Everywhere they insisted upon a high standard of honesty in business. A man who had no respect for his contract was struck off the list. They spread the every-day religion of the counting room. They were a welcome, unifying and civilizing force in the middle country. Samson Traylor was getting wealth and a reputation for good sense. He had made the plan on which the business had developed. He had proved himself a wise and far-seeing man. Sarah's friends had been out in Springfield for a visit. They had invested money in the business. Her brother had decided to bring his family West and settle in Sangamon County.

The lovers stopped in a grove at noon and fed their horses and Harry, who had a bundle of Joe's lucifer matches in his pocket—a gift from Samson—built a fire and made a broach of green sticks on which he broiled beef steak.

A letter from Harry to Sarah Traylor tells of the beauty of the day—of blue bells and scarlet lilies in the meadow grass, of the whistling quail, of pigeons and wild geese flying across the sky and of his great joy in seeing again the vast sunlit reaches of the level, virgin lands.

"It was my great day of fulfillment, all the dearer because I had come back to health and youth and beloved scenes out of those years shadowed with loneliness and despair," he writes. "The best part of it, I assure you, was the face I loved and that musical voice ringing like a bell in merry laughter and in the songs which had stirred my heart in the days of its tender youth. You—the dear and gentle mother of my later boyhood—are entitled to know of my happiness when I heard that voice tell me in its sweeter tone of the love which has endured through all these years of stern trial. We talked of our plans as we sat among the ferns and mosses in the cool shade sweet-

ened by the incense of burning fagots, over that re-
past to which we shall be returning often for refreshment in poorer days. We had thought of you and
of the man so well beloved of you and us in all these
plans. We shall live in Springfield so that we may
be near you and him and our friend, Honest Abe."

It is a long letter presenting minute details in the
history of that sentimental journey and allusion to
matters which have no part in this record. Its substance being fully in the consciousness of the writer,
he tenderly folds it up and returns it to the package—
yellow and brittle and faded and having that curious
fragrance of papers that have lain for scores of years
in the gloom and silence of a locked mahogany drawer.
So alive are these letters with the passion of youth in
long forgotten years that the writer ties the old rib-
bon and returns them to their tomb with a feeling of
sadness, finding a singular pathos in the contrast of
their look and their contents. They are turning to
dust but the soul of them has gone into this little history.

The young man and woman mounted their horses
and resumed their journey. It was after two o'clock.
The Grand Prairie lay ahead of them. The settlement
of Plain's End was twenty-one miles away on its farther side. They could just see its tall oak trees in the
dim distance.

"We must hurry if we get there before dark," said

the girl. "Above all we must be careful to keep our direction. It's easy to get lost down in the great prairie."

They heard a cat-bird singing in a near thicket as they left their camp. It reminded Bim of her favorite ballad and she sang it with the spirit of old:

> "My sweetheart, come along—
> Don't you hear the glad song
> As the notes of the nightingale flow?
> Don't you hear the fond tale of the
>   sweet nightingale
> As she sings in the valleys below?
> As she sings in the valleys below?"

They went on shoulder-deep in the tall grass on the lower stretches of the prairie. Here and there it gave Harry the impression that he was swimming his horse in "noisy, vivid green water." They startled a herd of deer and a number of wild horses. When they lost sight of the woods at Plain's End the young man, with his cavalry training, was able to ride standing on his saddle until he had got it located. It reminded him of riding in the Everglades and he told of his adventures there as they went on, but very modestly. He said not a word of his heroic fight the day that he and sixty of his comrades were cut off and surrounded in the "land of the grassy waters." But Bim had heard the story from other lips.

Late in the afternoon the woods loomed in front of

them scarcely a mile off. Near the end of the prairie they came to a road which led them past the door of a lonely cabin. It seemed to be deserted, but its windows were clean and a faint column of smoke rose from its chimney. There were hollyhocks and sunflowers in its small and cleanly dooryard. A morning-glory vine had been trained around the windows.

"Broad Creek is just beyond," said Bim. "I don't know how the crossing will be."

They came presently to the creek, unexpectedly swollen. A man stood on the farther shore with some seventy feet of deep and rapid water between him and the travelers.

"That man looks like Stephen Nuckles," said Harry.

"It is Stephen Nuckles," Bim answered.

"Hello, Steve!" the young soldier called.

"Howdy, boy!" said the old minister. "That ar creek is b'ilin' over. I reckon you'll have to swim the hosses."

"They're young city horses and not broke to deep water but we'll try them," said Bim.

They tried but Bim's horse refused to go beyond good footing.

"You kin light at that ar house an' spend the night but the folks have gone erway," the minister called.

"I guess you'll have to marry us right here and now," Harry proposed. "Night is coming and that house is our only refuge."

"Poor boy! There seems to be no escape for you!"
Bim exclaimed with a sigh. "Do you really and honestly want to marry me? If there's any doubt about
it I'll leave the horses with you and swim the creek.
You could put them in the barn and swim with me or
spend the night in the cabin."

He embraced and kissed her in a way that left no
doubt of his wishes.

"It's a cool evening and the creek is very wet," he
answered. "I'm going to take this matter in my own
hands."

He called to the minister: "Steve, this is the luckiest
moment of my life and you are just the man of all others I would have chosen for its most important job.
Can you stand right where you are and marry us?"

"You bet I kin, suh," the minister answered. "I've
often said I could marry any one half a mile erway if
they would only talk as loud as I kin. I've got the good
book right hyah in my pocket, suh. My ol' woman is
comin'. She'll be hyah in a minute fer to witness the
perceedin's."

Mrs. Nuckles made her appearance on the river bank
in a short time.

Then the minister shouted: "We'll begin by readin'
the nineteenth chapter of Matthew."

He shouted the chapter and the usual queries, knelt
and prayed and pronounced them man and wife.

The young man and woman walked to the cabin

and put their horses in its barn, where they found an abundance of hay and oats. They rapped at the cabin door but got no response. They lifted its latch and entered.

A table stood in the middle of the room set for two. On its cover of spotless white linen were plates and cups and saucers and a big platter of roasted prairie chickens and a great frosted cake and preserves and jellies and potato salad and a pie and a bottle of currant wine. A clock was ticking on the shelf. There were live embers in the fireplace and wood in the box, and venison hanging in the chimney.

The young soldier looked about him and smiled.

"This is wonderful!" he exclaimed. "To whom are we indebted?"

"You don't think I'd bring you out here on the plains and marry you and not treat you well," Bim laughed. "I warned you that you'd have to take what came and that the hospitality would be simple."

"It's a noble and benevolent conspiracy that has turned this cabin into a Paradise and brought all this happiness upon me," he said as he kissed her. "I thought it strange that Mr. Nuckles should be on hand at the right moment."

"The creek was a harder thing to manage," she answered with a smile. "I told my messenger to see that the gate of the reservoir was opened at four o'clock. So, you see, you had to marry or swim.

Now I've made a clean breast of it. I felt sure something would happen before you got back from Milwaukee. I was plum superstitious about it."

The young man shook with laughter and said: "You are the new woman born of the democracy of the West."

"I began to fear that I should be an old woman before I got to be Mrs. Needles."

"Whose house is this?" he asked in a moment.

"It is the home of Mr. and Mrs. Peter Lukins. Their land near Chicago is now used for a cattle yard and slaughter-house and is paying them a good income. They moved here some time ago. He looks after the reservoir. Mrs. Lukins is a famous cook as you will see. We can stay here as long as we want to. We shall find everything we need in the well, the chimney, the butt'ry and the cellar. And here is the wedding supper all ready for us and I as hungry as a bear."

"In the words of Mrs. Lukins 'it is very copasetic,' and I begin to feel that I have made some progress in the study of Bim Kelso. Come, let's have our supper."

"Not until you have broiled a piece of venison. It will take a lot of food to satisfy me. I'll get the cream and butter out of the well and make a pot of coffee. Hurry up, Harry, I'm starving."

Darkness fell upon the busy lovers and soon the firelight and the glow of many candles filled the homely cabin with flickering shadows and a soft beautiful color.

"Supper is ready," she said, when the venison steak had been deposited on the platter.

"Bim, I love you not as most men love," he said as they stood a moment by the side of the table. "From the bottom of my heart I do respect you for your honor and good faith and when I think of that and of all you have suffered for my sake I bow my head and ask God to make me worthy of such a helper."

They sat down to this unusual wedding feast and as we leave them the windows of the little cabin fling their light far out upon the level plain; we hear the sound of merry laughter and of the tall grasses rustling and reeling joyously in the breeze. The moon in mid-heaven and the innumerable host around it seem to know what is passing on the edge of the Grand Prairie and to be well pleased. Surely there is nothing that finds a quicker echo in the great heart of the world than human happiness!

CHAPTER XXV

BEING A BRIEF MEMOIR BY THE HONORABLE AND VEN-
ERABLE MAN KNOWN IN THESE PAGES AS JOSIAH
TRAYLOR, WHO SAW THE GREAT PROCESSION OF
EVENTS BETWEEN ANDREW JACKSON AND WOOD-
ROW WILSON AND ESPECIALLY THE MAKING AND
THE END OF LINCOLN.

Now, as I have done often sitting in the chimney
corner at the day's end, I look back at my youth and
manhood and tell, with one eye upon the clock, of those
years of fulfillment in the progress of our beloved pilgrim.   There are four and twenty of them that I shall
try to review in as many minutes.   At this distance I
see only the high places—one looming above another
like steps in a stairway.

The years of building and sentiment ended on the
fourth of November, 1842, when he and Mary Todd
were joined in marriage.   Now, like one having taken
note of the storm clouds, he strengthens the structure.

Mary tried to teach him fine manners.   It was a
difficult undertaking.   Often, as might have been expected, she lost her patience.   Mary was an excellent
girl, but rather kindlesome and pragmatic.   Like most

of the prairie folk, for instance, Abe Lincoln had been accustomed to reach for the butter with his own knife, and to find rest in attitudes extremely indolent and unbecoming. He enjoyed sprawling on the floor in his shirt-sleeves and slippers with a pillow under his head and a book in his hand. He had a liking for ample accommodation not fully satisfied by a bed or a lounge. Mary undertook to turn him into new ways and naturally there was irritation in the house, but I think they got along very well together for all that. Mary grew fond of him and proud of his great talents and was a devoted wife. For years she did the work of the house and bore him children. He milked the cow and took care of the horse when he was at home.

Annabel and I, having just been married, went with him to Washington on our wedding-tour in 1847. He was taking his seat in Congress that year. We were with him there when he met Webster. Lincoln was deeply impressed by the quiet dignity of the great man. We went together to hear Emerson lecture. It was a motley audience—business men, fashionable ladies and gentlemen, statesmen, politicians, women with their knitting, and lion-hunters. The tall, awkward orator ascended the platform, took off his top-coat and drew a manuscript from his pocket. He had a narrow, sloping forehead, a prominent nose, gray eyes and a skin of singular transparency. His voice was rich and mellow but not strong. Lincoln listened with rapt attention to his talk about Democracy.   It was a memorable night.   He spoke of it often.   Such contact with the great spirits of that time, of which he studiously availed himself in Washington, was of great value to the statesman from Illinois.   His experiences on the floor were in no way important to him, but since 1914 I have thought often of what he said there, regarding Polk's invasion of Mexico, unauthorized by Congress as it was:

"The Provision of the Constitution giving the war-making power to Congress was dictated, as I understand it, by the following reasons: kings had always been involving and impoverishing their people in wars, pretending generally that the good of the people was the object.   This our convention understood to be the most oppressive of all kingly oppressions and they proposed to so frame the constitution that no man should hold the power of bringing this oppression upon *us*."

The next year he stumped Massachusetts for "Zach" Taylor and heard Governor Seward deliver his remarkable speech on Slavery which contained this striking utterance:

"Congress has no power to inhibit any duty commanded by God on Mount Sinai or by His Son on the Mount of Olives."

On his return home Lincoln confessed that we had soon to deal with that question.

I was in his office when Herndon said:

"I tell you that slavery must be rooted out."

"What makes you think so?" Mr. Lincoln asked.

"I feel it in my bones," was Herndon's answer.

After that he used to speak with respect of "Bill Herndon's bone philosophy."

His term in Congress having ended, he came back to the law in partnership with William H. Herndon—a man of character and sound judgment. Those days Lincoln wore black trousers, coat and stock, a waistcoat of satin and a Wellington high hat. He was wont to carry his papers in his hat. Mary had wrought a great change in his external appearance.

They used to call him "a dead square lawyer." I remember that once Herndon had drawn up a fictitious plea founded on a shrewd assumption. Lincoln carefully examined the papers.

"Is it founded on fact?" he asked.

"No," Herndon answered.

Lincoln scratched his head thoughtfully and asked:

"Billy, hadn't we better withdraw that plea? You know it's a sham and generally that's another name for a lie. Don't let it go on record. The cursed thing may come staring us in the face long after this suit has been forgotten."

On the whole he was not so communicative as he had been in his young manhood. He suffered days of depression when he said little. Often, in good company, he seemed to be thinking of things in no way connected

John Mora & Adams

with the talk. Many called him a rather "shut-mouthed man."

Herndon used to say that the only thing he had against Lincoln was his habit of coming in mornings and sprawling on the lounge and reading aloud from the newspaper.

The people of the town loved him. One day as we were walking along the street together we came upon a girl dressed up and crying in front of her father's door.

"What's the matter?" Lincoln asked.

"I want to take the train and the wagon hasn't come for my trunk," said she.

Lincoln went in and got the trunk and carried it to the station on his back, with people laughing and throwing jokes at him as he strode along. When I think of him his chivalry and kindness come first to mind.

He read much, but his days of book study were nearly ended. His learning was now got mostly in the school of experience. Herndon says, and I think it is true, that he never read to the end of a law book those days. The study of authorities was left to the junior partner. His reading was mostly outside the law. His knowledge of science was derived from Chambers's *Vestiges of the Natural History of Creation.*

He was still afraid of the Abolition Movement in 1852 and left town to avoid a convention of its adherents. He thought the effort to resist by force the laws of Kansas was criminal and would hurt the cause of freedom. "Let us have peace and revolutionize through the ballot-box," he urged.

In 1854 a little quarrel in New York began to weave the thread of destiny. Seward, Weed and Greeley had wielded decisive power in the party councils of that state. Seward was a high headed, popular idol. His plans and his triumphant progress absorbed his thought. Weed was dazzled by the splendor of this great star. Neither gave a thought to their able colleague—a poor man struggling to build up a great newspaper. An office, with fair pay, would have been a help to him those days. But he got no recognition of his needs and talents and services. Suddenly he wrote a letter to Weed in which he said:

"The firm of Seward, Weed and Greeley is hereby dissolved by the resignation of its junior member."

When Greeley had grown in power and wisdom until his name was known and honored from ocean to ocean, they tried to make peace with him, but in vain.

Then suddenly a new party and a new Lincoln were born on the same day in 1856 at a great meeting in Bloomington, Illinois. There his soul was to come into its stateliest mansion out of its lower vaulted past. For him the fulness of time had arrived. He was prepared for it. His intellect had also reached the fulness of its

power. Now his great right hand was ready for the
thunderbolts which his spirit had been slowly forging.
God called him in the voices of the crowd. He was
quick to answer. He went up the steps to the platform.
I saw, as he came forward, that he had taken the cross
upon him. Oh, it was a memorable thing to see the
smothered flame of his spirit leaping into his face. His
hands were on his hips. He seemed to grow taller as he
advanced. The look of him reminds me now of what
the famous bronze founder in Paris said of the death-
mask, that it was the most beautiful head and face he
had ever seen. What shall I say of his words save that
it seemed to me that the voice of God was in them?
I never saw an audience so taken up and swept away.
The reporters forgot to report. It is a lost speech.
There is no record of it. I suppose it was scribbled
with a pencil on scraps of paper and on the backs of
envelopes at sundry times, agreeably with his habit, and
committed to memory. So this great speech, called by
some the noblest effort of his life, was never printed.
I remember one sentence relating to the Nebraska bill:

"Let us use ballots, not bullets, against the weapons
of violence, which are those of kingcraft. Their fruits
are the dying bed of the fearless Sumner, the ruins of
the Free State Hotel, the smoking timbers of the Her-
ald of Freedom, the Governor of Kansas chained to a
stake like a horse-thief."

In June, 1858, he took the longest step of all. The

Republican State Convention had endorsed him for the United States Senate. It was then that he wrote on envelopes and scraps of paper at odd moments, when his mind was off duty, the speech beginning:

"A house divided against itself must fall. Our Government can not long endure part slave and part free."

I was among the dozen friends to whom he read that speech in the State House library. One said of those first sentences: "It is a fool utterance." Another: "It is ahead of its time." Another declared that it would drive away the Democrats who had lately joined the party. Herndon and I were the only ones who approved it.

Lincoln had come to another fork in the road. For a moment I wondered which way he would go.

Immediately he rose and said with an emphasis that silenced opposition:

"Friends, this thing has been held back long enough. The time has come when these sentiments should be uttered, and if it is decreed that I shall go down because of this speech, then let me go down linked to the truth."

His conscience had prevailed. The speech was delivered. Douglas, the Democratic candidate, came on from Washington to answer it. That led to Lincoln's challenge to a joint debate. I was with him through that long campaign. Douglas was the more finished orator. Lincoln spoke as he split rails. His conscience was his beetle. It drove his arguments deep into the souls of his hearers. The great thing about him was his conscience. Unless his theme were big enough to give it play in noble words he could be as commonplace as any one. He was built for a tool of God in tremendous moral issues. He was awkward and diffident in beginning a speech. Often his hands were locked behind him. He gesticulated more with his head than his hands. He stood square-toed always. He never walked about on the platform. He scored his points with the long, bony, index finger of his right hand. Sometimes he would hang a hand on the lapel of his coat as if to rest it. Perspiration dripped from his face. His voice, high pitched at first, mellowed into a pleasant sound.

One sentence in Lincoln's speech at Ottawa thrust "The Little Giant" of Illinois out of his way forever. It was this pregnant query:

"Can the people of a United States territory in any lawful way and against the wish of any citizen of the United States exclude slavery from its limits prior to the formation of a state constitution?"

He knew that Douglas would answer yes and that, doing so, he would alienate the South and destroy his chance to be President two years later. That is exactly what came to pass. "The Little Giant's" answer was the famous "Freeport Heresy." He was elected to the Senate but was no longer possible as a candidate for the Presidency.

I come now to the last step in the career of my friend and beloved master. It was the Republican convention of 1860 in Chicago. I was a delegate. The New Yorkers came in white beaver hats enthusiastic for Seward, their favorite son. He was the man we dreaded most. Many in the great crowd were wearing his colors. The delegations were in earnest session the night before the balloting began. The hotel corridors were thronged with excited men. My father had become a man of wealth and great influence in Illinois. I was with him when he went into the meeting of the Michigan delegates and talked to them. He told how he came West in a wagon and saw the spirit of America in the water floods of Niagara and went on to the cabin village of New Salem and saw again the spirit of America in the life of the boy, Abe Lincoln, then flowing toward its manhood. When he sat down the Honorable Dennis Flanagan arose and told of meeting the Traylor party at the Falls when he was driving an ox-team, in a tall beaver hat; how he had remembered their good advice and cookies and jerked venison.

"Gentlemen," he said, "I am willing to take the word of a man whose name is hallowed by my dearest recollections. And believing what he has said of Abraham Lincoln I am for him on the second ballot."

The green Irish lad, whom I remember dimly, had

become a great political chieftain and his words had much effect. There was a stir among the delegates. I turned and saw the tall form of Horace Greeley entering the door. His big, full face looked rather serious. He wore gold-bowed spectacles. He was smooth-shaven save for the silken, white, throat beard that came out from under his collar. His head was bald on top with soft, silvered locks over each ear. He was a picturesque and appealing figure. They called on him to speak. He stepped forward and said slowly in a high-pitched drawl:

"Gentlemen, this is my speech: On your second ballot vote for Abraham Lincoln of Illinois."

He bowed and left the room and visited many delegations, and everywhere expressed his convictions in this formula. Backed by his tremendous personality and influence the simple words were impressive. I doubt not they turned scores of men from Seward to the great son of Illinois.

Then—the campaign with its crowds, its enthusiasm, its Vesuvian mutterings. There was a curious touch of humor and history in its banners. Here are three of them:

"Menard County for the Tall Sucker."

"We are for old Abe the Giant-Killer."

"Link on to Lincoln."

Then—those last days in Springfield.

He came to the office the afternoon before he left

and threw himself on the lounge and talked of bygone days with Herndon.

"Billy, how long have we been together?" he asked.

"Sixteen years."

"Never a cross word."

"Never."

"Keep the old sign hanging. A little thing like the election of a President should make no change in the firm of Lincoln and Herndon. If I live I'm coming back some time and then we'll go right on with the practice of the law as if nothing had happened."

Then—that Monday morning in Springfield when at eight o'clock on the eleventh of February the train bore him toward the great task of his life. Hannah Armstrong, who had foxed his trousers in New Salem, and the venerable Doctor Allen and the Brimsteads, and Aleck Ferguson, bent with age, and Harry Needles and Bim and their four handsome children, and my father and mother, and Betsey, my maiden sister, and Eli Fredenberg were there in the crowd to bid him good-by.

A quartet sang. Mr. Lincoln asked his friends and neighbors to pray for his success. He was moved by the sight of them and could not have said much if he had tried. The bell rang. The train started. He waved his hand and was gone. Not many of us who stood trying to see through our tears were again to look upon him. The years of preparation were ended and those of sacrifice had begun.

Now, we are at the foot of the last hill.   For a long time I had seen it looming in the distance.   Those days it filled my heart with a great fear.   Now, how beautiful, how lonely it seems!   Oh, but what a vineyard on that very fruitful hill!   I speak low when I think of it. Harry Needles and I were on our way to Washington that fateful night of April 14, 1865.   We reached there at an early hour in the morning.   We made our way through the crowded streets to the little house opposite Ford's Theatre.   An officer who knew me cleared a way for us to the door.   Reporters, statesmen, citizens and their families were massed in the street waiting with tear-stained faces for the end. Some of them were sobbing as we passed.   We were admitted without delay.   A minister and the doctor sat by the bedside.   The latter held an open watch in his hand.   I could hear it ticking the last moments in an age of history.   What a silence as the great soul of my friend was "breaking camp to go home."   Friends of the family and members of the Cabinet were in the room.   Through the open door of a room beyond I saw Mrs. Lincoln and the children and others.   We looked at our friend lying on the bed.   His kindly face was pale and haggard.   He breathed faintly and at long intervals.   His end was near.

"Poor Abe!" Harry whispered as he looked down at him.   "He has had to die on the cross."

To most of those others Lincoln was the great statesman.   To Harry he was still the beloved Abe who had shared his fare and his hardships in many a long, weary way.

The doctor put his ear against the breast of the dying man. There was a moment in which we could hear the voices in the street. The doctor rose and said: "He is gone."

Secretary Stanton, who more than once had spoken lightly of him, came to the bedside and tenderly closed the eyes of his master, saying:

"Now, he belongs to the ages."

We went out of the door. The sound of mourning was in the streets. A dozen bells were tolling. On the corner of Tenth Street a quartet of negroes was singing that wonderful prayer:

"Swing low, sweet chariot, comin' for to carry me home."

One of them, whose rich, deep bass thrilled me and all who heard it, was Roger Wentworth, the fugitive, who had come to our house with Bim, in the darkness of the night, long before.

THE END